Voodoos and Obeahs

Voodoos and Obeahs
Phases of West India Witchcraft
Author: Joseph J. Williams

Original publication: (1932)
Cover image: *Veve for the Sky Loa Damballah and his wife the Fertility Loa Ayida-Weddo*
Lay-out: www.burokd.nl

ISBN 978-94-92355-11-9

© 2015 Revised publication by:

VAMzzz Publishing
P.O. Box 3340
1001 AC Amsterdam
The Netherlands
www.vamzzz.com
contactvamzzz@gmail.com

VOODOOS
and OBEAHS
Phases of West India Witchcraft

Joseph J. Williams

Ph.D. (Ethnol.), Litt.D.
Fellow of the Royal Society of Arts;
Fellow of the Royal Geographical and the American
Geographical Societies;
Honorary Member of the Société Académique
Internationale (Paris) Member of the International Institute
of African Languages and Cultures (London);
Member of the Catholic Anthropological Conference;
Member of the American Folk-lore Society.

VAMzzz PUBLISHING

contents

Post Scriptum

Introduction

THE NEW YORK TIMES of August 14, 1925, printed the following news item:—

"SEIZE PRICE LISTS OF VOODOO DOCTOR—POLICE GET CIRCULARS OFFERING 'WISHING DUST' AND LUCKY CHARMS TO NEGROES AT $1 TO $1,000.—*Special to the New York Times.*-ATLANTIC CITY, Aug. 13.—Twelve thousand circulars said to have been sent to this city by a New York voodoo doctor were seized by the police here today as they were being distributed to negro homes on the north side by six negro boys.

"The circulars bore the address of D. Alexander of 99 Downing Street, Brooklyn, N.Y.

"All sorts of love powders, wishing dust, lucky charms and incantations are offered for sale in the circular, with prices ranging from $1 to $1,000.

"'Guffer Dust, New Moon, No. 1, good, $50; Happy Dust, $40; Black Cats' Ankle Dust, $500; Black Cat's Wishbone, $1,000; King Solomon's Marrow, $1,000; Easy Life Powder $100; Tying Down Goods, $50; Chasing Away Goods, $50; Boss Fix Powders, $15, and Buzzard Nest, $100,' were some of the goods offered."

"Inquiry developed that 'Bringing Back Powders' were designed to return an errant wife or husband to a grieving spouse, 'Tying Down Goods' were said to keep the subject of one's affections from departing, while 'Chasing Away Goods' had the opposite effect. 'Boss Fix Powders' keep one's employer in a friendly mind."

Four days after the appearance of the foregoing in The Times, we find this despatch from Cuba on the first page of The BOSTON POST:—

"SAVE CHILD FROM TORTURE—RESCUED DURING VOO-DOO DEATH RITES—HAVANA, Aug. 17.—Paula Cejes, a three-year-old white girl, was saved from a horrible death at the hands, of Voodoo worshippers at Aguacate, Havana Province, today, due to the rapidity of a search after she had disappeared.

"Paula, who lives with her parents on the Averhoff sugar plantation, was enticed away by Voodoo worshippers who bound and gagged her in a cane field and were in the act of performing their rites when a posse of searchers came upon them.

"Rural guards later captured a white man and a colored man who had in their possession articles used by voodooists in sacrificing life."

It may have been items such as these that inspired William Buchler Seabrook to go to Haiti with the set purpose of learning first hand whatever he could of Voodoo and kindred practices. At all events, after some stay in the island, he published in 1929 *The Magic Island* which at once became the centre of heated controversy. To some it was a weird conglomeration of fact and fancy worthy of little serious consideration and of even less credibility.[1]

On the other hand, the usually conservative LITERARY DI-GEST[2] apparently accepted it in its entirety as historic fact, and without question or cavil devoted five entire pages almost entirely to excerpts from its more startling passages and the reproduction of several photographs. One single reference to "the element of the occult which Mr Seabrook seems to believe" is the nearest approach to a guarded caution about the actuality of the most improbable details, a few of which may be mentioned in passing.

Thus, for example, at the "blood baptism," a truly voodooistic rite, when the author was to receive the "ouanga packet" prepared for him by Maman Célie, after the preliminary sacrifice of two red cocks and two black, an enormous white turkey and a pair of doves," in due course the sacrificial goat was led forth. "He was a sturdy brown young goat, with big, blue, terrified, almost human eyes, eyes which seemed not only terrified but aware and wondering. At first he bleated and struggled, for the odor of blood was in the air, but finally he stood quiet, though still wide-eyed, while red silken ribbons were twined in his little horns, his little hoofs anointed with wine and sweet-scented oils, and an old woman who had come from far over the mountain for this her brief part in the long ceremony sat down before him and crooned to him alone a song which might have been a baby's lullaby."[3]

After a further ritual with the goat, Catherine, the sixteen-year-old daughter of Maman Célie was led in by her brother Emanuel who "had to clutch her tightly by the arm to prevent her from stumbling when they brought her to the altar. Maman Célie hugged her and moaned and shed tears as if they were saying good-bye forever. The papaloi pulled them apart, and some one gave the girl a drink from a bottle. She began to protest in a dull sort of angry, whining way when they forced her down on her knees before the lighted candles. The papaloi wound round her forehead red ribbons like those which had been fastened around the horns of the goat, and Maman Célie, no longer as a mourning mother but as an officiating priestess, with rigid face aided in pouring the oil and wine on the girl's head, feet, hands and breast. All this time the girl had been like a fretful, sleepy, annoyed child, but gradually she became docile, somber, staring with quiet eyes, and presently began a weird song of lamentation."[4] The song itself is summed up in the last verse: "So I who am not sick must die!"[5] The author then continues: "And as that black girl sang, and as the inner meaning of her song came to me, I seemed to hear the voice of Jephtha's daughter doomed to die by her own father as a sacrifice to Javeh, going up to bewail her virginity on Israel's lonely mountain. Her plight in actuality was rather that of Isaac bound by Abraham on Mount Moriah; a horned beast would presently be substituted in her stead; but the moment for that mystical substitution had not yet come, and as she sang she was a daughter doomed to die."

"The ceremony of substitution, when it came, was pure effective magic of a potency which I have never seen equaled in Dervish monastery or anywhere. The goat and the girl, side by side before the altar, had been startled, restive, nervous. The smell of blood was in the air, but there was more than that hovering; it was the eternal, mysterious odor of death itself which both animals and human beings always sense, but not through, the nostrils. Yet now the two who were about to die mysteriously merged, the girl symbolically and the beast with a knife in its throat, were docile and entranced, were like automatons. The papaloi monotonously chanting, endlessly repeating, 'Damballa calls you,' stood facing the altar with his arms outstretched above their heads. The girl was now on her hands and knees in the attitude of a quadruped, directly facing the goat, so that their heads and eyes were in a level, less than ten inches apart, and thus they stared fixedly into each other's eyes, while the papaloi's hands weaved slowly, ceaselessly above their foreheads, the forehead of the girl and the forehead of the horned beast, each wound with red ribbons, each already marked with the blood of a white dove. By shifting slightly I could see the big, wide, pale-blue, staring eyes of the goat, and the big, black, staring eyes of the girl, and I could have almost sworn that the black eyes were gradually, mysteriously becoming those of a dumb beast, while a human soul was beginning to peer out through the blue. But dismiss that, and still I tell you that pure magic was here at work, that something very real and fearful was occurring. For as the priest wove his ceaseless incantations, the girl began a low, piteous bleeting, in which there was nothing, absolutely nothing, human; and soon a thing infinitely more unnatural occurred; the goat was moaning and crying like a human child. . .[6]

"While the papaloi still wove his spells, his hands moving ceaselessly like an old woman carding wool in a dream, the priestess held a twig of green with tender leaves between the young girl and the animal. She held it on a level with their mouths, and neither saw it, for they were staring fixedly into each other's eyes as entranced mediums stare into crystal globes, and with their necks thrust forward so that their foreheads almost touched. Neither could therefore see the leafy branch, but as the old mamaloi's hand trembled, the leaves flicked lightly as if stirred by a little breeze against the hairy muzzle of the goat, against the chin and soft lips of the girl. And after moments of breathless watching, it was the girl's lips which pursed up and began to nibble the leaves[7]

"As she nibbled thus, the papaloi said in a hushed but wholly matter-of-fact whisper like a man who had finished a hard, solemn task and was glad to rest, 'Ça y est' (There it is).

"The papaloi was now holding a machette, ground sharp and shining. Maman Célie, priestess, kneeling, held a gamelle, a wooden bowl. It was oblong. There was just space enough to thrust it narrowly between the mystically identified pair. Its rim touched the goat's hairy chest and the girl's body, both their heads thrust forward above it. Neither seemed conscious of anything that was occurring, nor did the goat flinch when the papaloi laid his hands upon its horns. Nor did the goat utter any sound as the knife was drawn quickly across the throat. But at this instant as the blood gushed like a fountain into the wooden bowl, the girl with a shrill, piercing, then strangled bleat of agony, leaped, shuddered, and fell senseless before the altar."[8]

But let us pass to an even more grewsome narrative. According to Seabrook, Celestine, the daughter of Antoine Simone,[9] "although under thirty, was reputed to be secretly the grande mamaloi of all Haiti, its supreme high priestess."[10] The author adds: "And not only Celestine herself but her father, Antoine Simone, president of the Republic, was reputed to be active in black sorcery. It was commonly said that magical rites and practices occurred even within the confines of the palace walls and probably they did."[11]

In explanation, then, of his chapter "Celestine with a Silver Dish," Seabrook writes: "The story of the silver dish is based on the evidence of two credible eye-witnesses, one a Frenchman who may still be seen and talked with at the Cape, the other a Haitian now dead. I talked with numbers of people about it and found none who questioned its approximate truth. It is current among the Haitians themselves; so they will forgive me for including it."... [12]

"One moonlight night in the Spring of 1909—it was during Easter week—the Frenchman who now lives at the Cape was sitting in one of the vine-covered summer-houses with his Haitian friend... Towards one o'clock in the morning they heard a tramping of feet from the direction of the palace, and presently saw a black sergeant with two squads of soldiers marching toward the stable yard, along a pathway of the deserted gardens.

They passed close to the summer house. Behind them, at a little distance, came Celestine. She was barefooted, in a scarlet robe, and carried in her hands a silver dish.

"In a small, open, moonlit glade, close to the summer house, the sergeant halted his eight men, and lined them up at attention, as if on a parade ground. Except for his low voiced commands, not a word was spoken. Celestine in her red robe which fell loose like a nightgown to her bare feet, laid the great silver platter on the grass.

"The sergeant handed Celestine a forked bent twig, a sort of crude divining-rod, and stepped back a little distance. Celestine, holding the wand loosely before her, facing the eight soldiers standing at attention, began a gliding, side-stepping dance, singing her incantations of mixed African and Creole in a low voice alternating from a deep gutteral contralto to a high falsetto, but never raised loudly, pointing the wand at each in turn as she glided to and fro before them.

"The men stood rigid, silent as if paralysed, but following her every movement with their rolling eyeballs as she glided slowly from end to end of the line.

"For a long ten minutes that seemed interminable, Celestine glided to and fro, chanting her incantation, then suddenly stopped like a hunting-dog at point before one man who stood near the center of the row. The wand shot out stiff at the end of her outstretched arm and tapped him on the breast.

"'Ou la soule, avant!' ordered the sergeant. (You there, alone, step forward.)

"The man marched several paces forward from the ranks, and halting at command, stood still. The sergeant, who seemed unarmed, drew the man's own knife-bayonet from its scabbard grasped the unresisting victim by the slack of his coat collar, and drove the point into his throat.

"While this was taking place, the other seven men stood silent obediently at attention. The victim uttered not a single cry, except a gurgling grunt as the point went through his jugular, and slumped to the grass, where he twitched a moment and lay still.

"The sergeant knelt quickly over him, as if in a hurry to get the job finished, ripped open the tunic, cut deep into the left side of the body just below the ribs, then put the knife aside, and tore out the heart with his hands.

"Black Celestine in her red robe, holding the gleaming platter before her, returned alone beneath the palm trees to the palace, bare-footed queen of the jungle, bearing a human heart in a silver dish."[13]

The general reaction on the author of such scenes, whether given as personal experiences or otherwise, is utterly appalling.

Thus he tells us in connection with the ceremony described a few pages back: "Not for anything, no matter what would happen, could I have seriously wished to stop that ceremony. I believe in such ceremonies. I hope that they will never die out or be abolished. I believe that in some form or another they answer a deep need of the universal human soul. I, who in a sense believe in no religion, believe yet in them all, asking only that they be alive—as religions. Codes of rational ethics and human brotherly love are useful, but they do not touch this thing underneath. Let religion have its bloody sacrifices, yes even human sacrifice if thus our souls may be kept alive. Better a black papaloi in Haiti with blood-stained hands who believes in his living gods than a frock-coated minister on Fifth Avenue reducing Christ to a solar myth and rationalising the Immaculate Conception."[14]

Of an earlier function at which he was present, he wrote: "And now the literary- traditional white stranger who spied from hiding in the forest, had such a one lurked near by, would have seen all the wildest tales of Voodoo fiction justified: in the red light of torches which made the moon turn pale, leaping, screaming, writhing black bodies, blood-maddened, sex-maddened, god-maddened, drunken, whirled and danced their dark saturnalia, heads thrown wierdly {sic} back as if their necks were broken, white teeth and eyeballs gleaming, while couples seizing one another from time to time fled from the circle, as if pursued by furies into the forest to share and slake their ecstacy.

"Thus also my unspying eyes beheld this scene in actuality, but I did not experience the revulsion which literary tradition prescribes. It was savage and abandoned, but it seemed to me magnificent and not devoid of a certain beauty. Something inside myself awoke and responded to it. These, of course, were individual emotional reactions, perhaps deplorable in a supposedly civilized person. But I believe that the thing itself— their thing, I mean—is rationally defensible. Of what use is any life without its emotional moments or hours of ecstasy?"[15]

We must not be surprised, then, that after watching the construction of the "ouanga packet" that was to preserve him "safe from all harm amid these mountains"[16], when bid to make a prayer, this should be the author's response: "May Papa Legba, Maitresse Exilee and the Serpent protect me from misrepresenting these people, and give me power to write honestly of their mysterious religion, for all living faiths are sacred."[17]

And how was this unholy pact carried out? Candidly, the glaring mistakes in ritual that the author makes in connection with his description of a Catholic funeral service,[18] which is open to the whole world to witness, does not inspire confidence in his exposition of the esoteric functions that are jealously reserved for the initiated alone.

As a matter of fact, Mr. Seabrook has divided his volume, perhaps of set purpose, into two distinct parts. First we have 282 pages devoted to the general story with weird fantastic drawings, more suggestive than illuminating, wherein the details are at variance with the text. Then follows, 52 pages under the general caption, "From the Author's Notebook" together with 27 photographs by the author. This second part is made up of quotations from standard authors and other references, with very few personal experiences and those of the most ordinary type.

While accepting, then, the latter portion of the book at its face value, it would seem safer to classify the earlier section as that sensational type of narrative that has become associated with the name of Trader Horn. This impression is strengthened by the fact that many passages in the story, especially those placed in the mouths of Louis and other informants, read almost as paraphrases from some of the authors who are mentioned later as references, and it seems as more than a coincidence that the quotation from Labat appearing on page 292 is probably copied without acknowledgment from Eugène Aubin,[19] as the same two variations from the original[20] appear in both places. The opening word has been changed from "*ces*" to "*les*" and "*ils*" has been omitted before "*conservent.*"

It is not at all surprising, then, that Dr. Price-Mars of Petionville, Haiti, whom Seabrook actually mentions in the course of his narrative[21] should publish an indignant reply to what he must needs consider a gross libel against his native island.

Of *Magic Island* as a whole, Dr. Price-Mars says: "This is nothing more than a chronicle, a rather long chronicle, if you will, but

throbbing, passionate, sensational. It contains whatever Mr. Seabrook has seen, or thinks that he has seen, in Haiti, during a few
months stay. I am forced to remark that this book is throughout
very amusing and very cruel—amusing, on account of the material
replete with savage humor, and abominable, because the American
reader, and even the Haitian who is not in a position to check up the
facts advanced, is drawn to ask himself: 'Is what he relates true? In
any case, these grewsome facts, such as are recorded, seem likely
if they are not true.'"[22]

Dr. Price-Mars further states: "From the very beginning, Mr.
Seabrook. . . . has grasped the two essential elements of Voodoo,
religion and superstition; religion, whoserites are preserved by oral
tradition alone, and superstition which is its grotesque caricature.
Not only is this distinction unknown to nine-tenths of the Haitians,
but most assuredly, as the writer expresses it, Voodoo is a cause of
astonishment, nay of a scandal, for most of us. And it is on account
of this disdain, of this fear of a fact, however important, in the life
of our plebian and rural masses, that our pitiful ignorance records
the sinister narratives of which we make ourselves the complacent
echo. And it is no less in this way, that, as a ripple of culture, our
mystic mentality displays itself. When, then, foreign writers arrive
among us, I mean above all journalists who as a rule are in quest of
sensational copy, they have only to imbibe at this fount of absurd
beliefs the most marvellous discourses and put them on the lips of
authentic individuals, to color them with an appearance of truth.
Their misconception or even evil intention is nothing in comparison

with the Haitian ignorance. How pitiful!"[23]

Dr. Price-Mars stamps the "Goat-Cry—Girl-Cry" episode as "A ceremony in which he pretends to have taken part. But to my way of thinking, this ceremony is a creation of his fertile imagination."[24] And again, he positively asserts: "As regards the ceremony of initiation, it is in every way false."[25]

Furthermore, after recounting the description of the "Petro Sacrifice" which Seabrook[26] claims to have attended, Dr. Price-Mars continues: "And was he, then, the spectator that he claims to be? I don't think so. It is probable that he did assist at Voodoo ceremonies. I personally sought to secure the opportunity for him, because, in the interviews that we had, I was made aware that he was familiar with the comparative history of religions, and the occasion seemed to me opportune to call attention to certain rites which indicate the antiquity of Voodoo, the solid foundation of my theory, to wit, that Voodoo is a religion. I was disappointed in my purpose, because I encountered a persistent distrust on the part of the peasants to whom I addressed myself, despite my long established and friendly relations with them. That Mr. Seabrook may have succeeded in winning the confidence of a Maman Célie. I am willing to concede to him, on the condition, however, that he does not dramatize the situation by depicting to us the peasant community whose guest he has been as a nook lost in the highest and most inaccessible mountains, isolated from all communication with urban centres. These conditions render his account absolutely improbable, because there is not a single peasant in a true rural centre who would consent to organize real Voodoo ceremonies for the sole pleasure of a stranger. On the other hand, the ceremony which he has described is only half true. At the very outset, he has committed a ritual absurdity in making the bull the principal sacrificial matter of the Petro. They sacrifice the bull as the fowl and the goat in nearly all the Voodoo ceremonies, but the victim proper to the Pedro is the pig. The absence of this animal in a ritual display of Pedro is equivalent to a blunder so stupid that it would falsify its meaning. Moreover, the sacrifice of the bull considered as a god, or symbol of a god, is totally unknown in Voodoo. It seems to me an invention or at least a very fantastic interpretation and which the footnote of Seabrook sufficiently explains."—This reference is to "the Bacchae" of Euripides.[27] Here we may leave Mr. Seabrook for the present.[28]

Just as fetishism was for a long time accepted as a generic term covering all that was nefarious in the customs of the West African tribes, so in the popular mind today, Voodoo and Obeah are interchangeable and signify alike whatever is weird and eerie in the practices of the descendants of these same tribes as they are found throughout the West Indies and the southern portion of the United States.

And yet technically, not only are Voodoo and Obeah specifically distinct, one from the other, both in origin and in practice, but if we are to understand the true force and influence which they originally exercised over their devotees, we must dissociate them from the countless other forms of magic, black or white, that have gradually impinged themselves upon them as so many excrescences.

Logically, then, we must begin our study, not in the West Indies but in Africa itself, going back as far as possible to the origins of the present day practices, and watching their development, both before and after their transplanting, through the medium of slavery, to new and fertile soil where they have become a rank, though exotic, growth.

The present writer first visited Jamaica in December, 1906, and he became at once intensely interested in the question of Obeah, and in a less degree in Voodoo. Since then he has made three other visits to the island and has spent there in all about six years. He has penetrated to the least accessible corners of mountain and "bush" and has lived for some time in those remote districts where superstitious practices are prevalent. He has steadily sought to extend his knowledge of the Black Man's witchcraft, both by conversation with the natives of every class and by seeking out its practitioners. He has conversed with professional Obeah men, whom, however, he has invariably found evasive and noncommittal. But despite this latter fact he has by chance, rather than by any prearrangement, had occasion at times to watch surreptitiously the workings of their gruesome art.

Meanwhile, for a quarter of a century he has culled the works of others and sought not only to familiarize himself with the smaller details of Voodoo and Obeah, but no less to discriminate judiciously between fact and fiction to the best of his ability. The result of his researches and observations are now set forth in the following pages.

CHAPTER I
African Ophiolatry

EDWARD B. TYLOR writing as long ago as 1871 observed: "Serpent worship unfortunately fell years ago into the hands of speculative writers, who mixed it up with occult philosophies, Druidical mysteries, and that portentous nonsense called the 'Arkite Symbolism,' till now sober students hear the very name of ophiolatry with a shiver."[1] Yet it is in itself a rational and instructive subject of inquiry, especially notable for its width of range in mythology and religion."[2]

Dr. C. F. Oldham, Brigade Surgeon of his Majesty's Indian Army, tells us in the Preface of his interesting little volume, *The Sun and the Serpent*:[3] "This work, which is based upon papers read before the Royal Asiatic Society in 1901, was at first intended to refer only to Indian serpent worship. It was soon found, however, that the serpent worship of India did not originate in that country but was, in fact, a branch of the worship of the Sun and the Serpent, which was once well-nigh universal. It became evident, therefore, that a history of the Indian cult would go far to explain the nature and origin of serpent worship, in other countries and in other times." While we cannot accept many of the views expressed in the course of this work, his final conclusion is most important, coming as it does from such a source. He says: "It would seem, moreover, that

the deification of totems, of kings, of ancestors, and of the heaven-
ly bodies, which furnish so many of the divinities associated with
the Sun-god; as also the human sacrifices and other abominations,
which occurred in some Sun-worshipping countries, all arose from
the corruption of the earlier worship of a supreme deity who was
believed to reside in the Sun. The Gayatri—the most sacred text of
the Veda, which must not be uttered so as to be overheard by profane
ears, and which contains the essence of the Hindu religion, is a short
prayer to the Sun-god, who is addressed as Savitri, the generator or
creator. The early Egyptians, and other ancient peoples also, seem to
have worshipped the Sun- god as the Creator."[4] in speaking of Africa,
however, Egypt, at least for the present must be excluded from our
consideration. For our question now deals with rites distinctively
belonging to the black tribes, whether we class them as Bantus or
Negroes in the strict sense of the word. And while at first glance it
seems but natural to assign an Egyptian origin for the cult, as far
as the dark continent is concerned, Wilfrid D. Hambly, Assistant
Curator of African Ethnology at the Field Museum of Natural History, Chicago, the first to produce a strictly scientific work on the
question of serpent worship in Africa[5] after a prolonged and careful
study, has adduced strong and convincing reasons to the contrary.
Hence his conclusion: "Examination of African Python worship in
relation to cults and beliefs from other parts of the world provides
no evidence that Africa received Python worship from extraneous
sources. On the contrary, the evidence is strongly in favour of an
indigenous origin of Python worship."[6] And again: "There is nothing
more than a superficial resemblance between the snake beliefs of

Africa and those of ancient Egypt."[7]

In any case, the subject does not really come within the scope of the present work. We are, it is true, in quest of the origin of Voodoo as a serpent cult, but precisely, as we shall see later, under the particular aspect of worshipping the non-poisonous python. We have nothing to do here directly with rainbow-snakes, or other like variants of the serpent cult.[8]

Canon Roscoe furnishes us with a description of the principal centre of serpent worship in East Africa. He tells this: "The python god, Selwanga, had his temple in Budu, by the river Mujuzi, on the shore of the lake Victoria Nyanza. . . . . The appearance of the new moon was celebrated by a ceremony extending over seven days; for this the people made their preparations beforehand, because no work was done during the festival. A drum was sounded as soon as the moon was seen, and the people gathered together to make their requests and to take part in the ceremonies. Those who wished to make any request brought special offerings, whilst the rest brought beer and food as they pleased. The priesthood of this deity was confined to members of the Heart Clan; the chief of the state upon which the temple stood was always the priest. His dress was the usual priestly dress, that is, it consisted of two barkcloths, one knotted over each shoulder, and two white goat-skins as a. shirt; round his chest he tied a leopard-skin decorated with beads and with seed of the wild banana, and in his hand he carried two fly-whisks made from the tails of buffalo. The priest first received the offerings for the god and heard the people's requests; then, going into the temple to the medium, he gave the latter a cup of beer and some of the milk from the python's bowl mixed with white clay. After the medium had drunk the beer and milk, the spirit of the python came upon him, and he went down on his face and wriggled about like a snake, uttering peculiar noises and using words which the people could not understand. The priest stood near the medium and interpreted what was said. During the time that the medium was possessed the people stood round, and the temple drum was beaten. When the oracle ended, the medium fell down exhausted, and would lie inanimate for a long time like a person in a deep sleep."[9]

To further clarify our position, we may at the outset accept Hambly's distinction between worship and cult as a scientific working basis. Thus he says: "The difficulty of supplying a rigid and logical definition of an act of worship is indisputable, but in practice confusion of thought may be avoided by using the word in connection with certain beliefs and acts. These might reasonably include ideas of a superhuman being, a priesthood, provision of a special house or locality, and also the employment of sacrifice and ritual procedure. The word 'cult' may be used to designate beliefs and acts whose nature is less clearly defined than is the case with concepts and ceremonies surrounding an act of worship. . . . The subject of serpent worship has suffered from hasty generalizations and a lack of classificatory treatment. Consequently there have been assumptions of similarities and identities where they do not exist."[10]

Of Africa in general, Hambly says: "The distribution of Python worship is clear. The main foci are the southwest shore of Lake Victoria Nyanza; also several centres in the coastal regions of the west, from Ashanti to the south of the Niger. Python worship was probably indigenous to an ancient possibly aboriginal Negro population, which was driven to the west by racial pressure in the cast. Eventually the python-worshipping people were forced into unfavourable situations in the Niger delta, where they are found at present. Around the main centres of python worship are python cults; also python and snake beliefs."[11]

Let us now follow Hambly's argument and see in a general way what facts have led him to this conclusion. "West Africa," he remarks, "undoubtedly yields evidence of python worship, especially in Dahomey and southern Nigeria. There is also supplementary evidence with regard to python cults and beliefs. . . . A geographical survey through the Congo, South Africa, and up the east is negative with regard to the existence of python worship.[12] Not until the region of Lake Victoria Nyanza is reached is there evidence of a definitely organized python worship with a sacred temple, a priesthood, and definite ritual acts including sacrifice. There appears to be no definite evidence of python worship in Cameroon, but the serpent design is often employed in wood carving and the equipment of medicine-men."[13]

Again: "There are two unquestionable areas of python worship, namely West Africa and a smaller region in Uganda, but there is no definite evidence of similar institutions in the great extent of country between the two centres. There are, however, usages which may be the residue of a decadent python cult. . . . The following factors are common to the East and West African forms of python worship:

(1) The python only, but no other snake, is selected for definite worship. This choice may be due to the impressive size of the large species of python. The reptiles are tractable and non-poisonous. All observers are agreed that the python rarely attacks a human being.

(2) Hut structures (temples) contain internal arrangements for feeding the reptiles.

(3) The python embodies a superhuman being, god of war, spirit of the water, patron of agriculture, or goddess of fertility.

(4) The king sends messengers and offerings. He asks for prosperity.

(5) Sacred groves are found in addition to temples.

(6) Acts of worship bring people who offer sacrifice and make requests.

(7) Priests and priestesses are employed; the latter are wives of the python. Both dance themselves into ecstatic trance in which they make oracular utterances which are given in a language not understood by the worshippers."[14]

Hambly later returns to the same point: "One of the most important questions is the possible relationship between the python worship of Uganda and that of West Africa. The points of comparison between these two centres have already been given in detail. Briefly they are: The acceptance of the python as a supernatural being; the honouring of the reptile, which is fed and generally cared for; the appointment of priests and priestesses who undergo special preparation; belief in the python as a source of productiveness in relation to human fecundity, agriculture, and fishing; making of petitions and the offering of sacrifice; ecstatic dances of priests and priestesses. These go into trance during which they prophesy and answer the requests of worshippers.

These points suggest relation rather than independent origin, though it has to be admitted that the points of resemblance are of a rather general nature. Zoological observations prove that the python is likely to be accepted anywhere as an object of adoration."[15] Despite the last assertion, then, Hambly would trace the python worship of Uganda and West Africa at least to a common source rather than ascribe them to independent origin.

He continues; "Knowledge of racial migrations in Africa points to the probability that python worship passed across the continent from east to west.[16] To a certain extent the movement of African races are understood; the defect of our knowledge lies in the absence of a chronology for the mass movements of races. It is known, however, that under Hamitic pressure in the Horn of Africa the primitive Negro of the Lake Region moved across the continent from east to west, sending branches of the migratory stem into the Congo area, in which the movement was from north to south and from east to west. There is not a fragment of evidence to suggest that the intrusive Hamites brought python worship with them. The most reasonable suggestion is that the worship is indigenous to the early Negroes of Uganda though the ritual is now practiced by people who are somatically and linguistically Hamitic. The migration of python worship was probably of a purely racial character. The forms of worship are found in their fullest structure and activity at both ends of the main racial migratory line; that is, in Uganda at the eastern end, and southern Nigeria and Dahomey at the western end of the line. . ...

When the main masses of migrants had passed across the continent, they were fifteen degrees north of the equator, that is, to the north of Dahomey, Ashanti, and Nigeria.

Owing to pressure from the Fulani and the Hausa, these Negro tribes from East Africa had to move south into the unfavourable coast regions of the area from Liberia to the mouth of the Niger. It is precisely in these non-Bantu regions that python worship, cults, and beliefs are found at present. They were exceptionally strong at Brass, the terminus of some of the oldest of these racial migrations."[17]

This theory of Hambly is amply supported by independent observations. Thus as regards East Africa, we may quote one or two in passing." A. L. Kitching published a work in 1912 of which he says himself: "This book embodies the experiences and observations of ten years spent among the outlying tribes of the Uganda Protectorate."[18] In the chapter on "Superstition" he writes: "While some of the tribes in Uganda may be said to know God in a certain sense, and to look to and pray to a Supreme Being, whose influence is expected to be benign and helpful, the religion of the majority . . . consists largely, in common parlance, of dodging evil spirits."[19] Then, speaking of the Gan' people of northwest Uganda, he states: "In the same vague fashion sacrifices are offered to demons on the rocks that abound throughout the district; the spot usually preferred is one where there is a hole in which dwells a snake. The demon, so I was informed, is supposed to reside in the body of the snake, a statement which has decided Biblical flavour, although there was no suspicion of Christian knowledge about my informer."[20]

Canon Roscoe writing of the Banyoro, or as he prefers to call them the Bakitara, located along the eastern shore of Lake Albert in Uganda, stresses the point that in the common estimation rivers and waterholes are usually under the guardianship of snakes to whom sacrifices are offered. Thus, for example, "At the Muzizi there was a medicine-man, Kaupinipini, who was in charge of the river and cared for the snake, to which he made offerings when people wished to cross. He affirmed that it was useless to attempt to build a bridge over the river for the snake would break it down, and the only means of crossing was by large papyrus rafts on which the people, after giving offerings to the medicine-man for the snake, had to be ferried over. The king sent periodical offerings of black cows to this snake and the medicine-man presented them to it with prayers that it would not kill men."[21] And again: "Pythons were held to be sacred, and in some places offerings were made regularly to them to preserve the people. A few men kept pythons in their houses, taming them and feeding them on milk with an occasional fowl or goat. It was said that these pythons did not kill children or animals in their own villages but went further afield for their prey. The king had a special temple at Kisengwa in which a priest dwelt with a living python which he fed on milk."[22]

It is well to note here what has been remarked by Hambly: "The Wa Kikayu regard the snake and some other animals as having a mysterious connection with spirits. When a snake enters the village the people offer it milk and fat. These snakes are not exactly the spirits themselves, but their messengers, who give warnings of future evils and come to indicate that an offering to the spirits will be opportune.[23]

Having thus sufficiently established the fountain-head of Negro Ophiolatry at Uganda, we may turn to West Africa for a more intimate and detailed study of its development at what Hambly calls the western end of the racial migratory line.

Major Arthur Glyn Leonard, writing in 1906, after ten years of personal contact with the natives of South Nigeria, came to the conclusion that here at least the Ophiolatry practiced was a form of ancestor worship. In his opinion the Nigerian venerates the snakes precisely because he believes that the spirits of his ancestors are embodied in them. Thus he states: "In Benin City, at Nembe, Nkwerri, and in various localities all over the Delta, Ophiolatry, so-called, exists and flourishes, as it has always done ever since man taught himself to associate the spirits of his ancestors with the more personal and immediate objects of his surrounding. And as snakes-living as they did in the olden days in caves and trees, and as they now do not only in the towns, but inside the houses, underground as well as in the thatched roofs-were very closely associated with man, it is no wonder that they were early chosen to represent ancestral embodiment."[24]

To one observation of Major Leonard we must draw particular attention. It is this: "Irrespective of tribe and locality, one fact in connection with these natives impressed me very forcibly, and that was that in every case, with regard to snakes, the emblem revered is the python, and not one of the poisonous varieties, such *e.g.* as the cobra or horned viper. . . . The snakes whose bite means death are looked on as representing the spirits of evil."[25]

In Northern Nigeria there are comparatively few vestiges of the serpent cult, which may formerly have existed there, as indicated by certain finds. Thus C. K. Meek reports in connection with the Bauchi Plateau:[26] "From a surface deposit at Rop there was discovered a representation in tin of a coiled snake. This evidently had some religious or magical significance, and once again points to the presence of a former people who knew how to work in tin, who had a developed artistic sense, and among whom the cult of the serpent was perhaps a feature of their religion."[27] And again, "The Hausa states were foreigners from the East and all belonged to the same racial stock. . . . The legend further suggests that the ancient people of Hausaland reverenced the snake. This we can readily believe, as certain snakes are still regarded as sacred by the Angas, whose language is closely allied to Hausa, and representations of snakes have been dug up on the Bauchi Plateau."[28] Later he adds: "Before the introduction of Islam, among the early peoples of the Hausa states various snakes were apparently common totem animals, especially among the people of Katsina and Daura. The Abayajidu invaders of the Daura traditions would appear to have slain the local snake and substituted their own sacred animal, *e. g.* the lion (zaki), or some other worship instead."[29]

Percy Amaury Talbot of the Nigerian Political Service published in 1912 the conclusions resultant of five years of intimate contact with the Ekoi who were located on both sides of the boundary between the Cameroons and Southern Nigeria. It is his suggestion that Ophiolatry reached Nigeria from Egypt and had its origin in the introduction "of non- poisonous snakes into granaries, in order to protect their contents from predatory rodents." He writes: "Possibly the cult of the snake and crocodile has come down from very ancient times. It is well known that both were honoured in Egypt as tutelar gods, and if the Ekoi have trekked, as seems likely, from the cast of Africa, it is probable that the original reason for deifying snake and cat, *i. e.* that these creatures were the principal scourges of the plague-carrying rat, lies at the back of the powerful snake cult, while traces of cat worship are still to be found. Rats are a great pest all over the land, and every possible means is taken to keep them down, though with little result. In Egypt the snake was not only the guardian of house and tomb, but a snake goddess presided over the harvest festival, held in the month of Pharmuthi or April. Doubtless among other attributes she was regarded as the protectress of the garnered grain, and her cult grew from the practice of introducing non-poisonous snakes into granaries, in order to protect their contents from predatory rodents."[30]

Fourteen years after the appearance of his first book, Talbot brought out a truly scholarly work in four volumes entitled, *The Peoples of Northern Nigeria*.[31] He was still of opinion that "The striking resemblance between the Nigerian cults and those of ancient Egypt and the Mediterranean area generally can only be explained by intercourse, direct and indirect."[32]

The following excerpts are of interest: "Minor deities often assume the form—or inhabit the bodies of snakes, some species of which, especially pythons, are held sacred throughout the region of marsh-lands and waters inhabited by the most ancient tribe of all, the Ijaw, while there are traces of Ophiolatry in many other parts."[33]

"The chief juju in the Badagri region used to be Idagbe, symbolized by a large python."[34]

"In some parts of the Brass country, the principal worship is that of Ogidiga which was apparently introduced from Benin by Isalema, the first settler at Nembe. He is represented by a python and is supposed by some to be identical with the Bini and Yoruba Olokun, God of the Sea."[35]

"The Elei Edda worship a male Alose named Aru-Nga, who resides in a very nimble snake, probably *Dandrapis augusticeps*. If anyone kills this, a chief dies. It lives in a grove near the town and comes out when the priest sacrifices to it; it is supposed to bite and kill any bad person."[36]

"The Ake-Eze Edda chiefly worship Ezi-Aku, 'the property of the Quarter,' to whom sacrifices are offered at the foot of a special tree. Snakes are called her children and no one may touch or hurt them."[37]

"Among the Ekoi the most usual name for juju is some form of Ndeum. . . . The Ejagham appear to confine the word to those spirits, usually female, who live in trees, though they manifest themselves at times in the shape of snake or crocodile."[38]

Finally after another six years, Talbot further enhances his reputation as the leading authority on Southern Nigeria by publishing his *Tribes of the Niger Delta*,[39] where we read: "There is a special snake called Adida, which is also worshipped at Tombia. This is said to be the wife of Simingi and may never be slain. Should any Oru-Kuru-Gbaw find one of these lying dead, she would give it burial just as the juju priests do for the Adumu serpents."[40]

That this serpent cult can have its disadvantages at times is evidenced by the following incident related by Talbot: "One evening, when staying in the rest house at Omi-Akeni, an Ibo town in Owerri District, Chief Gabriel Amakiri Yellow came to say that he had heard of a woman's juju named Ogugu, the shrine of which was near at hand. Our informant began: 'Ogugu is the chief juju of the women of this country, and is very powerful for the granting of children. . . . If anyone promises something to the juju and fail to give this, or swear on it name but does not carry out the thing, Ogugu always sends visitors to remind the person. Big snakes she sends to lie across the threshold of the house. At midnight, one will creep into bed, or coil by the head of the sleeper. Never, never does such a messenger leave again until the promise has been fulfilled.'"[41]

Before passing on, it should be remarked that despite the insistance of Mr. Talbot that the serpent cult of Nigeria probably owes its origin to Egypt, as he bases his supposition in great part on the fact that the Ijaws are ultimately from distant East Africa, so far from weakening Hambly's theory, he only strengthens it as the latter has already shown that the Ijaw derive their origin, in all probability, not from Egypt but from Uganda.

Stephen Septimus Farrow, in his thesis for the degree of Doctor of Philosophy in the University of Edinburgh, 1924, tells us: "Among the Ibo tribes of the Owerri District (near neighbours of the Yorubas) the boa-constrictor is worshipped. On the 27th day of each month a white cock is offered to him, with cowries, palm-oil or palm-nuts, white cloth and kola nuts. The sacrifice is deposited at cross roads, away from the town. There is, however, no reptile worship among the Yorubas, except in the case of crocodiles, belonging to Olosa the lagoon-goddess.[42]

Briefly, then, to sum up our present chapter. Prescinding from the question whether African Ophiolatry is a diffusion from abroad or of independent origin, we may accept Hambly's theory that as regards the Dark Continent itself, the local centre from which it eminated was in all probability in Uganda. Further we may accept his assertion that it was indigenous to distinctively Negro tribes which under pressure from Hamitic invasion, trekked across the continent, carrying with them their old tribal beliefs and customs. Thirdly, we agree that while the oppressors in East Africa assimilated in some small degree more or less of its principles, West and not East Africa gradually became its true centre of influence.

While the examples thus far cited in connection with the practice in West Africa have savoured rather of the cult than of the formal worship of the serpent in the strict sense of the word, still the following points are of value. Independently of Whydah, where in the next chapter we will find Ophiolatry practiced in detail, scattered around this centre we have all the requisites to satisfy our definition of serpent worship. True, it is, that they serve as confirmatory evidence and nothing more. But the very fact that they are scattered over many localities and not restricted to one place, adds to the strength of the argument. For local causes may at times lead to some particular introduction of a temporary cult, as in the instance related by Colonel Ellis, who writes: "Djwi-j'ahnu . . . was a god who formerly resided at Connor's Hill. Tradition says that the people of Cape Coast first discovered his existence from the great loss which the Ashantis experienced at this spot on the 11th of July, 1824. The slaughter was so great, and the repulse of the Ashantis so complete, that the Fantis, accustomed to see their foes carry everything before them, attributed the unusual result of the engagement to the assistance of a powerful local god. They accordingly sacrificed some prisoners to him, and sent to Winnebah to inquire of the priests of Bobowissi if their surmise was correct. The reply being in the affirmative, a regular cult was established, according to the directions of the priests of Bobowissi. At that time Connor's Hill was covered with usually dense bush, which swarmed with snakes. Indeed, even at the present day, when the bush is cleared every year, they are still very numerous, and large numbers are killed by the West India soldiers employed in his work. From this circumstance probably arose the idea that Djwi-j'ahnu ordinarily presented himself to his worshippers in the shape of a serpent— in the shape of the *cerastes*, one of the most deadly of the *ophidia*.[43] Other snakes accompanied him, and were regarded as his offspring or dependants. The first sacrifices offered were human victims, but in later times eggs became the ordinary offering. If the god did not present himself to his worshippers in his assumed form., it was imagined that one of their number had given him offence, and the priests then made inquiries to discover the offender. He, being found, would then be mulcted of a sheep, a white cloth, and some rum; and with this special propitiatory offering the worshippers would again proceed to the hill. If the god still remained invisible, it was assumed that he was still dissatisfied, that the atonement was insufficient; and additional offerings were enforced upon the guilty member till the god revealed himself. Djwi-j'ahnu was also believed to assume other shapes; and a leopard, which some thirty years ago haunted the vicinity of the hill, and became by its depredations the terror of the neighbourhood, was believed to be the god who had adopted this form. When undisguised, Djwi-j'ahnu was believed to be of human shape and black in colour, but of monstrous size. He was represented as bearing a native sword in his right hand. His worship has now been extinct for some twenty years, the acquisition of the hill by the Imperial Government, the clearing of the bush, and the building of huts for the accommodation of troops, having proved fatal to the continuance of this particular cult."[44]

Before going on to examine Ophiolatry as it existed at Whydah, we must accentuate one detail that already asserts itself, and that is the prevalence with which the veneration of the serpent, whether as a cult or worship, is associated with what is usually called ancestor worship. But even here, while the reptile may be regarded as the receptacle or dwelling place of the spirits, they in turn are only intercessors or messengers of the Supreme Being to whom the petitions or venerations ultimately tend.[45] It is not, then, idolatry, if we confine ourselves to the strict definition of the word, as was so frequently assumed by the early African travellers who came in contact with it and only too frequently described it in distorted terms.[46]

CHAPTER II
Serpent Cult at Whydah

PÈRE LABAT writing of the year 1698 in the Island of Martinique, recounts what he had personally heard from the lips of Père Braguez, who in turn had actually witnessed the serpent cult at Whydah when the King himself was in attendance to consult the oracle. This is probably the earliest recorded account of an eye-witness, before European contacts had modified the ritual. The narrative runs as follows: "The people on their knees and in silence were withdrawn some distance apart; the King alone with the Priest of the country entered the enclosure, where after prolonged prostrations, prayers and ceremonies, the priest drew near to a hole where supposedly he had a serpent. He spoke to him in behalf of the King and questioned him as regards the number of vessels that would arrive the following year, war, harvest and other topics. According as the serpent replied to a question, the priest carried the answer to the King who was kneeling a short distance away in an attitude of supplication. This by-play having been repeated a number of times, it was finally announced that the following year would be prosperous, that it would have much trade, and that they would take many slaves. The multitude expressed their joy by loud shouts, dancing and feasting." Père Braguez further stated that he had subsequently interviewed the officiating priest who assured him: "That the cult rendered to the serpent was only a cult in its relation to the Supreme Being, of whom they were all creatures. That the choice was not left to themselves, but that they had adopted it through obedience to the common Master's orders, which were always founded on sound principles. The Creator knew perfectly the dispositions of the creatures who had come from his hands, and appreciated only too well man's pride and vanity, not to take every means suitable to humble him; for which purpose nothing seemed more effective than to oblige him to bow down before a serpent, which is the most despicable and the vilest of all animals."[1]

Reynaud Des Marchais, the French navigator, went on his first voyage to Guinea in 1704. During the next twenty years, on recurrent visits, he made a close study of the customs and practices of the various kingdoms. In 1724 he sailed on his last voyage to the Coast and spent several months carefully revising his notes and checking up on his sketches.

Shortly before his death he gave his manuscript to Père Labat who published it in 1730.[2] In his Preface Père Labat accentuates the fact that on the voyage of 1724 Des Marchais had corrected "the observations which he had made on several earlier ones."[3] The narrative itself shows that Des Marchais was an eye-witness of the scenes that he describes concerning the serpent cult at Whydah and the dates on his sketches indicate that he attended these functions in different years.

Concerning the origin of this worship of the serpent at Why-dah he states: "The principal divinity of the country is the serpent, although it is not known just when they began to acknowledge him, to render him a cult. They only know as absolutely certain that this pretended divinity came from the Kingdom of Ardra. These Whydahs having undertaken to give battle to the Ardras, a large serpent left the enemy's army and came to deliver himself to that of Whydah. But he appeared so gentle, that instead of biting like the other animals of his species, he caressed and embraced everybody. The chief sacrificer made bold to take hold of him and raise him up on high to bring him in view of the entire army, which, astonished at the prodigy, pros-trated themselves before this compliant animal, and rushed on their enemies with such courage that they completely routed them. They did not fail to attribute their victory to this serpent. They respectfully carried him along, built him a house, brought him sustenance, and in a short time this new god eclipsed all the others, even the fetishes which were the first and oldest gods of the country."[4]

Des Marchais adds: "It is of particular note that the most thoughtful Negroes very seriously assert that the serpent which they venerate today is really the identical one which came to find their ancestors, and which enabled them to achieve this famous victory which freed them from the oppression of the King of Ardra."[5]

This would suggest that the centre of Ophiolatry at Whydah is of comparatively recent origin, and other indications point strongly in the same direction.

Up to the beginning of the nineteenth century the capital of Whydah is usually marked on the maps as Xavier or Sabi, also spelt Sabe, Saby, Savi, etc., and presumably a corruption of the word Xavier which alone appears on the D'Anville map of Guinea dated April, 1729. Des Marchais, also, heads his chapter on the subject merely as "The Town of Xavier."[6] It is hard to believe that at so early a date this name should have been applied anywhere except to a Jesuit Mission. As a matter of fact from about 1600 to 1617, one or more Jesuits were labouring continuously along the Guinea Coast with headquarters at Sierra Leone. In 1607 Fr. Balthasar Barreira, S. J. certainly visited Benin and in 1613 Fr. Emmanuel Alvarez, S. J. built a chapel at Lagos.[7]

Whether or not the Jesuits did actually establish a mission in Whydah and named it Xavier, this much is certain; that, in connection with their labours along the Guinea Coast, there is absolutely no mention of serpent worship in any form. And as the Jesuits in their Relations are proverbially so detailed in such matters, we have a strong presumption that it was non-existent within their field of activity at the beginning of the seventeenth century.

This presumption is strengthened by the fact that Charles Chaulmer in 1661, while describing the fetish practices of Guinea does not mention the subject."[8] Moreover Dr. O. Dapper who goes into great details about each of the Guinea Kingdoms and their religions in 1668,[9] as well as John Ogilby, two years later,[10] are both silent on this point of serpent worship.

From all this it is safe to conclude that in all probability the Ophiolatry of Whydah had its origin in the latter half of the seventeenth century as it was well established there before the century's close.

The whole story of the advent of the serpent, it must be admitted, if taken by itself savours somewhat of a mythological derivation of the cult from neighbouring Ardra. But this suggestion would be scarcely compatible with known facts, as we find no indication that Ophiolatry had any previous existence there. Actually Des Marchais takes care to point out that, in the fetishism of Ardra, it is the buzzard that is singled out for veneration, and that they show these birds "the same respect and the same attention as is had for the good serpents at Whydah."[11]

But even if we exclude this mythological aspect of the story, at least as far as Ardra is concerned, there is still a possibility that it may have reference to some migration from the east that brought to Whydah, together with Ophiolatry, much-needed succour in the time of some war against Ardra.

Before leaving Des Marchais, attention should be called to his minute description of the procession held on April 16, 1725, in honour of the serpent after the coronation of the King of Whydah.[12] He also goes into great detail about the recruiting and training of little girls for the future office of priestesses and their subsequent marriage to the serpent.[13]

We may now take up chronologically the principal accounts of the serpent worship at Whydah that have come down to us. The earliest detailed narrative and antedating even that of Des Marchais is from the pen of William Bosman, the Chief Factor for the Dutch at the Castle of St. George d'Elmina. Written originally in Dutch in 1700, it was quickly translated and circulated throughout Europe. Concerning Whydah, or as he calls it Fida, he declares: "It is certain that his country-men have a faint idea of the true God, and ascribe to him the attributes of Almighty and Omnipotent; they believe that he created the universe, and therefore vastly prefer him before their idol-gods: but yet they do not pray to him, or offer any sacrifices to him; for which they give the following reason. God, say they, is too high exalted above us, and too great to condescend so much as to trouble himself or think of mankind: wherefore he commits the government of the world to their idols; to whom, as the second, third and fourth persons distant in degrees from God, and our appointed lawful governors, we are obliged to apply ourselves. And in firm belief of this opinion they quietly continue. Their principal gods, which are owned for such throughout the whole country, are of three sorts. First, a certain sort of snakes, who possess the chief rank amongst their gods. . . . Their second-rate gods are some lofty high trees; in the formation of which Dame Nature seems to have expressed her greatest art. The third and meanest god or younger brother to the other is the sea. These three mentioned are the public deities which are worshipped and prayed to throughout the whole country.[14]

"They invoke the snake in excessive wet, or barren seasons:

on all occasions relating to the government and the preservation of their cattle, or rather in one word, in all necessities and difficulties in which they do not apply to their new batch of gods. And for this reason very great offerings are made to it, especially from the King.[15]

"The snake-house . . . is situated about two miles from the King's village, and built under a very beautiful lofty tree, in which, say they, the chief and largest of all the snakes resides. He is a sort of grandfather to all the rest; is represented as thick as a man, and of an unmeasurable length. He must also be very old, for they report that they found him a great number of years past; by reason of the wickedness of men, he left another country to come to them, at which being overjoyed, they welcomed their new-come god with all expressible signs of reverence and big veneration and carried him upon a silken carpet to the snakehouse, where he is at present."[16] This is a slight variation from the account of Des Marchais.

Bosman continues: "The reverence and respect which the Negroes preserve for the snake is so great that if a black should barely touch one of them with a stick, or any otherwise hurt him, he is a dead man, and certainly condemned to the flames. A long time past, when the English first began to trade here, there happened a very remarkable and tragical event. An English Captain having landed some of his men and part of his cargo, they found a snake in their house, which they immediately killed without the least scruple, and not doubting but they had done a good work, threw out the dead snake at their door, where being found by the Negroes in the morning, the English preventing the question who had done the fact, ascribed the honour to themselves; which so incensed the natives, that they furiously fell on the English, killed them all and burned their house and goods.[17]

"In my time an Aquamboean Negro took a snake upon his stick, because he durst not venture to touch it with his hands, and carried it out of the house without hurting it in the least, which two or three Negroes seeing, set up the same cry that is usual on account of fire, by which they can in a small time raise the whole country. . . . By these instances we are deterred from meddling with the accursed gods or devilish serpents, notwithstanding that we are frequently molested by them, since in hot sunshine weather, as if they were lovers of darkness, they visit us by five and six together, creeping upon our chairs, benches, tables, and even our beds, and bearing us company in sleep: and if they get a good place under our beds, and our servants out of laziness don't turn up our bedding, they some-times continue seven or eight days, where they have also cast their young. But when we are aware of these vermin and do not desire to be troubled with them any longer, we need only call any of the natives, who gently carries his god out of doors.[18]

"But what is best of all, is, that these idolatrous snakes don't do the least mischief in the world to mankind. For, if by chance in the dark one treads upon them, and they bite or sting him, it is not more prejudicial than the sting of the millepedes. Wherefore the Negroes would fain persuade us that it is good to be bitten or stung by these snakes, upon the plea that one is thereby secured and protected from the sting of any poisonous snake. But here I am somewhat dubious, and should be loth to venture on the credit of their assertions, because I have observed that the gods themselves are not proof against these venomous serpents, much less can they protect us from their bite. We sometimes observe pleasant battles betwixt the idol and venomous snakes, which are not wanting here.[19]

"The species of these idol serpents here are streaked with white, yellow and brown; and the biggest which I have seen here is about a fathom long, and the thickness of a man's arm."[20]

"If we are ever tired with the natives of this country, and would fain be rid of them, we need only speak ill of the snake, after which they immediately stop their cars and run out of doors. But though this may be taken from a European that they like; yet, if a Negro of another nation should presume to do it, he would run no small risk.[21]

"In the year 1697, my brother factor Mr. Nicholas Poll, who then managed the slave trade for our Company at Fida, had the diversion of a very pleasant scene. A hog being bitten by a snake, in revenge, or out of love to god's flesh, seized and devoured him in sight of the Negroes, who were not near enough to prevent him. Upon this the priests all complained to the King; but the hog could not defend himself, and had no advocate; and the priests, unreasonable enough in their request, begged of the King to publish a royal order, that all the hogs in his kingdom should be forthwith killed, and the swiny race extirpated, without so much as deliberating whether it was reasonable to destroy the innocent with the guilty."[22]

Twenty years after Bosman wrote his narrative, John Atkins, Surgeon in the Royal Navy, sailed from Spithead, February 5, 1720, on an expedition in quest of the pirates that were infesting the slave route from the Guinea Coast to the West Indies. Under the caption "Whydah" he wrote in his account of the voyage: "This country is governed by an absolute king, who lives in Negrish majesty at a town called Sabbee, six miles from the sea. His palace is a dirty large bamboo building, of a mile or two round, wherein he keeps near a thousand women, and divides his time in an indolent manner.... He is fattened to a monstrous bulk, never has been out since he became king (nigh twelve years)."[23]

Concerning the religion of the country, Atkins remarks: "The most curious of their customs, and peculiar to this part, is their snake worship, which, according to my intelligence, is as follows. This snake, the object of their worship, is common in the fields, and cherished as a familiar domestick in their houses, called deyboys; they are yellow, and marbled here and there, have a very narrow swallow, but dilatible (as all of the serpent kind are) to the thickness of your arm on feeding. It is the principal deity or fetish of the country, and brought into more regularity than others, by the superior cunning of their fetishers, who have one presiding over them, called the grand fetisher, or high priest, who is held in equal reverence with the King himself; nay, sometimes more, through gross supersitition and fear, for they believe an intercourse with the snake, to whom they have dedicated their service, capacitates them to stop or promote the plagues that infest them. He hath the craft by this means, to humble the King himself on all occasions for their service, and to drain both him and the people, in supplying their wants. It is death for a native to kill one of these snakes, and severe punishments to Europeans. When rains are wanted at seedtime, or dry weather in harvest, the people do not stir out after it is night, for fear of the angry snake, which, provoked with their disobedience, they are taught, will certainly kill them at those. times, if abroad, or render them idiots."[24]

All this was written on the eve of the destruction of Whydah as a nation. The Dahomans of the interior were bent on securing an outlet to the sea, that they might eliminate the coastal tribes from their position of middle-men in the lucrative slave trade. After the conquest of Ardra, Whydah alone stood between them and the consummation of their plan. Ordinarily a stout resistance might have been expected. But, as Atkins' description has shown us, the reigning king was devoid of the most fundamental qualities for directing affairs in such a crisis.

William Snelgrave who visited the country three weeks after the event, places the date of the destruction of Whydah by the Dahomans as March, 1727.[25] In this connection he writes: The King of Dahomey "was obliged to halt there by a river, which runs about half a mile to the northward of the principal town of the Whidaws, called Sabee, the residence of their King. Here the King of Dahomey encamped for some time, not imagining he could have found so easy a passage and conquest as he met with afterwards. For the pass of the river was of that nature, it might have been defended against the whole army, by five hundred resolute men: but instead of guarding it, these cowardly luxurious people, thinking the fame of their numbers sufficient to deter the Dahomans from attempting it, kept no set guard. They only went every morning and evening to the river side, to make fetiche as they call it, that is, to offer sacrifice to their principal God, which was a particular harmless snake they adore, and prayed to on this occasion, to keep their enemies from coming over the river.

"And as worshipping a snake may seem very extravagant to such as are unacquainted with the religion of the Negroes, I shall inform the readers of the reasons given for it by the people of Whi-daw. This sort of snake is peculiar to their country, being of a very singular make; for they are very big in the middle, rounding on the back like a hog, but very small at the head and tail, which renders their motion very slow. Their color is yellow and white, with brown streaks; and so harmless that if they are accidentally trod on (for it is a capital crime to do so wilfully) and they bite, no bad effect ensues; which is one reason they give for their worshipping of them. More-over, there is a constant tradition amongst them, that whenever any calamity threatens their country, by imploring the snake's assistance, they are always delivered from it. However this fell out formerly, it now stood them in no stead; neither were the snakes themselves spared after the conquest. For they being in great numbers, and a kind of domestic animal, the conquerors found many of them in the houses, which they treated in this manner. They held them up by the middle, and spoke to them in this manner: If you are gods, speak and save yourselves: Which the poor snakes not being able to do, the Dahomans cut their heads off, ripped them open, broiled them on the coals, and ate them. It is very strange, the conquerors should so far condemn the gods of the country, since they are so barbarous and savage themselves, as to offer human sacrifices whenever they gain a victory over their enemies."[26]

Another valuable witness is William Smith who was sent out by the Royal African Society of England which desired "an exact account of all their settlements on the coast of Guinea."[27] He arrived at Whydah. Road, April 7, 1727, that is, immediately after the snake incident. He adds many interesting details to Captain Snelgrave's account. Thus he tells us: "His Majesty of Whydah, who is the largest and fattest man I ever saw, thinking himself a little too bulky to fight, was, upon the first alarm, privately conveyed away by the main strength of a couple of stout lusty Negroes in a hammock, by which means he saved his life.[28]

"The city of Sabee was above four miles in circumference. The houses neatly built, though only mud-wall covered with thatch, having no stone in all that country nor even a pebble as big as a walnut."[29]

Concerning the serpent worship, Smith states: "They are all pagans and worship . . . a large beautiful kind of snake, which is inoffensive in its nature. These are kept in fittish- houses, or churches, built for that purpose in a grove, to whom they sacrifice greatstore of hogs, fowls, and goats, &c. and if not devoured by the snake, are sure to be taken care of by the fittish-men, or Pagan priests. . . . The laity all go in a large body by night with drums beating, and trumpets of elephant's teeth sounding, in order to perform divine worship, and implore either a prosperous journey, fair weather, a good crop, or whatsoever else they want. To obtain which from the snake, they then present their offering, and afterwards return home. They are all so bigoted to this animal that if any Negro should touch one of them with a stick, or otherwise hurt it, he would be immediately sentenced to the flames. One day as I walked abroad with the English Governor, I spied one of them lying in the middle of the path before us, which indeed I would have killed had he not prevented me, for he ran and took it up in his arms, telling me, that it was the kind of snake which was worshipped by the natives, and that if I had killed it, all the goods in his fort, and our ship would not be sufficient to ransom my life, the country being so very populous that I could not stir without being seen by some of the natives; of whom there were several looking at us that happened to be on their march home from their captivity at Adrah. They came, and begged their god, which he readily delivered to them, and they as thankfully received and carried it way to their fittish-house, with very great tokens of joy."[30]

The destruction of Whydah as a Kingdom did not put an end to the veneration of the serpent there. According to William Davaynes, who was one of the directors of the East India Company and who had left the Coast of Africa in 1763 after having resided there twelve years, eleven years as Governor at Whydah and the other at An-namboe, "The snake was the peculiar worship of the ancient people of Whydah, and when this province was conquered by the King of Dahomey, the worship of the snake was continued upon motives of policy. Formerly a person who killed a snake was put to death; but now a goat is sacrificed as an atonement."[31] The last statement must apply to the case of Europeans alone, for as we shall see the death penalty against natives who injured the sacred snake continued for some time to come.

Concerning the continuation of the serpent cult itself, Robert Norris states: "By Trudo's management (in tolerating his subjects with the free exercise of their various superstitions; and incorpo-rating them with the Dahomans by intermarriage if it may be so-called), no distinctions being made between the conquerors and the conquered, who were now become one people, many of those who had fled their native countries, to avoid the calamities of war, were induced to return and submit quietly to his government."[32] And "The remnant of the Whydahs who had escaped the edge of Guad-ja's sword, were abundantly thankful to him, for permitting them to continue in the enjoyment of their snake worship."[33]

Archibald Dalzel went out to Africa as a surgeon in the year 1763, and resided three years on the Gold Coast, some little part of the time as Governor, and four years as Governor of Whydah, returning to England in the year 1770. He was one of the witnesses who testified before the Committee of Council appointed for the consideration of all matters relating to trade and foreign plantations. Reference has already been made to the Report of this Committee which was published in 1789, and which contains the following statement: "With respect to the religion of the people at Whydah and the general object of their worship, Mr. Dalzel observed that in no part of Africa had he been able to understand the religion of the natives. At Whydah they pay a kind of veneration to a particular species of large snake, which is very gentle. In Dahomey they pay the same kind of veneration to Tigers. Thus veneration does not prevent people from catching and killing them if they please, but they must not touch the beard, which is considered as a great offence. They have a great number of men they call Fetiche men, or padres. The word fetiche is derived from a Portuguese word meaning witchcraft."[34]

For the condition at Whydah in the closing days of the eighteenth century, when throughout the British Empire the slave trade was coming to an end, we have the testimony of Dr. John M'Leod formerly of the British Navy who in 1803 served as surgeon on a ship, bound from London to the Coast of Africa, in the slave trade. On this occasion. he visited the centre of the serpent cult and tells us: "In Whydah, for some unaccountable reason, they worship their Divinity under the form of a particular specie of snake, called Daboa, which is not sufficiently large to be terrible to man, and is otherwise tameable and inoffensive. These Daboahs are taken care of in the most pious manner, and well fed on rat, mice and birds, in their fetish-houses or temples, where the people attend to pay their adoration, and where those also who are sick or lame apply to them for assistance."[35]

That the British abolition of slavery made little change in the serpent worship at Whydah, is evidenced by ample testimony. Thus, John Duncan in his journal records at Whydah in the Spring Of 1845: "The snake is also a fetish here; and houses are built in several parts of the town for the accommodation of the snakes, where they are regularly fed. These houses are about seven feet high in the walls, with conical roof, about eight feet in diameter, and circular. The snakes are of the boa-constrictor tribe, and are considered quite harmless, although I have my doubts upon it. They generally leave this house at intervals, and when found by any of the natives, are taken up and immediately conveyed back to the fetish-house, where they are placed on the top of the wall, under the thatch. It is disgusting to witness the homage paid to these reptiles by the natives.

When one of them is picked up by anyone, others will prostrate themselves as it is carried past, throwing dust on their heads, and begging to be rubbed over the body with the reptile. After taking the snake up, a very heavy penalty is incurred by laying it down, before it is placed in the fetish-house. Wherever a snake is found it must be immediately carried to the fetish-house, whether it has ever been placed there before or not. Snakes abound about Whydah; their average length is four feet and a half; head flat, and neck small in proportion."[36]

Another entry in Duncan's *Journal* is of particular interest, as it gives us in detail the punishment inflicted on the natives for even accidentally killing a sacred serpent.

Earlier writers merely indicate that such an individual was given to the flames. Here, however, we have a full description. Under date of May 1, 1845, he writes at Whydah: "Punishment was inflicted for accidentally killing two fetish snakes, while clearing some rubbish in the French fort. This is one of the most absurd as well as savage customs I ever witnessed or heard of. Still it is not so bad as it was in the reign of the preceding King of Dahomey, when the law declared the head of the unfortunate individual forfeited for killing one of these reptiles, even by accident. The present King has reduced the capital punishment to that described below. On this occasion three individuals were sentenced as guilty of the murder of this fetish snake. A small house is thereupon made for each individual, composed of dry faggots for walls, and it is thatched with dry grass. The fetish-men then assemble, and fully describe the enormity of the crime committed. Each individual is then smeared over, or rather has a quantity of palm-oil and yeast poured over them, and then a bushel basket is placed on each of the heads. In this basket are placed small calabashes, filled to the brim, so that the slightest motion of the body spills both the oil and the yeast, which runs through the bottom of the basket on to the head. Each individual carries a dog and a kid, as well as two fowls, all fastened together, across his shoulders. The culprits were then marched slowly round their newly prepared houses, the fetish-men haranguing them all the time. Each individual is then brought to the door of his house, which is not more than four feet high. He is there freed from his burthen, and compelled to crawl into his house on his belly, for the door is only eighteen inches high. He is then shut into this small space with the dog, kid and two fowls. The house is then fired, and the poor wretch is allowed to make his escape through the flames to the nearest running water. During his journey there he is pelted with sticks and clods by the assembled mob; but if the culprit has any friends, they generally contrive to get nearest to him, during his race to the water, and assist him, as well as hinder the mob in the endeavours to injure him. When they reach the water they plunge themselves headlong into it, and are then considered to be cleansed of all sin or crime of the snake-murder."[37]

Mr. Duncan subsequently returned to Whydah in 1849 as Vice Consul to the Kingdom of Dahomey,[38] and it was at his personal request that Commander Forbes was appointed to accompany him to the Court of Dahomey in the interests of the suppression of the slave trade. We may profitably cull some extracts from the Journal kept by Commander Forbes on this occasion.

Thus he writes: "The religion of Dahomey is a mystery only known to the initiated. There is no daily worship, but periods at which the fetish-men and -women dance. They who are initiated have great power and exact much in return. It is a proverb that the poor are never initiated. The Fetish of Abomey is the leopard, that of Whydah the snake. The human sacrifices at the See-que-ah-nee are neither to the invincible god 'Seh,' nor to the fetish 'Voh-dong,' but to the vitiated appetites of the soldiery. At the Cannah Customs there are sacrifices to the Voh-dong; and at the See-que-ah-nee there are sacrifices to the manes of their ancestors; the Dahomans, like the disciples of Confucius, looking to their departed ancestors for blessing in this life."[39]

March 8, 1849, he records: "The lions of Whydah are the snake fetish-house and the market. The former is a temple built round a huge cotton tree, in which are at all times many snakes of the boa species. These are allowed to roam about at pleasure; but if found in a house or at a distance, a fetish-man or woman is sought, whose duty it is to induce the reptile to return, and to reconduct it to its sacred abode, whilst all that meet it must bow down and kiss the dust. Morning and evening, many are to be seen prostrated before the door, whether worshipping the snake directly, or an invisible god, which is known under the name of 'Seh,' through these, I am not learned enough to determine."[40] In a supplementary chapter on "Religion," however, he states unequivocally: "The 'Voo-doong,' or fetish, represents on earth the supreme god 'Sell,' and in common with thunder and lightning,' Soh.'"[41]

Humour at times creeps into the *Journal*. On March 10th, Commander Forbes writes: "Called on the viceroy, and had a long conversation with him about trade. . . . On leaving a fetish-man was passing the gate, with two large snakes. State officers in most barbarous countries find it more convenient to remain at home, except when duty calls them abroad. The burly officer, was, according to custom, seeing me beyond his gate- and this was an opportunity not to be lost,-the fetish-man addressed him at great length, in praise of his extraordinary liberality to the fetish, for which be had no doubt to pay handsomely."[42] And again, on July 12th he records: "On leaving the British fort this morning, we learned that an extraordinary instance of the gorging of the fetish snake had taken place in the night. The reptile lay in the kitchen in dreadful pain, trying to force the hind legs and tail of a cat into his distended stomach, now in the shape of the half-swallowed victim. A fetish-woman arriving, carried the deity to the temple."[43]

It is not so surprising then, to find Father Lafitte, who arrived at Dahomey in 1861, and devoted eight years to missionary work, reporting that among those employed in the service of the sacred serpents was a physician, "charged especially to watch over the welfare of their laborious digestion."[44]

Another witness covering this same period is J. Leighton Wilson, who devoted eighteen years to missionary work in Africa and subsequently became a Secretary of the American Presbyterian Board of Foreign Missions. Of the sea-port town of Whydah, he says: "There is no place where there is more intense heathenism; and to mention no other feature in their superstitious practices, the worship of snakes at this place fully illustrates this remark. A house in the middle of the town is provided for the exclusive use of these reptiles, and they may be seen here at any time in very great numbers. They are fed, and more care is taken of them than of the human inhabitants of the place. If they are seen straying away they must be brought back; and at the sight of them the people prostrate themselves on the ground, and do them all possible reverence. To kill or injure one of them is to incur the penalty of death. On certain occasions they are taken out by the priests or doctors, and paraded about the streets, the bearers allowing them to coil themselves around their arms, necks, and bodies."[45]

This brings us to Richard F. Burton of Arabian Nights fame, who, writing in 1864, more than a century and a quarter after the event, thus details the debacle of the over-trustful devotees of the serpent-god at Whydah. "The infatuated "Whydahs," he says, "instead of defending their frontier line, were contented to place with great ceremony Danh, the fetish snake, Dan-like, in the path. Agaja had retired to levy his whole force, leaving the field army under his general. The latter seeing only a snake to oppose progress ordered 200 resolute fellows to try the ford. They not only crossed it unimpeded, but were able to penetrate into the capital."[46] He has already said: "When the Dahomans permitted serpent worship to continue, the Whydahs abundantly thankful, became almost reconciled to the new stern rule."[47]

The serpent revered as sacred in Burton's day was clearly of identical species with that first described by visitors to Whydah. For he says: "The reptile is a brown yellow-and- white-streaked python of moderate dimensions; and none appear to exceed five feet.

The narrow neck and head tapering like the slow-worms, show

it to be harmless; the Negro indeed says that its bite is a good defence against the venomous species, and it is tame with constant handling. M. Wallon saw 100 in the temple, some 10 feet long, and he tells his readers that they are never known to bite, whereas they use their sharp teeth like rats. Of these 'nice gods' I counted seven, including one which was casting its slough; all were reposing upon the thickness of the clay wall where it met the inner thatch. They often wander at night, and whilst I was sketching the place a Negro brought an astray in his arms; before raising it, he rubbed his right hand on the ground and duly dusted his forehead, as if grovelling before the king. The ugly brute coiled harmlessly round his neck, like a 'doctored' cobra in India or Algeria. Other snakes may be killed and carried dead through the town, but strangers who meddle with the Danhgbwe must look out for 'palavers' which, however, will probably now resolve themselves into a fine."[48] Then follows a description, differing only slightly in detail from Duncan's account of two decades earlier. Thus: "In older times death has been the consequence of killing one of these reptiles, and if the snake be abused, 'serious people' still stop their ears and run away. When under former reigns, a native killed a Danhgbwe, even accidentally, he was put to death; now the murderer is placed somewhat like the Salamanders of old Vauxhall, in a hole under a hut of dry faggots thatched with grass which has been well greased with palm-oil. This is fired, and he must rush to the nearest running water, mercilessly belaboured with sticks and pelted with clods the whole way by the Danhgbwe-no, or fetish-priests. Many of course die under the gauntlet."[49]

Of the "Boa Temple" he observes: "It is nothing but a small cylindrical mud hut-some fetish-houses are square-with thick clay walls supporting a flying thatch roof in extinguisher shape. Two low narrow doorless entrances front each other, leading to a raised floor of tamped earth, upon which there is nothing but a broom and a basket. It is roughly whitewashed inside and out, and when I saw it last a very lubberly fresco of a ship under full sail sprawled on the left side of the doorway. A little distance from the entrance were three small pennons, red, white and blue cotton tied to the top of tall poles."[50] And again: "On the other side of the road the devotees of the snake are generally lolling upon the tree roots in pretended apathy, but carefully watching over their gods. Here, too, are the fetish schools, where any child touched by the holy reptile must be taken for a year from its parents—who 'pay the piper'—and must be taught the various arts of singing and dancing necessary to the worship. This part of the system has, however, lost much of the excesses that prevailed in the last century when at the pleasure of the strong-backed fetish-men, even the king's daughters were not excused from incarceration and from its presumable object. The temple is still annually visited by the Viceroy, during the interval after the Customs and before the campaigning season. He takes one bullock, with goats, fowls, cloth, rum, meal, and water to the priest, who holding a bit of kola nut, prays aloud for the king, the country, and the crops."[51]

Burton relates one incident which shows what a hold the fanaticism had on the people at large even in his day. Speaking of the Catholic Mission Station at Whydah which was located in what was known as the Portuguese "Fort": "In March, 1863, the fort was struck by the lightning-god, Khevioso, the Shango of the Egbas; and they are not wanting who suppose that the fetishers, having been worsted in dispute by the Padres, took the opportunity of a storm to commit the arson. As the inmates impiously extinguished the fire, they were heavily fined; and, on refusing to pay, the Father-Superior was imprisoned. In June of the same year occurred another dispute, about a sacred snake that was unceremoniously ejected from the mission premises, and doubtless this anti- heathenism will bring them to further grief."[52]

Pierre Bouche who spent seven years on the Slave Coast, was resident at Whydah in 1868, where, as he tells us, he witnessed this scene: "One day I was on my way to visit a sick person. The boy who accompanied me suddenly cried out: 'Father, a fetiche!' I turned quickly, and saw a large serpent which had passed by me. Before it, a black prostrated himself, placing his brow in the dust and bowing low. His prayer deeply distressed me: 'You are my father, you are my mother,' said he to the reptile; 'I am all yours . . . my head belongs to you! . . . Be propitious to me!' And he covered himself with dust as a mark of humiliation."[53]

Writing of the same period, E. Desribes tells us: "The cult of living serpents is in vogue at many points along the Coast; but no where have they temples and regular sacrifices as at Whydah. . . . At Grand Popo not far from Whydah, the serpents have no temple, it is true, but they receive a cult even more revolting. There is there a species of large, very ferocious reptiles; when one of these serpents encounters small animals, he mercilessly devours them; and the more voracious it is, the more it excites the devotion of its worshippers. But the greatest honours, the greatest blessings are bestowed on it when, finding a young child it makes a meal of it. Then the parents of the poor victim prostrate themselves in the dust, and give thanks to one so divine as to have chosen the fruit of their love to make of it a repast."[54] We shall have occasion to refer to this incident later.

Our next witness is J. A. Skertchley who tells us: "In the early part of 1871 I left England with the object of making zoological collections on the West Coast of Africa."[55] On account of local wars, he was unable to penetrate the interior at Assinee and Accra and so proceeded to Whydah, where he was induced to visit King Gelele at Aborney, where he was detained as a "guest" for eight months. Incidentally he relates: "Opposite Agauli, hidden from profane eyes by a thick grove of fig trees which form but a mere undergrowth when compared with several tall bombaxes in their midst, is the far-famed snake house, or 'Danh-hweh,' as it is usually called. The name is derived from Daub, a snake, and Hweh, a residence. It is sometimes called Vodun-hweh, i. e. the fetiche house; and again, 'danhgbwe-hweh,' or the big snake (python) house. I was much disappointed at this renowned fetiche, for instead of a respectable temple, I found nothing but a circular swish hut, with a conical roof; in fact, an enlarged model of the parian inkstands to be seen in every toyshop. There was a narrow doorway on the eastern side[56] leading to the interior, the floor of which was raised a foot above the street. The walls and floors were whitewashed, and there were a few rude attempts at reliefs in swish. From the roof there depended several pieces of coloured yarn, and several small pots containing water were distributed about the floor. The roof was raised above the circular walls by short projecting pieces of bamboo; and coiled up on the top of the wall, or twining round the rafters, were twenty-two pythons. The creatures were the ordinary brown and pale yellow reptiles, whose greatest length is about eight feet. They were the sacred Danhgbwes whose power was relied upon to save the kingdom from the conquering armies of Agajah. It was the tutelary saint of Whydah, and when that kingdom was conquered, was introduced into the Dahoman pantheon. As recent as the late King's reign, if a native had the misfortune to accidentally (for no one would have had the temerity to purposely) kill a Danhgbwe, he was at once sacrificed, and his wives and property confiscated to the church. At the present time the defaulter has to undergo a foretaste of the sufferings of his portion hereafter."[57] Then follows a description of the ordeal by fire which has already been described.

Incidentally, Skertchley gives indication of a decadence having set in, at least as regards external discipline. That reverence for the sacred serpent, as regards the populace, is becoming subservient to greed oil the part of the custodians of the temple, is evidenced by the following passage: "The doorway being always open, the snakes frequently make excursions after nightfall. Should an unfortunate person of either sex meet the strolling deity, he is obliged to prostrate himself before it, and then, taking it tenderly in his arms, carry it to the priests. Of course he is rewarded by these gentlemen for taking care of the god, says the reader. No such thing! He is fined for meeting the snake, and imprisoned until it is paid to the last cowrie."[58]

Eight years after Skertchley, Colonel Ellis visited Whydah and thus describes his experience: "While at Whydah I stayed at the French Factory, and there I had a rather unpleasant adventure on the night of my arrival. It was a very close night, and I was sleeping in the grass hammock slung from the joists of the roof, when I was awakened by something pressing heavily on my chest. I put out my hand and felt a clammy object. It was a snake, I sprung out of the hammock with more agility than I have ever exhibited before or since, and turned up the lamp that was burning on the table. I then discovered that my visitor was a python, from nine to ten feet in length, who was making himself quite at home, and curling himself up tinder the blanket in the hammock. I thought it was the most sociable snake I had ever met, and I like snakes to be friendly when they are in the same room with me, because then I can kill them the more easily; so I went and called one of my French friends to borrow a stick or cutlass with which to slay the intruder. When I told him what I purposed doing he appeared exceedingly alarmed and asked me anxiously if I had yet injured the reptile in any way. I replied that I had not, but I was going to. He seemed very much relieved, and said that it was without doubt one of the fetish snakes from the snake-house, and must on no account be harmed, and that he would send and tell the priests, who would come and take it away in the morning. He told me that a short time back the master of a merchant vessel had killed a python that had come into his room at night, thinking he was only doing what was natural, and knowing nothing of the prejudices of the natives, and had in consequence got into a good deal of trouble, having been imprisoned for four or five days and made to pay a heavy fine.

"Next morning, I went to see the snake-house. It is a circular but with a conical roof made of palm branches,[59] and contained at that time from 200 to 250 snakes. They were all pythons, and of all sizes and ages; the joists and sticks supporting the roof were completely covered with them, and looking upwards one saw a vast writhing and undulating mass of serpents. Several in a state of torpor, digesting their last meal, were lying on the ground; and all seemed perfectly tame, as they permitted the officiating priest to pull them about with very little ceremony.

"Ophiolatry takes precedence of all other forms of Dahoman religion, and its priests and followers are most numerous. The python is regarded as the emblem of bliss and prosperity, and to kill one of these sacred boas is, strictly speaking, a capital offence, though now the full penalty of the crime is seldom inflicted, and the sacrilegious culprit is allowed to escape after being mulcted of his worldly goods, and having 'run-a-muck' through a crowd of snake-worshippers armed with sticks and fire-brands."[60] Evidently the ordeal of the burning huts has been mitigated, still another indication of the decadence in ritual.

Ellis continues: "Any child who chances to touch, or to be touched by one of these reptiles, must be kept for a space of one year at the fetish-house under the charge of the priest, and at the expense of the parents, to learn the various rites of Ophiolatry and the accompanying dancing and singing."[61]

Abel Hovelacque, writing in 1889, thus depicts the formal nuptial ceremonies with the serpent which the priestess undergoes when she has attained the marriage age of about fourteen or fifteen years: "They are brought to the temple. On the following night they are made to descend into a vaulted cellar, where it is said that they find two or three serpents who espouse them in the name of the great serpent. Until the mystery is accomplished, their companion and the other priestesses dance and sing with the accompaniment of instruments. They are then known under the name of wives of the great serpent, which title they continue to carry all their lives."[62]

During the last half of the nineteenth century a rapid decay set in as regards the veneration of the serpent at Whydah, due no doubt to increasing contacts with the white man and consequent European influences. Thus Édouard Foà, a resident in Dahomey from 1884 to 1890, describes conditions as they existed at the time of the French occupation which was completed in 1894. Remarking the extraordinary prestige which Dangbe enjoyed, he tells us: "One being alone, however, makes exception to the rule: it is the pig. When he meets the god (which happens at every step in Dahomey and Popo) without regard for the veneration of which it is the object, kills it, eats it up, or at least tramples it under foot when he has sufficiently gorged himself with the kind."[63] And apparently there are now no retaliatory measures on the part of the devotees of the serpent.

Finally M. Brunet, who was the delegate of Dahomey at the World Exposition of 1900, while stating that no mother would dare rescue her own child if seized by one of the sacred snakes, asserts later that for some years the cult of the serpent has been on the decline, and adds: "Today, when a black has accidentally killed or injured a reptile, they are content to have the culprit flogged."[64]

The evidence adduced in the present chapter shows conclusively that the Ophiolatry as practiced by the Whydahs was worship in the strict sense of the word. Its ultimate object is a superhuman being: we find a well organized priesthood; the snake-house or temple is described by all visitors; sacrifices are certainly employed and there is ritual procedure.

When we first come in contact with the worship of the serpent at Whydah towards the end of the seventeenth century, we find it well organized and in full vigour. Still there are indications that it had not been long established there. Certainly, all traditions point to the fact that it is not indigenous and that it has come presumably from the cast. This is in conformity with the supposition that Uganda is the fountainhead of African Ophiolatry.

After the destruction at Sabee of the original centre of Whydah

Ophiolatry, it springs up again and is extended to other localities. For the most part, it follows closely at first the old ritual, but as time goes on and European contacts assert themselves, modifications gradually creep in, and we find at one centre at least, Grand Popo, the introduction of a decadent variant. A human child becomes a victim when the sacred serpent sees fit to appropriate one for the purpose. Thus while the worship of the serpent was well regulated and clearly defined, should a child come in contact with one of the sacred reptiles, it was regarded as a sign of vocation to its service, and the little one was immediately attached to the school estab-lished for the purpose, where the service of the deity was formally taught. In the decadent days, however, as witnessed independently by Desribes and Brunet, mothers readily yielded up their children not merely to the service of the sacred snakes, but as a living holocaust should one of these reptiles appropriate the little one for the purpose.

We must also notice, that especially in the earlier accounts of the worship at Whydah there is no question of idolatry. The serpent itself is not the object of adoration, it is merely a medium of giving worship to the Supreme Being, whatever concept in the native mind this term may represent. In the present work we are excluding all theological considerations and we must leave to a later volume the analysis of what the real divinity was that was usually honoured by the title of Creator or Maker.

Furthermore, there are indications, as noted by Forbes, that the superhuman being to whom the Whydah addressed himself was probably the ancestral spirits, and that these were in some way connected with the sacred pythons.

The Reverend Robert Hammill Nassau, a Presbyterian minister, with a Doctorate both in Medicine and in Sacred Theology, was for forty years a missionary in French Congo, and published in 1904 a work on fetishism in West Africa, wherein he gives us the fruit of his life-study of native customs and superstitions.

Mary H. Kingsley gives due credit to Mr. Nassau for much valuable information on fetish, and then playfully takes him to task for not having thrown open to science the mass of valuable material collected in long years of research. Thus she writes: "I am quite aware that Dr. Nassau was the first white man to send home gorilla's brains: still I deeply regret he has not done more for science and geography. Had he but had Livingstone's conscientious devotion of taking notes and publishing them, we should know far more than we do at present about the hinterland from Cameroons to Ogowe, and should have for ethnological purposes, an immense mass of thoroughly reliable information about the manners and religions of the tribes therein, and Dr. Nassau's fame would be among the greatest of the few great African explorers-not that he would care a row of pins for that."[65] All unknown to Miss Kingsley, Dr. Nassau had been taking the necessary notes and the publication of his book repaired the other shortcoming referred to by his critic who had been so deeply impressed by the Doctor's "immense mass of thoroughly reliable information about the manners and religion of the tribes" he had visited.

Dr. Nassau, it is true, is treating of the Bantu tribes situated for the most part south of the equator, but much that he says is also applicable to the Negroes in the strict sense of the word, namely, those tribes from which the bulk of the slaves were drawn, and which go by the generic term of West Africans.

Quite possibly, Miss Kingsley, if asked, might not have given to the finished book the same encomium which she extended to the material in hand. Still as she was like Ellis, whose writings carry great weight with her, to a certain extent a professed follower of Spencer, her general approval of Dr. Nassau's conscientiousness and ability in his scientific researches, should lend considerable support to the facts adduced as well as to the conclusions drawn.

Dr. Nassau is unreserved in his assertion: 'I see nothing to justify the theory of Menzies[66] that primitive man or the untutored African of today, in worshipping a tree, a snake, or an idol, originally worshipped those very objects themselves, and that the suggestion that they represented, or were even the dwelling-place of, some spiritual Being is an after-thought up to which we have grown in the lapse of ages. Rather I see every reason to believe that the thought of the Being or Beings as an object of worship has come down by tradition and from direct original revelation of Jehovah Himself. The assumption of a visible tangible object to represent or personify that Being is the after- thought that human ingenuity has added. The civilized Romanist claims that he does not worship the actual sign of the cross, but the Christ who was crucified on it; similarly, the Dahoman in his worship of the snake."[67]

Again Dr. Nassau asserts: "The evil thing that the slave brought with him was his religion. You do not need to go to Africa to find the fetich. During the hundred years that slavery in our America held the Negro crushed, degraded, and apart, his master could deprive him of his manhood, his wife, his child, the fruits of toil, of his life; but there was one thing of which he could not deprive him,-his faith in fetich charms. Not only did this religion of the fetich endure under slavery—it grew. None but Christian masters offered the Negro any other religion; and by law, even they were debarred from giving them any education. So fetichism flourished. The master's children were infected by the contagion of superstition; they imbibed some of it at the Negro foster-mother's breasts. It was a secret religion that lurked thinly covered in slavery days, and that lurks today beneath the Negro's Christian profession as a white art, and among the non-professors as a black art; a modern memory of the revenges of his African ancestors; a secret fraternity among slaves of far distant plantations, with words and signs,—the lifting of a finger, the twitch of all eyelid,—that telegraphed from house to house with amazing rapidity (as today in Africa) current news in old slave days and during the late Civil War; suspected, but never understood by the white master; which, as a superstition, has spread itself among our ignorant white masses as the 'Hoodoo,' Vudu, or Odoism, is simply African fetichism transplanted to American soil."[68]

Père Baudin, while labouring as a missionary among the Dahomans, writes: "Their traditions and religious doctrines suggest a people more civilized than the blacks of Guinea of the present day. And on the other hand, many customs, usages, and industries show clearly that they are a people in decadence. The wars, particularly the civil wars, which have laid waste, and still continue to lay waste, these countries, have caused them to lose what they had preserved of their ancient civilization, which was in great part Egyptian, as indicated by many customs and usages. . . .

"Though scattered over an immense extent of country, these fetish-worshippers have a certain uniformity of religious belief; their divinities are identical, differing only in name; and the particular details which we give of the blacks of the Slave Coast of Yoruba, Dahomey, Benin, and other neighbouring kingdoms apply to all fetish- worshipping nations."[69]

Of "The Religious System of the Negroes of Guinea," he asserts: "The religion of the blacks is an odd mixture of monotheism, polytheism, and idolatry. In these religious systems the idea of a God is fundamental; they believe in the existence of a Supreme Primordial Being, the Lord of the Universe, which is His work. Monotheism recognizes at the same time numbers of inferior gods and subordinate goddesses. Each element has its divinity who is as it were incorporated in it, who animates and governs it, and is the object of adoration. After the gods and goddesses there are infinite numbers of good and evil genii; then comes the worship of heroes and great men who were distinguished during their lives. The blacks also worship the dead, and believe in metempsychosis, or the migration of souls into other bodies. They believe in the existence of an Olympus, where dwell the gods and celebrated men who have become fetishes, and in an inferior world, the sojourn of the dead, and finally in a state of punishment for great criminals.

They have also their metamorphosis, their sacred animals, their temples and their idols, etc. In a word, their religion is similar in all things to the old polytheism of the ancients; and notwithstanding the abundant testimony of the existence of God, it is practically only a vast pantheism, a participation of all the elements of the divine nature, which is as it were diffused throughout them all."[70]

He then proceeds to go into details: "The idea of God—Although deeply imbued with polytheism, the blacks have not lost the idea of the true God; yet their idea of Him is very confused and obscure. . . . They represent that God, after having commenced the organization of the world, charged Obatala with the completion and government of it, retired and entered into an eternal rest, occupying Himself only with His own happiness; too great to interest Himself in the affairs of this world. He remains like a Negro king, in a sleep of idleness.

"Thus the black renders no worship whatever to God, completely neglecting Him, to occupy themselves with the gods and goddesses and the spirits to which they believe themselves indebted for their birth, and their fate in this life and the next. However, although they seem to expect nothing from God, the Negroes by instinct naturally address themselves to him in sudden danger or in great afflictions. When they are victims of injustice, they take God to witness their innocence."[71] This last statement nullifies in great part what he. has just said about God being unconcerned about the affairs of the blacks, and their reciprocal neglect of Him. Elsewhere this condition certainly does not exist. As we shall see among the Ashanti, for example, he actually has his temple and his priesthood.

As regards the demi-gods, Père Baudin gives us the following explanation: "A family establishes itself near a river, a forest, a rock, or a mountain; imagination aided by the fetish-priests soon creates a belief in a demi-god, a tutelary genius of the place, and thus a new divinity makes its appearance in the Negro pantheon, and it is not long before it has its legend also.[72]

"The worship of the dead has greatly aided in augmenting the number of the gods. joined to the worship of nature is that of humanity. The descendants from generation to generation offer presents and sacrifices on the tomb of their ancestor, and end by adoring him as a local divinity, the origin of which becomes more and more obscure and consequently more and more venerable. This occurred at Porto-Novo in the case of the chiefs of families in various parts of the city, of whom the inhabitants are the real descendants."[73]

Concerning the lesser spirits, Père Baudin writes: "After the gods and the demi-gods come: the spirits or genii. The genii are very numerous; some are good and some bad spirits. A certain number serve as messengers to the gods and demi-gods, some are considered nearly as powerful as the gods themselves and have authority over lesser spirits who are their messengers, and these in turn command others, forming a hierarchy which is not very defined. The more ordinary spirits dwell in the forests and deserts."[74]

One of these lesser spirits has its own interest for us. We are told: "Audowido, the rainbow, is a genius, held in great veneration at Porto-Novo. In Yoruba he is called Ochumare. The temples dedicated to this genius are painted in all the colors of the rainbow, and in the middle of the prism a serpent is drawn. This genius is a large serpent; he only appears when he wants to drink, and then he rests his tail on the ground and thrusts his mouth into the water. He who finds the excrement of this serpent is rich forever, for with this talisman he can change grains of corn into shells which pass for money."[75]

CHAPTER III
Voodoo in Haiti

THE REPORT of the Lords of the Committee of Council appointed for the consideration of all matters relating to trade and foreign plantations, published in London, in 1789, states, "Mr. Dalzell supposes that the number of slaves exported from the Dominions of the King of Dahomey amounts to 10,000 or 12,000 in a year. Of these, the English may export 700 to 800, the Portuguese about 3,000, and the French the remainder." This will explain how the Dahomans with their serpent cult became so centred in the French islands of the West Indies, and especially in Haiti.

William Snelgrave who, as we have seen, was the first to visit Whydah, after the conquest by the Dahomans, says of the slavery there: "And this trade was so very considerable, that it is computed, while it was in a flourishing state, there were above twenty thousand Negroes yearly exported thence, and the neighbouring places, by the English, French, Dutch, and Portuguese."[1] As he was in the trade himself, he may be regarded as speaking with authority.

It is with good reason, then, that Colonel Ellis states: "In the southeastern portions of the Ewe territory, the python deity is worshipped, and this vodu cult, with its adoration of the snake god was carried to Haiti by slaves from Ardra and Whydah, where the faith still remains today. In 1724 the Dahomies invaded Ardra and subjugated it; three years later Whydah was conquered by the same foe. This period is beyond question that in which Haiti first received the vodu of the Africans. Thousands of Negroes from these serpent-worshipping tribes were at the time sold into slavery, and were carried across the Atlantic to the eastern island. They bore with them their cult of the snake. At the same period, Ewe-speaking slaves were taken to Louisiana."[2]

Elsewhere Ellis remarks: "That the term vodu should survive in Haiti and Louisiana, and not in the British West India Islands, will surprise no one who is acquainted with the history of the slave trade. The Tshi-speaking slaves (the Ashanti and kindred tribes) called Coromantees in the slave-dealer's jargon, and who were exported from the European fort on the Gold Coast, were not admitted into French and Spanish colonies on account of their dispositions to rebel and consequently they found their way into the British colonies, the only market open to them, while the French and Spanish colonies drew their chief supply from the Ewe-speaking slaves exported from Whydah and Badogry."[3]

Richard F. Burton had already asserted positively: "I may observe that from the Slave- Coast 'Vodun' or Fetish we may derive the 'Vaudoux' or small green snake of the Haitian Negroes, so well known by the abominable orgies enacted before the (Vaudoux King and Queen) and the 'King Snake' is still revered at S'a Leone."[4] He had previously stated: "Vodun is Fetish in general. I hardly know whether to write it Vodun or Fodun, the sound of the two labials is so similar."[5]

There is extent but one detailed account of Haitian Voodoo as it existed in the days of slavery, but that description, being by an experienced eye witness is invaluable for our present purpose. In fact it would be difficult to find a man better qualified than Moreau de Saint-Méry to place before us the true picture of the period. His youth in Martinique, his years as a legal practitioner and later as a Magistrate in Haiti, his executive and administrative ability as shown in the most trying days of the outbreak of the Revolution in France, all mark him out as a witness of the utmost reliability.[6]

Moreau de Saint-Méry classified Voodoo among the various dances of Haiti which he thus describes.[7] "What enraptures the Negroes, whether they were born in Africa or America was their cradle, is the dance. There is no amount of fatigue which can make them abandon going to very great distances, and some times even during the dead of night, to satisfy this passion.[8]

"One Negro dance has come with them from Africa to San Domingo, and for that very reason it is common also to those who are born in the colony, and these latter practice it almost from birth, they call it the Calenda.

"To dance the Calenda, the Negroes have two drums made, when possible from the hollow trunk of a tree in a single piece. One end is open and they stretch over the other a skin of sheep or nan-ny-goat. The shorter of these drums is named Bamboula, because it is sometimes formed out of a very thick bamboo. Astride of each drum is a Negro who strikes it with wrist and fingers, but slowly for one and rapidly for the other. To this monotone and hollow sound, is joined that of a number, more or less great, of little calabashes half-filled with small stones, or with grains of corn, and which they shake by striking them on one of the hands by means of a long haft which crosses them. When they wish to make the orchestra more complete, they add the Banza, a kind of Bass viol with four strings which they pluck. The Negresses arranged in a circle regulate the tempo by clapping their hands, and they reply in chorus to one or two chanters whose piercing voice repeats or improvises ditties. For the Negroes possess the talent of improvising, and it gives them an opportunity for displaying especially their tendency to banter.

"The dancers male and female, always equal in number, come to the middle of a circle (which is formed on even ground and in the open air) and they begin to dance. Each appropriates a partner to cut a figure before her. This dance which has its origin on Mt. Atlas, and which offers little variation, consists in a movement where each foot is raised and lowered successively, striking with force, some-times the toe and sometimes the heel, on the ground, in a way quite similar to the English step. The dancer turns on himself or around his partner who turns also, and changes place, waving the two ends of a handkerchief which they hold. The dancer lowers and raises alternately his arms, while keeping the elbows near the body, and the hand almost closed. This dance in which the play of the eyes is nothing less than extraordinary, is lively and animated, and an exact timing lends it real grace. The dancers follow one another with emulation, and it is often necessary to put an end to the ball, which the Negroes never abandon without regret.[9]

"Another Negro dance at San Domingo, which is also of African origin, is the Chica, called simply Calenda in the Windward Isle, Congo at Cayenne, Fandango in Spanish, &c. This dance has an air which is especially consecrated to it and wherein the measure is strongly marked. The proficiency in the dance consists in the perfection with which she can move her hips and lower part of the back while preserving the rest of the body in a kind of immobility, that even the slightest movement of the arms which balance the two ends of a handkerchief or her petticoat does not make her lose. A dancer approaches her, all of a sudden he leaps into the air, and lands in measured time so as almost to touch her. He draws back, he jumps again, and excites her by the most seductive play.

The dance becomes enlivened and soon it presents a tableau, of which the entire action at first voluptuous afterwards becomes lascivious. It would be impossible to depict the Chica in its true character, and I will limit myself to saying that the impression which it produces is so strong, that the African or Creole, it does not matter of what shade, who comes to dance it without emotion, is considered to have lost the last spark of vitality.

"The Calenda and the Chica are not the only dances in the Colony derived from Africa. There is also another which has been long known there especially in the western part, and it is called Voodoo.

"But it is not merely as a dance that Voodoo deserves consideration, or at least it is accompanied by circumstances which ranks it among those institutions where superstition and bizarre practices have a considerable part.

"According to the Negro Aradas,[10] who are the real devotees of Voodoo in the Colony, and who keep up its principles; and rules, Voodoo signifies an all powerful and supernatural being on whom depends whatever goes on in the world. But this being is the non-poisonous serpent, or a kind of adder, and it is under its auspices that all those assemble who profess the same doctrine. 'Knowledge of the past, realization of the present, foreknowledge of the future, all pertain to this adder, which, however, agrees to communicate its power, and make known its wishes, only through the medium of a high priest whom its devotees select, and even more so through that of the Negress, whom the love of the other has raised to the rank of high priestess.

"These two ministers who claim themselves inspired by their god, or in whom the gift of inspiration is really manifested for the devotees bear the pompous names of King and Queen, or the despotic ones of master and mistress, or finally the touching titles of papa and mama. They are, for life, the chiefs of the grand family of

Voodoo, and they have the right to the limitless respect of those who compose it. It is they who determine if the adder approves of the admission of a candidate into the society, it is they who prescribe the obligations, the duties which he must fulfil; it is they who receive the gifts and presents which the god expects as a just homage; to disobey them, to resist them, is to resist God himself, and expose oneself to the greatest misfortunes.

"This system of domination on the one side, and of blind obedience on the other, once well established, they meet at fixed intervals at gatherings where King and Queen Voodoo preside, according to those usages which they may have brought from Africa, and to which Creole customs have added many variants and traits which disclose European ideas; for example, the scarf or the rich belt which the Queen wears in this assembly, and which she sometimes varies.

"The reunion for the true Voodoo, that which has least lost its primitive purity, never takes place except secretly, when the night casts its shadows, and in a secure place, and under cover from every profane eye. There each initiated puts on a pair of sandals and fastens around the body a more or less considerable number of red handkerchiefs or at least of handkerchiefs in which this colour is strongly predominant. The Voodoo King has more beautiful handkerchiefs and in greater numbers and one which is entirely red and which he binds around his brow is his crown. A girdle, usually blue, puts the finishing touch to display his striking dignity.

"The Queen clad with a simple luxury, shows also her predilection for the colour red, which is most frequently that of her sash or belt.

"The King and Queen take their place at one end of the room near a kind of altar on which is a box where the serpent is kept and where each member can see it through the bars.

"When they have made sure that no busy-body has gained admission to the enclosure, they begin the ceremony with the adoration of the adder, by protestations to be faithful to its cult and submissive to whatever it may prescribe. With hands placed in those of the King and Queen, they renew the promise of secrecy which is the foundation of the association, and it is accompanied by everything horrible that delirium has been able to devise to make it more impressive.

"When the devotees of Voodoo are thus disposed to receive the impressions which the King and Queen desire to make them feel, they finally take the affectionate tone of compassionate father and mother, boasting to them of the good-fortune which is attached to whoever is devoted to the Voodoo; they urge them to confidence in it, and to give proof of this by following their advice as to the way they are to conduct themselves in the most important circumstances.

"Then the crowd scatters, and each according to his needs, and following the order of seniority in the sect, come to implore the Voodoo. For the most part they, ask of it talent to direct the mind of their masters; but this is not enough. One asks for more money, another the gift to please an unresponsive one; this one wishes to recall a faithless mistress; that one desires a speedy cure, or a long life. After these, an old hag comes to conjure the god to end the disdain of him whose happy youth she wishes to captivate. A maid solicits eternal love, or she repeats the malediction with which hate inspires her against a preferred rival. There is no passion which does not utter a vow, and even a crime does not always disguise those who have for object its success.

"At each of these invocations, the Voodoo King is wrapped in thought; the spirit is working in him. All of a sudden he takes the box wherein the adder is, places it on the ground and makes the Voodoo Queen stand upon it. As soon as the sacred ark is under her feet, the new pythoness is possessed by the god. She shivers, her entire body is in a convulsive state, and the oracle speaks by her lips. At times she flatters and promises happiness, again she inveighs and breaks out in reproaches; and according to her heart's desire, or her own interests, or her caprice, she dictates as obligatory without appeal whatever it pleases her to prescribe, in the name of the adder, to the imbecile crowd which opposes not even the smallest doubt to the monstrous absurdity, and which only knows to obey all that is despotically prescribed.

"After all the questions have received some sort of an ambiguous answer from the oracle, they form. a circle, and the adder is replaced on the altar. This is the time when they bring to it a tribute, which each one has tried to make most worthy of it, and which they place in a covered hat, that a jealous curiosity may not cause anyone to blush. The King and Queen promise to make this acceptable to it. It is by the profits of these offerings that they pay the expenses of the assembly, that they obtain help for members absent or present, who are in need, or from whom the society expects something for its glory or its renown. Suggestions are made, measures are determined, actions are prescribed which the Voodoo Queen always declares to be the will of god, and which have not as invariably good order and public tranquillity as an object. A new oath, as execrable as the first, engages each one to silence as regards all that has passed, to give assistance to whatever has been determined, and sometimes a vessel wherein is the blood of a goat, still warm, goes to seal on the lips of the congregation the promise to suffer death rather than reveal anything, and even to inflict it on anyone who forgets that he is thus solemnly bound to secrecy.

"After that, there begins the dance of the Voodoo.

"If there is a candidate to be received, it is with his admission that the ceremony begins. The Voodoo King traces a large circle with some substance that blackens, and places therein the one who wishes to be initiated, and in his hands he puts a packet of herbs, horse-hair, pieces of horn, and also other disgusting objects. Tapping him lightly, then, on the head with a little wooden wand, he intones an African chant which those who surround the circle repeat in chorus; then the candidate begins to tremble and to dance; this is what is termed to 'make Voodoo.' If by mischance the excess of his transport makes him leave the circle, the chant ceases at once, the Voodoo King and Queen turn their backs on him to avert misfortune. The dancer recovers himself, reenters the circle, begins anew, drinks, and finally becomes convulsive. Whereupon the Voodoo King orders him to stop by tapping him lightly on the head with his wand, or stirring stick, or even with a blow of the voodooistic whip if he judges it fitting. He is conducted to the altar to take the oath, and from that moment he belongs to the sect.

"The ceremonial finished, the King places his hand or his foot on the box wherein is the adder, and soon he becomes agitated. This condition he communicates to the Queen, and by her the commotion is spread around, and each one goes into contortions in which the upper part of the body, the head and the shoulders seem to be dislocated themselves. The Queen above all is a prey to the most violent agitations; she goes from time to time to seek new frenzy from the Voodoo serpent; she shakes the box, and the little bells with which it is decorated produce the effect of a fool's bauble. The delirium increases. It is even further aroused by the use of spiritous liquors which in the intoxication of their imagination the devotees do not spare, and which in turn keeps them up. Fainting fits, swoonings follow for some, and a kind of madness for others; but with them all there is a nervous trembling which they seem unable to control. They ceaselessly whirl around. And finally it comes about that in this sort of Bacchanalia, they tear their clothes and bite their own flesh; others who become senseless and fall to the floor, are carried, without interrupting the dance, to a nearby room, where in the darkness a disgusting prostitution holds the most horrible sway. Finally, weariness puts an end to those demoralizing scenes, but for a renewal of which they have taken good care to fix a time in advance.

"It is most natural to believe that Voodoo owes its origin to the serpent cult, to which are particularly addicted the inhabitants of Juida (Whydah), who it is said come originally from the Kingdom of Ardra, of the same Slave Coast, and when one has read to what an extreme these Africans carry the superstition for this animal, it is easy to recognize it in what I am about to relate.

"What is unquestionably true, and at the same time most remarkable in Voodoo, is that sort of magnetism which prompts those who are assembled to dance to insensibility.

The prepossession in this regard is so strong that even the Whites found spying on the mysteries of this sect, and touched by one of the members who have discovered them, are sometimes set to dancing, and have agreed to pay the Queen Voodoo, to put an end to this punishment. Nevertheless, I cannot refrain from remarking that never has any man of the constabulary who has sworn to fight Voodoo, felt the power which forces one to dance, and which has doubtlessly preserved the dancers themselves from the necessity of taking flight.

"Without doubt, to assuage the fears which this mysterious

cult of Voodoo causes in the Colony, they pretend to dance it in public, to the sound of drums and with the clapping of hands; they even have it follow a repast where they eat nothing but poultry. But I affirm that this is nothing more nor less than a scheme to escape the vigilance of the magistrates, and the better to assure the success of these dark conventicles which are not a place of amusement and pleasure, but rather a school where feeble souls go to deliver themselves to a domination which a thousand circumstances can render baneful.

"One cannot believe to what an excess extends the dependence in which the Chiefs of the Voodoo hold the other members of the sect. There is not one of these latter who would not choose anything in preference to the misfortune with which he is threatened if he does not go regularly to the assemblies, if he does not blindly obey whatever the Voodoo commands him. One has seen that the fear of it has been sufficiently aroused to deprive them of the use of reason, and those who, in a fit of frenzy, have uttered shrieks, shun the gaze of men and excite pity. In a word, nothing is more dangerous, by all accounts, than this cult of the Voodoo, founded on this extravagant idea; but of which one can make a truly terrible force where the 'ministers of being' whom they have honoured with the name, know and can do everything.

"Who will believe that Voodoo gives place to something further, which also goes by the name of dance? In 1768, a negro of Petit-Goave, of Spanish origin, abusing the credulity of the Negroes, by superstitious practices, gave them an idea of a dance, analagous to that of the Voodoo, but where the movements are more hurried. To make it even more effective the Negroes place in the rum, which they drink while dancing, well crushed gun-powder. One has seen this dance called Dance to Don Pédro, or simply Don Pédro, induce death on the Negroes; and the spectators themselves, electrified by the spectacle of this convulsive exercise, share the drunkenness of the actors, and hasten by their chant and a quickened measure, a crisis which is in some way common to them. It has been necessary to forbid dancing Don Pédro under grave penalty, but sometimes ineffectually."[11]

According to Moreau de Saint-Méry, then, four kinds of dances were indulged in by the Haitian slaves before the insurrection. The Calenda and the Chica have accompaniments of drums, etc. and the Voodoo and Don Pédro in which there is no mention of such instruments. In fact, drums and the clapping of hands are actually introduced at the pretended Voodoo which was invented as "a scheme to escape the vigilance of the Magistrates and the better to assure the success of these dark conventicles which are not a place of amusement and pleasure," as we are expressly told. Here we have the first main distinction-the presence or absence of drums.

Don Pédro, being an outgrowth from Voodoo with even the year of its origin, 1768, clearly defined, may be passed over for the present with the single remark that in place of the goat of Voodoo, the pig becomes the particular animal of sacrifice.

Voodoo itself as described by Moreau de Saint-Méry bears a close resemblance to its prototype of Whydah, making due allowance for local conditions, and it clearly satisfies all our requisites to be classed as worship in the strict sense of the word, as distinct from a mere Cult.[12] Furthermore, despite the rankling controversy concerning modern Voodoo in Haiti, all disputants seemingly accept Moreau de Saint-Méry's account, at least substantially. We are safe, then, in making this our starting point in our study of Haitian Voodoo.

It is also generally agreed, that the slave insurrection was fostered and made possible by nocturnal assemblies that have been commonly ascribed to Voodoo.

This uprising of the slaves which resulted in the first massacre of the Whites in Haiti, in 1791, is thus described by Dr. Dorsainvil: "It was then that Boukman entered on the scene and determined to arouse the imagination and the senses. Born in Jamaica, Boukman was a N'Gan or priest of Voodoo, the principal religion of the Dahomans. His tall statue, his herculean strength, had attracted the attention of the Master of the Plantation, Turpin, who had him appointed successively an overseer and a coachman. Over all the slaves who came in contact with him he exercised an ascendancy which became extraordinary.

"To put an end to all hesitation and to arouse complete devotion, he gathered together on the night of August 14, 1791, a large number of slaves in a clearing in the Caiman woods, near Morne-

Rouge. All were assembled when a tempest broke. The jagged flashes of lightning illuminating a sky of low and sombre clouds. In a few minutes a torrential rain flooded the ground; at length under the repeated assaults of a violent wind, the trees of the forest writhed, moaned, and even their heavy branches, torn away, fell with a crash.

"In the midst of this impressive setting, the bystanders, motionless, seized with holy terror, saw an old Negress arise, her body shaking with prolonged shivers; she chants, spins around, and whirls a large cutlass above her head. Rigid stance, gasping breath, silence, blazing eyes fixed on the Negress, the audience is fascinated. Then is brought in a black pig, whose grunting is lost in the uproar of the storm. With a quick movement, the inspired priestess plunges her cutlass into the throat of the animal. The blood gurgles forth, it is collected foaming, and distributed round about to the slaves, all drink of it, all swear to carry out the orders of Boukman."[13]

Since Boukman was a Jamaican it would be reasonable to suppose that he introduced Jamaican features into the cult as he practiced it. In all probability he had been banished from Jamaica for complicity in previous unrest there. His administering of the solemn fetish oath bears resemblance to the Myalistic ceremonial that will be discussed in a later chapter. In any case the sacrificial victim was a pig, the rite strictly speaking belonged to the Don Pédro and not to Voodoo proper. This fact alone suggests that Don Pédro, which had started only twenty-three years previously, in its very origin, may have been devised precisely in preparation for such an uprising.

Very little notice was paid to Haitian Voodoo by the outside world until 1884, when there appeared a book which has caused no end of controversy from that day to this. It was entitled *Hayti or the Black Republic*, and the author was Sir Spencer St. John. His claim to credibility was based on the following facts. Before becoming her Majesty's Envoy Extraordinary and Minister Plenipotentiary to Mexico, he had been England's Resident and Consul-General in Haiti for more than two decades. Secondly, as he says himself, he had personally known "the Haitian Republic above twenty-five years."[14] Again writing from. Mexico, November 13, 1888, in the introduction to his Second Edition, he says of his original work: "The most difficult chapter to write was that on 'Vaudoux-worship and Cannibalism.' I have endeavoured to paint them in the least sombre colours, and no one who knows the country will think that I have exaggerated: in fact, had I listened to the testimony of many experienced residents, I should have described rites at which dozens of human victims were sacrificed at a time. Everything I have related has been founded on evidence collected in Haiti, from Haitian official documents, the press of Port-au-Prince, from trustworthy officers of the Haitian Government, my foreign colleagues, and from residents long established in the country,—principally, however, from Haitian sources."[15] And: "As my chapter on Vadoux-worship and Cannibalism excited considerable attention both in Europe and the United States, and unmitigated abuse in Haiti, I decided again to look into the question with the greatest care. The result has been to convince me that I underrated the fearful manifestations; I have therefore rewritten these chapters, and introduced many new facts which have come to my knowledge."[16] In view of this last statement all our quotations will be taken from this Second Edition of the work.

Let us, then, carefully weigh the testimony of Sir Spencer St. John. At the very outset, he states: "I must notice that there are two sects which follow the Vaudoux-worship—those who only delight in the flesh and blood of white cocks and spotless white goats at their ceremonies, and those who are not only devoted to these, but on great occasions call for the flesh and blood of 'the goat without horns,' or of human victims. It is a curious trait of human nature that these cannibals must use a euphemistic term when speaking of their victims, as the Pacific Islanders have the expression of 'long pig.'"[17]

We must here remark the careful distinction between the cults in Haiti, and while the author does not also distinguish them by name, the legitimate cult, if we may so term it, is Voodoo proper, while the cannibalistic element belongs to Don Pédro. Further, it should be noted that while the human sacrifice is called the "goat without horns" it is really substituted, not for the goat of Voodoo, but for the pig of Don Pédro: just as in those Pacific Islands that are referred to, where the term "long pig" is used.

But to resume St. John's narrative: "When Haiti was still a French Colony, Vaudoux- worship flourished, but there is no distinct mention of human sacrifice in the accounts transmitted to us. In Moreau de Saint-Méry's excellent description of the island, from whose truthful pages it is a pleasure to seek for information, he gives us a very graphic account of fetishism. as it existed in his day, that is, towards the close of the last century." He means of course the eighteenth century. Then follows a lengthy citation from the very passage that we have already quoted.

At the close of the quotation, St. John observes: "In studying this account, freely taken from Moreau de Saint-Méry, I have been struck how little change, except for the worse, has taken place during the last century. Though the sect continues to meet in secret, they do not appear to object to the presence of their countrymen who are not yet initiated. In fact, the necessity of so much mystery is not recognized, since there are no longer any French magistrates to send these assassins to the scaffold."[18]

A few pages further on, we read: "After studying the history of Haiti, one is not astonished that the fetish worship continues to flourish. The Negroes imported from the west coast of Africa naturally brought their religion with them, and the worship of the serpent was one of its most distinguishing features. Saint-Méry writes of the slaves arriving with a strange mixture of Mohammedanism and idolatry, to which they soon added a little Catholicism. Of Mohammedanism I have not myself observed the faintest trace. When the Negroes found the large, almost harmless serpent in Haiti, they welcomed it as their god, and their fetish priests soon collected their followers around them. The French authorities tried to put down all meetings of the Vaudoux, partly because they looked upon them as political, but they did not succeed. Many of the tribes in Africa are to this day cannibals, and their ancestors no doubt imported this taste into the French colony."[19]

Sir Spencer St. John had already remarked, "I have been informed on trustworthy testimony that in 1887 cannibalism was more rampant than ever,"[20] and now in the body of his work he writes: "There are in Haiti, as I have before noticed, two sects of Vaudoux-worshippers; one, perhaps the least numerous, that indulges in human sacrifices;-the other, that holds such practices in horror, and is content with the blood of the white goat, and the white cock. ... In the country districts the Catholic priests say these fetish-worshippers call themselves 'Les Mystères,' and that they mix Catholic and Vaudoux ceremonies in a singular manner; the name probably refers to the rites they practice."[21] And, "I have been informed that, besides the goat and cock, the Vaudoux priests occasionally sacrifice a lamb. ... It is carefully washed, combed, and ornamented with bunches of blue ribands before being sacrificed."[22]

Let us come now to a spectacle that is even more revolting than any of those already described-one, in fact, where we are told that the rites actually included human sacrifice. The following letter appeared in the NEW YORK WORLD of December 5, 1886. The writer of it is personally vouched for by Sir Spencer St. John who quotes the letter in full.

"I spent some weeks in Cap Haitien, one of the largest and most important cities in Haiti, and while there I met a number of

Dominican gentlemen, who for various reasons had been compelled to spend a long time in the sister republic. These gentlemen talked a great deal about the existence of cannibalism, and insisted that its existence was not, as all Haitians claim, merely in the minds of the writers who desire to publish sensational stories. I had shut my eyes and ears to the customs of the country people, and moreover I never allowed myself to think it possible that such horrible practices, as these gentlemen assured me were common, existed. Therefore I tried in every way to disabuse them of the illusions which I thought they entertained. Among these Dominicans was one who, irritated by my constant denials, determined to prove to me that his assertions were true. In April (1886) the workers on one of the coffee- plantations near Le Cap intended to have some kind of demonstration in honour of one of their superstitious observances, and my friend learned that, incidental to the Vaudoux-worship (which by the way, unaccompanied by human sacrifices no Haitian will deny exists), there would be a human sacrifice. In some manner my friend had ingratiated himself with certain of the Negro labourers who were to attend the sacrifices, and induced them to allow him and me to be present, also. On the evening of April 19 he came to my house, where both of us dressed ourselves in the ordinary country working-man's costume, and then had our hands and faces well blacked by the Negro who was to conduct us to the Vaudoux temple. To reach the temple we rode out over the smooth wagon-road which runs to and through the place called Haut-du-Cap, and when we had gotten about three miles beyond the little tavern on that place, where everybody stops for refreshments, our conductor suddenly left the highway, and by a little winding bridle-path led us up the big mountain to a spot about half-way up the side.

"Here the Negroes had constructed a rude wooden shanty among the trees and where it could be hardly noticed by any passer-by, if such there might be in that lonely quarter. Into this miserable hut we were ushered by our guide, who to obtain admittance, uttered some signal words to the two brawny Negroes who stood guard at the entrance, and who closely interrogated every person who entered. We were apparently a little late. In the single room there was a motley crowd of Negroes, men and women, congregated round a sort of wooden throne erected in the centre of the room. On this throne arranged in many coloured long gowns and adorned with tawdry finery, there sat on chairs draped with flaming red cloth, a mail and a woman. They were the Papaloi and Mamanloi, or priest and priestess, of the order of the Vaudoux. At their feet was the box which contained the 'holy serpent,' which was being worshipped by this ungodly assemblage. Behind the throne was stretched across from wall to wall a red cloth partition, which divided the room, or rather which made another and smaller apartment behind it. As we entered the people were singing a chant low and monotonous, and at a sign from our mentor, we, my friend and I, joined it. When this chant had been finished, there succeeded an interval of deathly quiet during which the worshippers appeared to be engaged in prayer. Suddenly the silence was broken by the priest, who with violent gestures, and almost shrieking his words, harangued his audience for ten or fifteen minutes. He told them there was but one thing to do by which they might obtain spiritual as well as temporal reward, to adore the serpent and obey implicitly and without question its slightest order. The attitude of the people showed that they comprehended the injunction and would obey. When he had wrought the crowd to a sufficiently high pitch of enthusiasm, the priest suddenly dropped his talk, and bursting into a chant again, was immediately joined by the others. A weird dance followed, the people singing as they danced, and gradually becoming almost delirious in their fervour. The place was soon in ail awful tumult, some of the women, who especially seemed to have lost all control over themselves, even climbing up to the rafters, wriggling their bodies, hissing, and trying in every way to imitate the movements of the snake.

"This ghastly dance was continued for two hours more, when silence was again produced by the appearance from behind the red curtain of two men leading by the hand a little trembling Negro boy in white robes. The child was led to the throne, and mounting it, he prostrated himself twice before the man and woman seated there. The Papaloi, holding his hands over the boy's head, blessed him in the name of the sacred serpent, and then asked him in pompous language what he most desired in the world. The little fellow, glancing up into the faces of his two conductors, replied (and the reply had evidently been taught him), 'That object above all other objects in the world which l most desire is the possession of a little virgin.' Hardly had he spoken when from the encurtained apartment came two women leading a Negro girl of four or five years, also dressed in the purest white. The second child was led to the throne and stood confronting the boy. Again the boy was asked what he most desired, and when he had repeated his former answer, both he and the girl were at once thrown down on their backs and bound band and foot.

"A burly Negro, knife in hand, separated himself from the crowd, who had been watching the proceedings with breathless interest, and mounted the throne. Reaching the boy, he said something to the men, who with their hands over his mouth was trying to stop the little fellow's cries, and they held their victim by the feet up in the air. With a single slash across the little throat, the brutal executioner killed the child, and the others held him whilst the life-blood gushed into the receptacle placed below to receive it.

"At this moment an involuntary exclamation of horror escaped me, and immediately all eyes were turned towards me, looking with distrust and suspicion. The horrible proceedings on the throne were suspended, and a hasty consultation was held among the people on it. Fearing for my life, and obeying a slight signal from our guide, I somehow got out of the door, mounted my horse and rode as hard as I could to the town. The worshippers did not suspect that I was a white man. They assumed probably that I was a novice and not yet hardened to the sight. At any rate I was not pursued, and my friend was not interfered with. He remained until the end, joined me that night, or rather morning, and told me that the little girl had been killed in the same manner as the boy, and that then the bodies had been cut up, cooked, and eaten by the wretches.

The whole awful orgy was ended only when every person present had become helplessly intoxicated."[23]

James Anthony Froude, writing in 1888, refers to Sir Spencer St. John's account, "Which," he says, "they cry out against with a degree of anger which is the surest evidence of its truth."[24]

Of his own visit to Port-au-Prince, he writes:—"Immorality is so universal that it almost ceases to be a fault, for a fault implies an exception, and in Haiti it is the rule. . . . So far they are no worse than in our own English islands, where the custom is equally general; but behind the immorality, behind the religiosity, there lies active and alive the horrible revival of the West African superstitions; the serpent worship, and the child sacrifice, and the cannibalism. There is no room to doubt it. A missionary assured me that an instance of it occurred only a year ago within his own personal knowledge. The facts are notorious; a full account was published in one of the local newspapers, and the only result was that the president imprisoned the editor for exposing his country. A few years ago persons guilty of these infamies were tried and punished, now they are left alone, because to prosecute and convict them would be to acknowledge the truth of the indictment."[25]

Two years later the accusation was renewed by Hesketh Prichard in the following words: "Vaudoux, according to its more elect disciples, is an all-powerful deity, but the idea of the masses does not rise above the serpent, which represents to them their god and which presides, in its box, over all their services . . . Vaudoux is cannibalism in the second stage, In the first instance a savage eats human flesh as an extreme form of triumph over an enemy; so the appetite grows until this food is preferred to any other. The next stage follows naturally. The man, wishing to propitiate his god, offers him that which he himself most prizes. Add to this sacrifice the mysteries and traditions of the ages, and you have the Vaudoux of today. . . . Cannibalism has been brought as a very general accusation against the Haitians, but although there is no doubt that the child sacrificed in the worst Vaudoux rites is afterwards dismembered, cooked, and eaten, I do not think of recent years the practice of cannibalism, unconnected with sacrifice, is in any degree prevalent, although it is equally certain that scattered instances do still come to light. Haiti is the sole country with any pretence to civilization where a superstition contaminated by such active horrors exists."[26]

Such scathing accusations, whether true or false, could not fail to attract the notice of friends of Haiti, and many official and unofficial answers or rather refutations have been attempted. Notable among these defenders of the reputation of the Black Republic may be cited J. N. Léger, who, while Envoy Extraordinary and Minister Plenipotentiary of Haiti to the United States, in 1907 published simultaneously in French and English a work entitled *Hayti. Her History and Her Detractors*.[27] However, his partisan and exaggerated view is betrayed by his statement: "The island which is now called Haiti is the only one in the West Indies where cannibalism has never prevailed."[28] No doubt his ire has been provoked by the assertion of

Prichard, "Haiti is the sole country with any pretence to civilization where a superstition contaminated by such active horrors exists," which we have recently quoted. But in any case, the very aspersion which he so indignantly repudiates in the case of his native island, he gratuitously cast against all the rest of the West Indies. This in itself might well make us cautious about accepting his reliability as a witness. And further on the very page where we find this bald accusation, he admits on the authority of Moreau de Saint-Méry[29] that of the Blacks imported to the Island of Haiti as slaves, one tribe at least was anthropophagous. This he terms "the small tribe of the Mondongues," but seeks to show that the gentle influence of the Congo Negroes entirely tamed this unnatural instinct and blotted out the practice. But where has it been recorded of savages, that those of gentler traits prevailed over the warlike and the blood-thirsty?

To Sir Harry H. Johnston more attention must be paid when he comes forward as a defender of Haiti's fair name and reputation. He writes: "At least two out of the three millions of Haitian Negroes are only Christians in the loose statistics of geographers. They are still African pagans, with a vague recognition of the Cross as an unexplained but potent symbol. They believe in a far off scarcely heeding Deity and a multitude of spirits, ancestral and demiurgic. Magic or empirical medicine ('Wanga') is, of course, believed in; and ranges in scope from genuine therapeutics to sorcery, mesmerism, and poisonings. As to Vuduism, much exaggeration and untruth have been committed to paper on this subject, so far as it affects Haiti. Snake worship is of doubtful occurrence, owing to the rarity of snakes in Haiti.[30] Such harmless snakes as do exist are tolerated in some villages or fetish temples for their rat-killing propensities. The idea has therefore got abroad that they are 'kept' as sacred animals by the Vudu priests or priestesses.

Sacrifices of eggs, rum, fowls, possibly goats (white fowls or white goats preferred) are offered to ancestors or minor deities presiding over the fertility of crops, rainfall (nature forces in fact), and various small animals (perhaps even human remains) are deemed useful in sorcery. . . . Isolated instances—about four or five—of cannibalism (the killing and eating of children) have occurred in the criminal records of Haiti during the last twenty years, but the convicted were, in nearly all cases, punished with death; the one or two not executed had been proved to be mad, and were confined in prison or asylum. These acts of cannibalism were mostly examples of mad religious exaltation.

Haiti 'Vuduism' has absorbed elements of Freemasonry and Christianity. It predicts the future, investigates crime, arranges love affairs. . . . The 2,500,000 Haitian peasants are passionately fond of dancing, will even sometimes dance almost or quite naked. And following on this choreographic exercise is much immorality. It is for these dances and not for mystic 'Vudu' purposes that the drums may be heard tapping, tapping, booming, rattling at night. No secret is made, nor is any shame felt about these village dances, in which many young people take part."[31]

Of the neighboring island of Cuba, Johnston writes: "The white Cubans charge the Negroes with still maintaining in their midst the dark Vudu or Hudu mysteries of West Africa. There seems to be no doubt that the black people of Cuba (not the mulattoes) do belong, to a number of secret or Masonic societies, the most widely-heard-of being the NYANNEGO; and it is possible that these confraternities or clubs are associated with immoral purposes. They originated in a league of defence against the tyranny of the masters in the old slavery days. Several of them (as described to me) sounded as harmless as our United Order of Buffaloes. But those seeking after scientific truth should discount much that may be read on Vuduism. This supposed Dahomean or Niger cult of the python or big serpent (Monitor, lizard, crocodile or leopard), with which are associated frenzied dancing, mesmerism, gross immorality, cannibalism or corpse eating, really exists (or existed) all over West Africa, from Sierra Leone to Tanganyika, and no doubt was introduced by Inner Congo, Niger Delta or Dahomey slaves into Haiti, Cuba, Louisiana, South Carolina, Jamaica, the Guianas and Brazil. Where Christianity of a modern type has obtained little or no influence over the Negro slaves and ex-slaves, these wild dances and witchcraft persist.[32] They are fast becoming a past phase in the life-condition of the American Negro, and much of the evidence to the contrary is out of date, or is manufactured by sensation-mongers for the compilation of magazine articles."[33]

Of the kindred cult in Cuba, Johnston further states: "The last vestige of noxious witchcraft lingering among the Cuban Negroes is (said to be) the belief that the heart's blood of the heart of a white child will cure certain terrible diseases if consumed by the sufferer. The black practitioners who endeavour to procure this wonderful remedy are known as 'Brujos' or 'Brujas' (*i. e.* male or female sorcerers). At the time I was in Cuba (December, 1908), there were four or five Negroes awaiting trial on this charge at Havana. Other cases—said to have been proved beyond a doubt—have occurred in Eastern Cuba within the last two or three years. But all these stories and charges are vague hearsay, and during the short time at my disposal I was not able to get proof of one. There is little doubt that occasionally in the low quarters of the old Spanish towns little white girls do disappear. It is too readily assumed that the Negro is at fault."[34]

Scarcely had these words of Johnston in defence of Haiti been written before a new attack was launched. Stephen Bonsal asserts without hesitation: "The truth is, that while you need have no fear whatever of eating human flesh in Haiti disguised as roast or as a round of beef, there is no place in the world where you could so easily satisfy a cannibalistic craving as in this land. . . .

"Voodoo is not a written creed over which a house of bishops presides publicly, a fact which should account for the many and extremely varied versions of its practices which are in circulation through the world. It is certainly not a mere veneer or an old garment from the Congo days of the black race which has not yet been cast away. But it is a substantial edifice of West African superstition, serpent worship, and child sacrifice which exists in Haiti today, and which undoubtedly would become rampant throughout the island were it not for the check and control upon native practices which the foreign residents exercise.

"Several Roman Catholic priests, who have long resided in the heart of Haiti, told me that one of the hardships and difficulties of the combat against African darkness upon which they are engaged, is the extreme reticence not only of the active Voodooists themselves, but of all blacks in regard to the fetish-worshipping rites.

"A Haitian is often absolutely lacking in that form of self-respect which is the last to depart from the most ignoble white. 'All will confess the most despicable crimes,' said my priestly informant, 'and admit having sunk to the lowest form of human degradation, but even should you see him at the dance under the sablier tree at night, all smeared with the blood which may have flowed in the veins of a cock, or goat, or even a human child, he will deny having anything in common with the Voodoo sectaries."[35]

Again: "Of course, the real charge against Haitian civilization is not that children are frequently stolen from their parents and are often put to death with torture, and subsequently eaten with pomp at a Voodoo ceremony, but that Haitians officials, often the highest in the land, not only protect the kidnappers, but frequently take part in the cannibalistic rites which they make possible. This is the charge which I bring and which I am prepared to substantiate in every particular upon evidence which appears to me, and to many others to whom I have submitted it, to be absolutely unimpeachable."[36]

Finally: "Every moonlight night in Haiti you hear in the woods the tom-toming of the Voodoo drums and you know that the devil's priests are astir. On the horizon burns a great campfire, and around it dance weird and shadowy forms. Now and again a piercing shriek rends the air, whether of joy or pain or uttered at the sight of death, you know not, and your friend and mentor, acclimated by twenty years of residence and sophisticated by much study of this strange people, takes you by the hand and says, at least so did mine; 'It is time, high time, to go now.'

"So I never saw the dark frenzy of the African rites descend to the level of the cannibalistic feast which, at least in the last generation, became so frequently a matter of court record, and I believe that today there is only one white man in Haiti, a French priest, who has seen the Voodoo rites carried out to their ghastly conclusion. The little green serpent, the ruling spirit of the abject Guinea coast sect, is often worshipped and the feast terminates in scenes of the most vile debauchery, the 'goat without horns,' however, is not always being sacrificed.

"The cannibalistic feed is only indulged in on rare occasions and at long intervals, and is always shrouded in mystery, and hedged about with every precaution against interlopers; for, be their African ignorance ever so dense, their carnal fury ever so unbridled, the papalois and mamalois, the head men and head women of the serpent worshippers never seem to forget that in these vile excesses there should perhaps be found excuse enough for the interference of the civilized world to save the people of the Black Republic from the further degradation which awaits them.

"Within the last fifteen years human victims have been sacrificed to the great god Voodoo in the national palace of Haiti. Last February there was assembled in the national palace what might justly be called a congress of serpent worshippers. During the life of Mme. Nord, which came to an end in October, 1908, not a week passed but what a meeting of the Voodoo practitioners was held in the executive mansion, and her deathbed was surrounded by at least a score of these witch doctors.

"General Antoine Simon, who recently achieved the presidency, may be the intelligent man he is represented to be by not a few White residents who have come in close contact with him during the years of his government of the southern arrondissements of the island. But one thing is quite sure: if he wishes to remain in the Black House and rule, he must share his sovereignty with the Voodoo priests. If he should exclude them from power and banish them from his presence, his term of office will be of short duration." This prophecy was only too well verified. President Simon ruled about two years and a half, from December 17, 1908 to August 2, 1908, when he made his escape to Jamaica.

Bonsal continues: "There is generally, in fact invariably, much diversity of opinion in Haiti about things Haitian and a host of contradictory counsellors, but upon this point there is practical unanimity. No government can stand in Haiti unless it is upheld by the Voodoo priests or by foreign bayonets. At least two governments in the last fifty years, that of Geffrard and that of Boisrond-Canal, have tried to dispense with the priestly poisoners of men's minds and bodies without at the same time inviting the active support of the civilized world, and in each instance these governments ended in disaster and in bloodshed which lasted for years.

"But while few, if any, of the white men who are at present residents of the island have witnessed the sacrifice of the 'goat without horns,' it is the easiest thing in the world to assist at the preliminaries at least of a Voodoo feast. While my two visits to Haiti, taken altogether, do not cover quite a month, I have without great difficulty attended Voodoo feasts in town and country, in the open air under the moonlit heavens, and in the slums of the capital under the, pallid glare of the electric light."[37]

This would almost indicate that even as visitors to Chinatown are said at times, to be allowed to visit some stage-set opium dive, where the actors for the occasion play up to the part with grewsome reality, so too, perchance the Haitian brethren of the cult may not be averse to turn an honest penny by staging, in the hopes of a small consideration, a Voodoo spectacle to satisfy the demands of tourists who in all good faith fancy that they have been admitted to the most secret mysteries. This would explain much that Seabrook has reported.

Bruce W. Merwin, Assistant Curator at the University of Pennsylvania Museum, writes in THE MUSEUM JOURNAL,[38] under the caption "A Voodoo Drum from Hayti" as follows: "During the first three centuries of colonization of the New World many of the native customs and beliefs of West Africa were introduced and retained by the slaves. Of these fetish worship with considerable development or modification survives even to the present time. In Haiti, as the Voodoo cult with its human sacrifices, this worship is the most primitive and degraded in the two Americas. Attention was drawn to the cult recently by a Voodoo priest's drum presented to the University Museum by Mr. J. Maxwell Bullock, who had received it from 'Major Alexander Williams of the United States Marines. During the insurrection in 1916 in Haiti it had been confiscated and its head punctured because the beating of a drum was the signal to assemble the Voodoo devotees and to incite them to a religious race war." This statement must be accepted with restrictions. The term Voodoo is here employed not technically but in its broadest possible sense. Moreover, anyone familiar with the famous talking drums of Africa might suspect here that during the Haitian troubles messages were actually transmitted through the island by drum language. While I have never found among West Indies the slightest vestige of what must now be a lost art among them, certainly their ancestors were most proficient in this regard and it is still actively practiced in Africa. This much, however, is certain; that the average drummer of the West Indies is as proficient as any army bugler in the conveying of conventional calls and commands.

Merwin further states: "The incessant booming of the drum, the sight and taste of blood, and the great amount of rum drunk cause a religious form of hysteria to sweep over the audience. At the close of the sacrificial ceremony the worshippers begin a dance called the 'loiloichi,' or stomach dance, which is well known in West Africa. The dance gets wilder and. wilder and more degraded until it ends in an orgy of the worst description which lasts until daylight. . . . In Haiti the basis of Voodooism is the frank worship of the sacred green snake that must be propitiated in order to keep off the evil duppies."[39]

We have here to all appearances the Chica dance of slave days with a title that combines the old name with the Voodoo "loi." Hence we may conclude that it was presumably a Voodoo feast at which the Chica was danced.

George Mannington, in 1925 published a work on the West Indies in which he tries to sum up the whole question dispassionately. His book boasts a Foreword by the Rt. Hon. Baron Olivier, a former Governor of Jamaica. The following statement is of interest: "Voodooism or serpent worship, is a degraded form of religion commonly practiced by the ancestors of the present Negroes in the forests of Africa, and was the only religion known to the slaves in the early days. It is said to be followed still in the remoter parts of some of the islands-especially Haiti. It is only fair to say, however, that the more

118

self- respecting of the people indignantly deny that such practices are now followed even among the most backward of the race. But reports to the contrary still persist. It is certain that the Haitian Negroes still assemble in groves or clearing in the forests and dance until they are exhausted to the accompaniment of tom-toms and wild chantings; rum-drinking adds zest to the proceedings. These scenes are occasionally witnessed by spectators concealed from view; it would not be safe to show themselves openly.

Whether or not the more degraded forms of Voodooism are associated with these gatherings cannot be positively stated, though such an assertion is made by many. The belief of the Voodoo (or Vaudoux) votaries appears to be that an all-powerful non- venomous serpent controls all human events, knows all things past, present and future, and communicates his power and will to the priest and priestess who administer the rites, and who are called Papaloi and Mamaloi, loi being the equivalent of the French roi and stands in the Negro terminology—which is without gender—for both king and queen. This 'deity' is supposed to require the sacrifice of 'a goat without horns.' Accordingly the sacrifice of goats accompanied by incantations was the common practice, the animals being afterwards cooked and eaten. It is alleged that the phrase 'goat without horns' was also interpreted to mean a child, that small children were killed and eaten in secret groves, and that the mothers were proud that their children should be chosen for sacrifice. The victim's blood was mixed with rum and drunk."[40]

Dr. Price-Mars, whom we quoted at length when considering Seabrook's *Magic Island*, gives us an extended view of Voodoo as be sees it. Being a devoted and loyal son of the little isle that was once so glorious as the proudest boast of Colonial France, he maybe partial in his views at times, but his sincerity cannot be questioned.

Of the rise of the Haitian community, he tells us: "We know, it is true, what elements have made up the Haitian community. We know that a drove of slaves, imported to San Domingo from the far-stretched western coast of Africa, presented in its entirety a microcosm of all the black races of the continent. We know how from the promiscuous intercourse of the white with his black concubine, and from the artificial conditions of a society governed by the law of castes, there developed a group intermediate between the master and the body of slaves. We know further how the clash of interests and passions, how the confronting of egoisms, and how the principles evoked by the strange revolution, all brought about the insurrection which led the erstwhile slaves to found a nation. Such in a few words is the origin of our people."[41]

Concerning the days that preceded the slave uprising, Dr. Price-Mars writes: "We have at hand two documents whence we may gather valuable information. The first is entitled *L'Essai sur l'Esclavage et Observations sur l'État Présent des Colonies*. It treats of the anxiety which was aroused among the whites by the frequent nocturnal gatherings of the slaves, where they fomented their plots, against the colonial regime. In this connection, the author makes the following remark: 'Their designs would have been undiscoverable if they had not been betrayed by the women concubines of the whites to whom they were generally very much attached. The dance called at Surinan, *Water Mama*, and in our Colony the *Mere de l'eau*, is rigidly forbidden. They make it a great mystery and all that can be said of it is this, that it greatly excites the imagination. They work themselves up to debauchery when they keep the mind fixed on evil purposes. The leader of the conspiracy goes into an ecstasy so as to lose all consciousness; on returning to his senses, he pretends that his god has spoken to him and has commanded some undertaking, but, as they do not adore the same god, they hate him and they spy one on another,—and their projects are nearly always denounced.'

"From this curious document may be drawn an important conclusion. It is that at the period to which it makes reference, probably about 1760, the religion of the slaves had not yet been unified, and without questioning the fact, the author of the Essay gives the reason when he informs us that the Negroes do not adore the same god."[42]

Dr. Price-Mars goes on to state that while at this time, probably about 1760, there could have been no uniformity of religious cult among the Negro slaves, yet "less than thirty years later, we find under the name of 'Voodoo' a religious establishment of which Moreau de Saint-Méry was the first to give a detailed analysis and which has remained famous, and has become the theme, enlarged and borrowed, of most of the accounts which have been given of the cultural ceremonies of Voodoo by writers who have not themselves had the occasion of observing them."[43]

Dr. Price-Mars remarks elsewhere: "The great mass of Negroes gathered from different parts of Africa and brought to San Domingo were from pious races attached to Mohammedanism, Dahoman religion, and a few Catholics."[44]

However, "With many of the slaves Christianity was little more than an external formality to be observed during the hours of the day. By night they met in small groups to practice surreptitiously their old tribal Customs."[45] Gradually "These nocturnal meetings became regular occurrences under the indomitable influence of tile Aradas, the Ibos and the Dahomans."[46]

Showing that during the long formation period there steadily developed a composite religious cult by a process of assimilating the various animistic beliefs of Africa, Islamism included, he observes: "But there was only one religion which retained a solid framework of disciplinary traditions, a sacredotal hierarchy, capable of imposing some of its rites upon the composite beliefs, and this was the Dahoman."[47]

In connection with his criticism of Seabrook's *Magic Island*, Dr. Price-Mars asks a question and then answers it: "Is there a Voodoo initiation whereby a neophyte, it matters not who he is, thanks to the good will of the hougan,[48] may be admitted to the congregation? It seems not. Listen, however. If anyone believes in the rites of

Voodoo and he desires actually to take part in some ceremony, rites of exorcism, of annual commemoration, expiatory rites, etc., be he white or black, he has only to address himself to the first hougan met, who will give him the mode of procedure. As a general rule, the one officiating will not trouble himself to find out how far the applicant is sincere. His mere application is sufficient guarantee of good faith. Seabrook was in a position to make such an application, and I believe that nothing more unusual was done for the sake of making sport.

"On the contrary, is the individual a menial who is ignorant of his own prerogatives? I mean to say supposing that he is an individual, who thus far has been shut out from all participation in the ritual obligations of the Voodoo, and who has suddenly become aware of them, and has been inspired by 'the mysteries.' He may wish 'to renounce,' to wit, to make up the arrears due to the gods, and take a more intimate part in the congregation. Then the hougan proceeds to those ceremonies which are more or less the rites of initiation-baptism of 'loi bossales,' and of the 'hounsis' and of the 'hougainikons.'

"But these initiations are all esoteric. They are accomplished only by degrees. In the case suggested, the first order of the hougan to the neophyte, is a severe penance, sexual and dietary abstinence, penance as regards clothing; then there is the rigorous retreat and the fast, followed by the ceremony of initiation and finally the trials.

"As regards this part of the rite, the initiation is in every way secret. Moreover the ceremony allows variations. Sometimes the hougan keeps himself in a darkened room where he has a pool, the candidates, clothed in white, are stretched on couches in the adjacent room, having each a wide-mouthed pitcher full of water which is supposedly ready to receive the 'Mystery' with which the hougan is going to converse. In fact, the congregation outside the enclosure can hear at a given moment a kind of conversation between the one officiating and the pretended 'Mystery' which, having come at his call, may converse with the subject whom he has honoured with a fellow-feeling towards him, the 'Mystery.' To my mind, this conversation—a probable effect of ventriloquism—is the boldest of trickeries and it is on that account that there is so much need of obscurity and of solitude as is claimed by the hougan. When, at last, the 'Mysteries' have taken possession of the elect, these come forth from the enclosure in procession, carrying their pitchers on head and shoulder, make the round of the arbour where the bulk of the congregation is gathered, taking part in the feverish ecstasy of the dances and submitting to the ordeal of the 'Canzo' which consists in plunging the hand into a boiling pot of mess intended for the cult meal. The aroused congregation cries out at this moment: 'Aie Bobo! Aie Bobo!'

"At other times, it is at a spring, or occasionally on the bank of a river, or, if in a locality where there is neither water course nor Spring, it is beside a large cistern, or even a half-cask that the hougan establishes a 'shrine,' made of a trellis of reed, on which are spread large white cloths. There the gods are thought to establish their temporary domicile. The one officiating enters alone. By his interpretation, the gods, whom certain ones who have died 'serve,' constrain the voice of the dead to converse with their kindred, their friends among the congregation which is kept at a respectful distance. In this variant, the rite assumes a character, half-expiatory, half -initiatory, as it is assumed that the hougan can transfer to the living 'the Mystery' of his departed parent."[49]

Throughout these initiation functions, we notice in clothing and draperies the entire absence of red, which is the characteristic colour of Voodoo. If the rites described really belong to present-day Voodoo, then a marked change has been effected in the whole cultural ritual. As a matter of fact, the entire ceremony as described by Dr. Price-Mars suggests Ashanti origin rather than Dahoman or Whydah.

After a lengthy quotation from Moreau de Saint-Méry, Dr. Price-Mars observed in his earlier book: "This page of Moreau de Saint-Méry assumes in our eyes an importance of the very first order, not only because it is the only authentic document which contains serious facts on the religious manifestations of the Negroes of San Domingo, but on account of the fulness of details, the precision of delineation, the character of the whole work, one recognises at once the evidence of the truth. Well does the author tell us that the sect was secret—and it is still so in our day—his relation actually gives us the impression of a deposition of an eye-witness. However, if as we believe, and as we shall prove later, the ritual of cult is sensibly modified since the colonial epoch, many of the distinctive details in the celebrated description have remained unchanged even today. They help us to establish the primordial elements of Voodoo."[50]

Dr. Price-Mars now makes a very serious mistake by assuming that Voodoo, as he sees fit to portray it at the present day, is substantially unchanged in one hundred and fifty years, and that it is specifically the same rite as it was in slave times. Rather, since he admits that Moreau de Saint-Méry has described accurately the real Voodoo of Colonial times, it would be more profitable to us if he had simply pointed out the present variants; perhaps, however, it would be more accurate to say that it has been so radically changed that the term Voodoo can be applied to it only by an extension, if not distortion, of its meaning. That is, of course, providing that Dr. Price-Mars is actually describing present-day Voodoo to us and not some kindred rite, when he says: "Of these traits the most characteristic is the state of trance in which the individual possessed by the god finds himself enthralled." This is certainly more like an Ashanti function than one from Whydah as noted previously. "The second trait," we are told, "which gives its tone to the ceremony is the dance, a rhythmic dance, to the sound of a trio of long drums to the cadence of the 'assons,' executed on the syncopated airs which a leader improvises, his voice being echoed multifold by the enthusiastic congregation." Drums at a Voodoo ceremony! And what of his assertion that "the initiation is in every way secret." And: "Well does the author tell us that the sect was secret—and it is still so in our day." What secrecy, or even privacy can be had with the blatant summoning of the drums?

"As regards the rest," he continues, "what seems to be the essential of the belief—we speak of the adoration of the adder—this part of the rite has been eliminated from Voodoo or relegated altogether to the background of the ceremonial. We believe it is almost abolished. On this point we may be permitted to give our personal testimony. In the course of our investigations, we have had occasion to assist at numerous Voodoo ceremonies-a hundred at least—of which some were celebrated in the most remote districts, we have never seen, not even once, homage rendered to the adder. And, a remarkable coincidence, the writers either Haitians or foreigners, who have seriously devoted themselves to the question, are unanimous in remarking the same, whether they say it explicitly or they fail to make mention of such a ceremony."[51] With all due respect to the experience of Dr. Price-Mars, one cannot refrain from making the reflection:—Either he was fully initiated into the cult, or he was not. If he was, then he has taken the oath to conceal the true facts; if he was not, then from his own statements, being an uninitiated, he would never be admitted to the full ceremonies.[52]

Furthermore, if the present state of Voodoo in Haiti, is precisely as Dr. Price-Mars describes it, with the serpent eliminated, there must have been a very radical change quite recently. Some twenty years ago, I was assured personally by Haitians in Jamaica, whom I certainly considered worthy of credence, that to their own knowledge, the mixture of Voodoo and Catholicism in Haiti had given rise to many altars with regular tabernacles, such as are commonly found in Catholic churches, but in each case the tabernacle was reserved by the owner for the use of the serpent.

This view is further confirmed by the personal experience of one who spent many years in Haiti and Jamaica. While not free to disclose the name of the party in question, whom we may refer to as Madam X., the writer can unreservedly attest her honesty and sincerity. She was a lady of education and refinement, and the exemplary mother of a family. Of her stay in Haiti she subsequently told a missionary in Jamaica: "When I first moved there, I was told that I must be very careful about my baby, because the natives often stole babies, white babies especially, to use them in their obi rites or services." By obi is here meant witchcraft in its generic form; though, of course, Voodooism would be specifically more correct. Madam X. continues: "Soon after I arrived, a woman living next door, whose husband had been a notorious Obeah man and had died just a short time before, came to visit me. She was very friendly, and when she saw my chapel, she said; 'You know I have a chapel, you must come over and see me and see my chapel which I have for my services; my husband was a great Obeah man and all the great people came to him.' When I went to see her, she showed me a room generously fixed up like a chapel; there was a box corresponding to our tabernacle, an altar and two statues. . . . There was a white goat there which was used in Obeah rites, she used to dress up this goat in the most costly robes; there was a barrel in which was a large snake which was dressed in ribbons. She showed me lots of costly presents which had been given her by rich people, costly robes for the goat, wine, jewels, etc. After her husband's death she had kept up his work. She said that all the people from the president down, even practical Catholics, went to the ignorant Obeah men and women. She added, that in order to get sacred particles the Obeah men and women used to go to communion, keep the Hosts dry in their month, and bring them home to their Obeah chapel and keep them in their tabernacles."[53]

Despite his perfervid descriptions, Seabrook has much of real value and particularly as already noted in the second portion of his book. Thus for example: "Voodoo in Haiti is a profound and vitally alive religion .... Voodoo is primarily and basically a form of worship, and ... its magic, its sorcery, its witchcraft (I am speaking technically now), is only a secondary, collateral, sometimes sinisterly twisted by-product of Voodoo as a faith."[54] And "Voodoo is not a secret cult or society in the sense that Freemasonry or the Rosicrucian cult is secret; it is a religion, and secret only as Christianity was secret in the catacombs, through fear of persecution. Like every living religion it has its inner mysteries, but that is secretness in a different sense. It is a religion toward which whites generally have been either scoffers, spyers, or active enemies, and whose adherents, therefore, have been forced to practice secrecy, above all where whites were concerned. But there is no fixed rule of their religion pledging them to secrecy, and Maman Célie was abrogating nothing more than a protective custom when she gave me her confidence."[55]

Again he says: "Although Damballa, the ancient African serpent god remains enthroned as its central figure, this Voodoo ceremony is not the old traditional ritual brought over from Africa, but rather a gradually formalized new ritual which sprang from the merging in earliest slave days of the African tradition with the Roman Catholic ritual, into which the slaves were all baptized by law, and whose teachings and ceremonials they willingly embraced, without any element of intended blasphemy or diabolism, incorporating modified parts of Catholic ritual—as for instance the vestments and the processional—into their Voodoo ceremonials, just as they incorporated its Father, Son, Virgin, and saints in their pantheistic theology."[56]

We rather suspect that the following passage is, partially at least, ascribable to Dr. Price- Mars from whom much of Seabrook's technical information was gathered. "The worship of the snake in Haiti," he declares, "is by no means so literal as commentators have supposed. It is true that on every Petro altar in Haiti there is a serpent symbol, sometimes painted on the wall, sometimes carved of wood and elevated on a staff. It is true also that living snakes are regarded as sacred objects, not to be injured or molested. One of the commonest and handsomest is a harmless green tree snake which grows to three or four feet in length, but all snakes are held sacred. But the serpent is worshipped symbolically, and not because they believe he has any power of his own; he represents the great god Damballa. . . . So far as I am aware no living serpent is kept 'in a box' or otherwise on any Voodoo altar to-day in Haiti. A negro friend has told me, however, of an Obeah ceremony which he had seen in Cuba in which a living snake was the central object. He said that a large, non-poisonous snake was kept in a big earthern jar on an altar, that some ten or fifteen negroes made a sort of circular endless chain beginning and ending at the rim of the jar by lacing their arms around each others shoulders: that the snake was then drawn from the jar and induced to crawl over their shoulders, making the circuit and returning to the jar."[57]

Finally Seabrook tells us: "It is not my intention to gloss over the fact that actual human sacrifice is also an occasional integral part of the Voodoo ritual in Haiti. . . . That human sacrifice in Voodoo to-day may seem strange and to many persons horrible, but only, I think, because they consider it in terms of 'time.' . . . I have described no human sacrifices on the pages of this book solely for the reason that I never saw one. If I had lived for many years instead of months with Maman Célie in the mountains, it is probable that I should have seen one. Such sacrifices, however, Maman Célie tells me, are rare and performed only under stress of seeming necessity. That they never reach the courts or public notice is due to the fact that when they are pure authentic Voodoo, the sacrificial victim is never kidnapped, stolen, or procured by other criminal means, but always voluntarily offered from within tile religious group. Occasionally also, however, occurs some extraordinary criminal abuse of this practice, followed by denunciation and prosecution. In this category was the case of Cadeus Bellegarde which occurred in 1920. He was a papaloi turned criminal, a pathological monster."[58]

Dr. J. C. Dorsainvil, a Haitian physician of standing, in an address to the Historical and Geographical Society of Haiti stated in 1924: "Ten years ago, in a study published by the review HAITI MEDICALE, we asserted that Voodoo in its psycho-physiological effects consists in this, it is a racial psycho-nervous disorder, of a religious character bordering on paranoia. Our opinion has in no way changed. But as you see the question was then viewed from a medical standpoint.[59]

"We are permitted today to present to you the same question under another aspect, the philological viewpoint. This will be nothing else but a study chapter wherein we trace our origins.

"As much if not more than our revolution, Voodoo has tended to destroy the reputation of our country. The imagination of well-meaning chroniclers, such as St. John our latest visitor, to pass over Alaux, Texier and others, who does his utmost to discover in the frequently inoffensive ceremonies of this cult, the most repugnant scenes of cannibalism and orgies. Some of our journalists even speak of it with that inconsideration and absence of study, with which one can too frequently reproach them.

"We have then a deep interest in shedding the clearest light on the origins of this mysterious cult. This work is easy today, for the activity of investigators has left unturned no corner of the vast moral world of humanity."[60]

Taking up the meaning of the word, Dr. Dorsainvil asserts:

"Voodoo . . . is simply a generic term of the fongbe dialect. . . It is the most important word of the dialect since it includes nearly the whole moral and religious life of the Fons and is the origin, or rather it is the invariable root, of an entire family of words. What is the precise meaning of the world in fongbe? It designates the spirits, good or evil, subordinate to Mawu and, by extension, the statue of one of these spirits, or every object that symbolizes their cult or their power, protective or malevolent."[61] Again, "The most celebrated expression of the religion of the Voodoo is the cult of the serpent or of the adder Da, pronounced Dan, incarnating the spirit Dagbe, pronounced Dangbe." He is writing as a Frenchman. "The two principal sanctuaries of this cult were found in the sacred woods of Somorne near Allada and at Whydah. Among us by contraction, the Dahoman expression Dangbe Allada has become the loa (a Congo word) Damballah, of which the symbol still remains an adder."[62]

Of the establishment of the cult in Haiti, Dr. Dorsainvil has this to say: "By comparison with other African tribes, the Aradas, Congos, Nagos, etc. the Fons have been very much in the minority in San Domingo. How, then, explain the strong religious impress with which they have marked the people? It is here that shows forth all the importance of the Voodoo cult in San Domingo. Whether it is pleasing or not, Voodoo is a great social factor in our history. The colonials tolerated all the noisy dances of the slaves, but feared the Voodooistic ceremonies. They instinctively dreaded this cult with its mystical movements, and felt in a confused way that it could become a powerful element of cohesion for the slaves. They were not mistaken, for it was from the heart of these Voodooistic ceremonies that the great revolt of the slaves of San Domingo developed.

Toussaint himself knew this so well that when he became the first authority of the colony, he no longer tolerated this kind cult"[63] He adds later: "Religion so hierarchic, so enshrouded in mystery, should, it is clear, exercise a powerful attraction in the other African tribes represented in San Domingo. It offered them a body of religious beliefs which were not in the least to be found in the superstitions practiced by themselves. But in branching out, Voodoo divested itself of its original characteristics. It overburdened itself with parasitic beliefs, Aradean, Congoleon, etc."[64]

Dr. Parsons thus begins her article on the Spirit Cult of Haiti, "During a recent folk-tale collecting tour to the south coast of Haiti, I had opportunities to observe combinations in cult of African paganism and French Catholicism of much interest to the student of acculturation, as well as to West Indian folklorist or historian. That this cult has heretofore passed undescribed in Haiti is probably due to the diversion of interest to one of its reputed features, ritual cannibalism or, in journalistic term, voodoo human sacrifice, the folklore of which is wide-spread among all foreigners, white and coloured, in Haiti, as well as among Caribbean neighbours. Some St. Lucia boys shipwrecked in San Domingo told me there that they had become afraid of going on to Haiti, as they once thought of doing, since they had heard how they killed and ate people in Haiti. It was the same story I had heard fifteen years before from the French wife of a Syrian merchant at the Haitian town of Ganaives. This lady felt outraged against the Island 'sauvages.' . . . If human sacrifice occur or has ever occurred in Haiti, it is in connection with the Taureau Criminel, the Criminal Bull, one of the spirits or loi of which there is a large number, both Catholic and African. Between patron saint and West Indian fetish no distinction is made in the cult which may be described as a theory and practice of possession by spirits. There is little or no philosophic or religious expression of the theory to be heard in Haiti, but descriptive details of the practice abound."[65]

Perhaps the most dispassioned account of Voodoo comes from the pen of one who had lived for years in Haiti towards the close of the last century and had sought to study the question scientifically. Eugène Aubin, in giving the results of his researches, dissociates himself from the partisans of every phase of sentiment. His narrative is simple and to the point."[66] Thus: "In the settlement as in the home, Negro life is dominated by old African superstitions, that is to say by the Voodoo cult. Although they point out many traces of it in the United States and in certain islands of the Antilles, it is nowhere more prevalent than in Haiti where its development remains unimpeded. Elsewhere it restricts itself to the exploitation of witchcraft for the profit of some shrewd individuals, which they call Obeah in the English colonies. The historic development of San Domingo is sole cause for the difference in Haiti. Whereas in the other islands fetishism tends, if not to disappear, at least to disguise itself under the influence of Christianity, supported by external force; the independence of Haiti encourages parallel progress, even the confusion of the two beliefs. . . .

"The study of Haitian fetishism is not easy. Those who treat of the subject do so with prejudice or inaccurately. The Fathers Du Terte and Labat scarcely touch on it. The latter restricts himself to a mere expression of distrust. 'The Negroes,' he writes, 'do without scruple what the Philistines attempted; they associate the ark with Dagon and secretly preserve all their old idolatrous worship, with the ceremonies of the Christian religion.' A 'trusty and intelligent Negress' understood little of anything at Descourtelz. As ever Moreau de Saint-Méry was the best informed of colonial writers. The educated creoles pretend complete ignorance of things so gross; unconsciously there survives in them the old prejudices of times when the planter felt himself insecure in his isolation among the Negroes, dreaded their mysterious cult, their secret meetings, their witchcraft and their poisons. For his part, the Negro remains attached to his practices, observant of his initiations.—Z'affe mouton pas z'affe cabrite.—The affairs of the sheep are not those of the nanny-goat, says the creole proverb; the things of the blacks do not concern the whites.

"However uncouth may seem the cult sprung from Haitian fetishism the fault is in no way due to the fundamental principle of their beliefs, which restrict themselves to seeking out the manifestations of the Divinity in the forces of nature. It is a pantheism, as any other, classified by the same standard as ancient paganism or the religions of India. The great wrong of the Negroes was to over-indulge life, in exaggerating the evil character of the supernatural world and in conceiving the universe as peopled with predominantly evil spirits, among which the lois and the ancestors freely enjoyed an aggressive rôle as regards suffering humanity. They came to the conclusion that it was necessary to conjure these evil influences by witchcraft, gifts and sacrifices; to the papalois or sorcerers, people well versed in the mysteries, fell the charge and the profit of these conjurations. . . .

"According to the tribe, the rites and the traditions differ. just as the Negroes of San Domingo came in great numbers from all coasts of Africa, Haitian Voodoo results from the confusion of all the African beliefs. However, there stands out two principal rites, each constituting a distinct cult, the rite of Guinea and the 'Congo rite.' Although the blacks of this colony came in greater numbers from Congo than from Guinea, the followers are divided about equally, according to the origin or the convenience of the families. But, nevertheless, the superstitions of Guinea exercise a prepondering influence on the actual doctrines of Voodoo. In each of the two rites, experts remark a series of subdivisions, corresponding to the different tribes of the north and of the middle coast of Africa. Arada, Nago, Ibo belong to the rite of Guinea; it seems that the north coast has had more agreeable fetishism and freely admits good spirits. The Arada would be the simplest and purest cult of all, knowing nothing whatever of witchcraft.

The spirits venerated on the southern coast are more frequently wicked: these latter frequent the subdivision of the Congo rite, the Congo Franc, the Petro, and the Caplaou.

"The scenes of cannibalism which occur even now at times (an example of this kind was tried in 1904 by the criminal court of Port-au-Prince) would be the work of the adherents, fortunately few in number, of the particular divisions of the Petro and the Caplaou; some may be ascribed to the Mondongue, of which the character is a little out of the ordinary, although belonging to the Congo rite.

"The paraphernalia of all these rites have created a veritable mythology in Haitian Voodoo. The lois, saints, the mysteries found in nature, have received the names of ancient African kings or indeed of the localities where they have been deified. They add the title of Master, Papa or Mister. Legba, Dambala, Aguay, Guede, derived from the rite of Guinea, are the object of an almost universal cult; Master Ogoun, Loco, Saugo, Papa Badère . . . and they have also no end of others. The King of Engole (Angola) and the King Louange (Loango) belong to the Congo rite. . . .

"All the lois wish to be 'served'; and their service belongs to the papalois. Do these ministers restrict themselves to the good lois, namely to the rite of Guinea and to those elements of the Congo, as they say 'who serve with one hand alone'? 'To serve with two hands' implies no less the cult of the evil lois, pitiless deities, craving for blood and vengeance. The houmforts, sanctuaries of these multiple spirits, are on every hand in the plains, where the people, better circumstanced, take care to surround their fetishism with elaborate ceremonies, unknown in the uplands.

"The papaloi is a man versed in the rites, by heredity or study, who has gradually risen in the Voodoo hierarchy. He has sometimes attended the famous houmforts of the plains of Leogane and Arcahaye, received the most secret initiations and undergone the ordeal of an ordination. When these final ceremonies are concluded, the new papaloi presents himself to the faithful, and possessed by the spirit, he intones the chant proper to the loi who, during his life, will be the Maître-caye, the Maître-tête, and to whom will be consecrated the houmfort which he is about to enter.

"The foundation of the Voodoo cult is found in the family. Each familyhead, clothed with a family priesthood, honors the spirit of the ancestors and their protecting lois."[67]

To our way of thinking, then, Voodoo as first found in Haiti was substantially the serpent worship of Whydah; and in the beginning at least, it was but slightly modified by local conditions.

As the children of the African "bush" were ruthlessly torn away from their native haunts, they naturally carried with them the practices and superstitions that served as cherished memories of the past, and thus introduced to their new surroundings the diverse forms of perverted worship or sorcery, as the case might be, and for a time at least clung to their own peculiar customs.

Those who had practiced Ophiolatry in Africa, had a great advantage over the rest. Seemingly they had not lost their deity after all. For the non-poisonous python was waiting their arrival in Haiti. It was the one familiar object to meet their gaze. It was the one connection with the past. Naturally any of the priests and priestesses who were among them would not be slow to put the incident to good account.

In any case, Voodoo quickly became the dominant form of worship among the slaves, but as was to be expected it gradually suffered modifications and even split tip into various sects according to the whim and fancy of some new leader who gained influence among the general body of the slaves.

Thus in 1768, Don Pédro came into being, as seems probable, directly as a means of stirring up the slaves to insurrection. At Whydah the serpent was consulted about the undertaking of war, and in a sense represented the god of war. But now something more aggressive and emotional was required. The serpent naturally was retained, but in the ritual not only were the dances quickened in their tempo, but the pig was substituted for the goat as the sacrificial animal.

With the arrival of Broukman from Jamaica, the Don Pédro cult in Haiti developed further, as it began to take on more and more the form of sorcery. Its religious element is gradually transferred from the service of the good spirits to that of evil spirits, and in course of time it becomes the cult of blood par excellence and finds its climax, at least on rare occasions, in human sacrifice and cannibalistic orgies.

As regards Voodoo proper, the account of Moreau de Saint-Méry, it must be admitted, might seem to indicate that the cult had become formal idolatry. But we should remember that the atheistic tendencies of that day would probably influence the point of view of one who subsequently was to take such an active part in the events that led up to the French Revolution.

There are equally strong indications from the testimony of later observers, thatVoodoo in the nineteenth century could still be classed as formal worship, substantially unchanged though modified in many details.

However, it appears that the religious element in the cult was gradually yielding to social influences. Voodoo feasts are introduced, probably at first as a disguise for the secret session that will follow later. But in time, more and more is made of the accompanying dance, with the consequences that Voodoo in the strict sense of the word begins to wane. And unless Dr. Price-Mars is entirely wrong in his estimate of conditions, the present century finds the cult so modified and changed that it is now Voodoo in name only.

Meanwhile we have a general conglomeration of all the old cults, combined with dances of every description, all imbued with every form of witchcraft and sorcery, posing under the generic term of Voodoo. The religion of the Whydahs has become the witchcraft of the Haitians!

As regards the much resented accusation of human sacrifice and cannibalism, the weight of evidence would indicate that while these abuses are by no means common in Haiti, nevertheless, at times there are sporadic outbreaks. And it would be strange if the orgies of nerve-racking debauchery and dissipation so peculiar to tropical dances when the strong arm of the law does not intervene, did not at times evolve a paranoiac state of irrational craving, and subsequent surreptitious gratification of the lowest instincts in degraded human nature-the animal-like gratification of the "goat without horns" in Haiti and the "long pig" in the distant Pacific Islands.

It must not be supposed, however, that these disgusting orgies are countenanced by the present Government authorities, or that they are of frequent occurrence. Certainly within the coastal districts which are watched over by the American Marines, public Voodoo is non-existent. But back in the hills there must still be many a secretgathering as in the days of slavery, where Voodoo and even Don Pédro at times find outlets for pent-up energy and orgiastic excesses.

Nor on the other hand must this abnormality on the part of a few be held as a reflection on the Haitians as a people. The chapters of recent crimes in our own country, which may bespeak degeneracy and moronism on the part of individuals, would not ascribe these reproaches to the entire nation.

CHAPTER IV
Origin of Obeah

JUST AS in the case of Voodoo there is a fundamental document that has served as a starting point for all writers on the subject, so we have a similar source of information as regards Obeah. This is the *Report of the Lords of the Committee of the Council appointed for the consideration of all matters relating to Trade and Foreign Plantation*, London, 1789.[1] Part III is entitled: *Treatment of slaves in the West Indies, and all circumstances relating thereto, digested under certain heads*, and begins with a consideration of Jamaica, and as noted, the information is furnished by "Stephen Fuller, Agent for Jamaica, and assisted by Mr. Long and Mr. Chisholm. Questions 22 to 26 are as follows:—

"Whether Negroes called Obeah men, or under any other denomination, practicing Witchcraft, exist in the Island of Jamaica?

"By what arts or by what means, do these Obeah men cause the deaths, or otherwise injure those who are supposed to be influenced thereby; and what are the symptons {*sic*} and effects that have been observed to be produced in people, who are supposed to be under the influence of their practice?

"Are the instances of death and diseases produced by these arts or means frequent?

"Are these arts or means brought by the Obeah men from Africa, or are they inventions which have been originated in the islands?

"Whether any or what laws exist in the island of Jamaica for the punishment, and what evidence is generally required for their conviction?" The answer to this questionnaire follows.

"The term Obeah, Obiah, or Obia (for it is variously written), we conceive to be the adjective, and the Obe or Obi the noun substantive; and that by the words Obiah-men and women, are meant those who practice Obi. The origin of the term we should consider of no importance in our answer to the questions proposed, if, in search of it, we were not led to disquisitions that are highly gratifying to curiosity. From the learned Mr. Bryant's ' Commentary on the word Oph, we obtain a very probable etymology of the term: 'A serpent, in the Egyptian language, was called Ob or Aub.'—'Obion is still the Egyptian name for a serpent."—Moses, in the Name of God, forbids the Israelites even to enquire of the daemon Ob, which is translated in our Bible, charmer or wizard, divinator aut sortilegus.'—'The woman at Endor is called Oub or Ob, translated pythonissa, and Oubaios (he cites from Horus Apollo) was the name of the basilisk or royal serpent, emblem of the sun, and an ancient oracular deity of Africa."[2]

"This derivation which applies to one particular sect, the remnant probably of a very celebrated religious order in remote ages, is now become in Jamaica the general term to denote those Africans who in the island practice witchcraft or sorcery, comprehending also the class of what are called Myal men, or those who by means of a narcotic potion made with the juice of a herb (said to be the branched calalue or species of solarium) which occasions a trance or profound sleep of a certain duration, endeavour to convince the deluded spectators of their power to reanimate dead bodies.

"As far as we are able to decide from our own experience and information when we lived in the island, and from concurrent testimony of all the Negroes we have ever conversed with on the subject, the professors of Obi are, and always were, natives of Africa, and none other, and they have brought the science with them from thence to Jamaica, where it is so universally practiced, that we believe there are few of the larger Estates possessing native Africans, which have not one or more of them. The oldest and most crafty are those who usually attract the greatest devotion and confidence, those whose hoary heads, and something peculiarly harsh and diabolic in their aspect, together with some skill in plants of the medicinal and poisonous species, have qualified them for successful imposition upon the weak and credulous. The Negroes in general, whether Africans or Creoles, revere, consult, and abhor them; to these oracles they resort and with the most implicit faith, upon all occasions, whether for the cure of disorders, the obtaining of revenge for injuries or insults, the conciliating of favour, the discovery and punishment of the thief or the adulterer, and the predicting of future events. The trade which these wretches carry on is extremely lucrative; they manufacture and sell their Obies adapted to different cases and at different prices. A veil of mystery is studiously thrown over their incantations, to which the midnight hours are allotted, and every precaution is taken to conceal them from the knowledge and discovery of the white people. The deluded Negroes, who thoroughly believe in their supernatural power, become the willing accomplices in this concealment, and the stoutest among them tremble at the very sight of the ragged bundle, the bottle or the eggshells, which are stuck to the thatch or hung over the door of the hut, or upon the branch of a plantain tree, to deter marauders. In case of poison, the natural effects of it are by the ignorant Negroes ascribed entirely to the potent workings of Obi. The wiser Negroes hesitate to reveal their suspicions, through a dread of incurring the terrible vengeance which is fulminated by the Obeah men against any who should betray them; it is very difficult therefore for the white proprietor to distinguish the Obia professor from any other Negro upon his plantation; and so infatuated are the blacks in general, that but few instances occur of their having assumed courage enough to impeach these miscreants. With minds so firmly prepossessed, they no sooner find Obi set for them near the door of their house, or in the path which leads to it. than they give themselves up for lost. When a negro is robbed of a fowl or a hog, he applies directly to the Obiah- man or woman; it is then made known among his fellow Blacks, that Obi is set for the thief; and as soon as the latter hears the dreadful news, his terrified imagination begins to work, no resource is left but to the superior skill of some more eminent Obiah-man of the neighbourhood, who may counteract the magical operations of the other; but if no one can be found of higher rank and ability, or if after gaining such an ally he should still fancy himself affected, he presently falls into a decline, under the incessant horror of impending calamities. The slightest painful sensation in the head, the bowels, or any other part, any casual loss or hurt, confirms his apprehensions, and he believes himself the devoted victim of an invisible and irresistible agency. Sleep, appetite, and cheerfulness, forsake him, his strength decays, his disturbed imagination is haunted without respite, his features wear the settled gloom of despondency; dirt, or any other unwholesome substance, becomes his only food, he contracts a morbid habit of body, and gradually sinks into the grave. A Negro who is ill, enquires of the Obiah-man the cause of the sickness, whether it will prove mortal or not, and within what time he shall die or recover? The oracle generally ascribes the distemper to the malice of some particular person by name, and advises to set Obi for that person; but if no hopes are given for recovery, immediate despair takes place, which no medicine can remove, and death is the certain consequence. Those anomalous symptoms, which originate from causes deeply rooted in the mind, such as terrors of Obi, or from poisons whose operation is slow and intricate, will baffle the skill of the ablest physician.

"Considering the multitude of occasions which may provoke the Negroes to exercise the powers of Obi against each other, and the astonishing influence of this superstition upon their minds, we cannot but attribute a very considerable portion of the annual mortality among the Negroes of Jamaica to this fascinating mischief.

"The Obi is usually composed of a farrago of materials most of which are enumerated in the Jamaica Law (Act 24, Sect. 10, passed 1760), viz. 'Blood, feathers, parrots beaks, dogs teeth, alligators teeth, broken bottles, grave dirt, rum, and eggshells.' ...

"It may seem extraordinary, that a practice alleged to be so frequent in Jamaica should not have received an earlier check from the Legislature. The truth is that the skill of some Negroes in the art of poisoning has been noticed ever since the colonists became much acquainted with them. Sloane and Barham, who practiced physic in Jamaica in the last century, have mentioned particular instances of it. The secret and insidious manner in which this crime is generally perpetrated, makes the legal proof extremely difficult.

Suspicions therefore have been frequent, but detections rare. These murderers have sometimes been brought to justice, but it is reasonable to believe that a far greater number have escaped with impunity. In regard to the other and more common tricks of Obi, such as hanging up feathers, bottles, eggshells, &e. &c. in order to intimidate Negroes of a thievish disposition from plundering huts, hog-styes, or provision grounds, these were laughed at by the white inhabitants as harmless stratagems, contrived by the more saga-cious for deterring the more simple and superstitious Blacks, and serving for much the same purpose as the scarecrows which are in general use among our English farmers and gardeners. But in the year 1760, when a very formidable insurrection of the Koromantin or Gold Coast Negroes broke out in the parish of St. Mary, and spread through almost every other district of the Island; an old Koromantin Negro, the chief instigator and oracle of the insurgents in that Parish, who bad administered the fetish or solemn oath to the conspirators, and furnished them with a magical preparation which was to render them invulnerable, was fortunately apprehended, convicted, and hung up with all his feathers and trumperies about him; and this execution struck the insurgents with a general panic, from which they never afterwards recovered. The examinations which were taken at that period first opened the eyes of the public to the very dangerous tendency of the Obiah practices, and gave birth to the law which was then enacted for their suppression and punishment.

But neither the terror of the Law, the strict investigation which has ever since been made after the professors of Obi, nor the many examples of those who from time to time have been hanged or transported, have hitherto produced the desired effect. We conclude, therefore, that either this sect, like others in the world, has flourished under persecution, or that fresh supplies are annually introduced from the African seminaries. . .

"We have the following narratives from a planter in Jamaica, a gentleman of the strictest veracity, who is now in London, and ready to attest the truth of them.

"Upon returning to Jamaica in the year 1775, he found a great many of his Negroes had died during his absence; and that of such as remained alive, a least one-half were debilitated, bloated, and in a very deplorable condition. The mortality continued after his arrival, and two or three were frequently buried in one day, others were taken ill, and began to decline under the same symptoms. Every means were tried by medicines, and the most careful nursing, to preserve the lives of the feeblest; but in spite of all his endeavours, the depopulation went on for above a twelvemonth longer, with more or less intermission, and without his being able to ascertain the real cause, though the Obiah practice was strongly suspected, as well by himself as by the doctor and other white persons upon the plantation, as it was known to have been very common in that part of the island. Still he was unable to verify his suspicions, because the patients constantly denied having anything to do with persons of that order, or any knowledge of them. At length a Negress who had been ill for some time, came one day and informed him, that feeling that it was impossible for her to live much longer, she thought herself bound in duty before she died, to impart a very great secret, and acquaint him with the true cause of her disorder, in hopes that the disclosure might prove the means of stopping that mischief which had already swept away such a number of her fellow- slaves. She proceeded to say, that her step-mother (a woman of the Popo[3] country, above eighty years old, but still hale and active) had put Obi upon her, as she had also done upon those who had lately died, and that the old woman had practiced Obi for as many years past as she could remember.

"The other Negroes of the plantation no sooner heard of this impeachment, than they ran in a body to their master, and confirmed the truth of it, adding that she had carried on this business sit-ice her arrival from Africa and was the terror of the whole neighborhood. Upon this he repaired directly with six white servants to the old woman's house, and forcing open the door, observed the whole inside of the roof (which was of thatch), and every crevice of the walls stuck with the implements of her trade, consisting of rags, feathers, bones of cats, and a thousand other articles. Examining further, a large earthen pot or jar, close covered, was found concealed under her bed.—It contained a prodigious quantity of round balls of earth or clay of various dimensions, large and small, whitened on the outside, and variously compounded, some with hair and rags and feathers of all sorts, and strongly bound with twine; others blended with the upper section of the skulls of cats, or stuck round with cats teeth and claws, or with human or dogs teeth, and some glass beads of different colours; there were also a great many eggshells filled with a viscous or gummy substance, the qualities of which he neglected to examine, and many little bags stuffed with a variety of articles the particulars of which cannot at this distance of time be recollected. The house was instantly pulled down, and with the whole of its contents committed to the flames, amidst the general acclamation of all the other Negroes. In regard to the old woman, he declined bringing her to trial under the Law of the island, which would have punished her with death; but from a principle of humanity, delivered her into the hands of a party of Spaniards, who (as she was thought not incapable of doing some trifling kind of work) were very glad to accept and carry her with them to Cuba. From the moment of her departure, his Negroes seemed all to be animated with new spirits, and the malady spread no further among them. The total of his losses in the course of about fifteen years preceding the discovery, and imputable solely to the Obiah practice, he estimates, at the least, at one hundred Negroes. . . .

"The following paper relating to the Obeah man in Jamaica, was delivered by Mr. Rheder.

"Obeah men are the oldest and most artful Negroes; a peculiarity marks them, and every Negro pays the greatest respect to them, they are perfectly well acquainted with medicinal herbs, and know the poisonous ones, which they often use. To prepossess the stranger in favor of their skill, he is told that they can restore the dead to life; for this purpose he is shown a Negro apparently dead, who, by dint of their art, soon recovers; this is produced by administering the narcotic juice of vegetables. On searching one of the Obeah men's houses, was found many bags filled with parts of animals, vegetables, and earth, which the Negroes who attended at the sight of, were struck with terror, and begged that they might be christened, which was done, and the impression was done away. In consequence of the rebellion of the Negroes in the year 1760, a Law was enacted that year to render the practice of Obiah, death.

"The influence of the Professors of that art was such as to induce many to enter into that rebellion on the assurance that they were invulnerable, and to render them so, the Obeah man gave them a powder with which they were to rub themselves.

"On the first engagement with the rebels nine of them were killed, and many prisoners taken; among the prisoners was a very sensible fellow, who offered to discover many important matters, on condition that his life should be spared, which was promised. He then related the part the Obeah man had taken, one of whom was capitally convicted and sentenced to death.

At the place of execution he bid defiance to his executioner, telling him that it was not in the power of white people to kill him; and the Negro spectators were astonished when they saw him expire. On the other Obeah men, various experiments were made with electrical machines and magic lanterns, which produced very little effect; except on one who, after receiving many severe shocks, acknowledged his master's Obeah exceeded his own.

"I remember sitting twice on trials of Obeah men, who were convicted of selling their nostrums, which had produced death. To prove the fact, two witnesses are necessary, with corroborating circumstances."

As regards Barbados in this same Report, Mr. Braithwaite, Agent for the Assembly of the Island, stated: "Negroes formerly called Obeah men, but now more commonly called Doctors, do exist in Barbados, but I understand that they are not so many at present as formerly, and that the number has diminished greatly in the course of the last twenty years." The Council of the Island answered the same question: "There is hardly any estate in the island in which there is not some old man or woman who affects to possess some supernatural power. These are called Obeah Negroes, and by the superstitious Negroes much feared." As regards the origin of Obeah, Mr. Braithwaite answered: "Most undoubtedly imported with them from Africa." The Council replied: "It has been so long known here, that the origin is difficult to trace, but the professors are as often natives as Africans."

The investigation concerning Antigua elicited the information that a few Obeah men were still to be found there though in decreasing numbers. Also that "the arts and means they use seem to operate on the mind rather than on the body; for though it has been supposed that they have occasionally been guilty of administering poison, Dr.

Adair has never had just ground for believing that any disease could be traced to this cause, though he does not deny the probability of it."

Mr. Spooner, the Agent for the Islands of Grenada and St. Christopher, testified: "Obeah among the Negroes must be considered in the same light as witchcraft, second-sight, and other pretended supernatural gifts and communication among white men, with this difference only, that in proportion as the understanding of the Negroes are less cultivated and informed, and consequently weaker than those of white men, the impressions made on their minds by Obeah are much stronger, more lasting, and attended with more extraordinary effects." And further: "Obeah has its origin in Africa, and is practiced entirely by natives from thence: the creole Negroes, seldom, if ever, laying any pretensions to it."

Strange as it may seem, even at the date of this Report, 1789, practically nothing was known of Obeah which had already begun to threaten the white rule in Jamaica. They were satisfied to accept it as the remnant of "a very celebrated religious order in remote ages." It was a reflection of the distant Egyptian Ob of antiquity, etc.

The Council of Barbados alone was awake to the fact that Obeah is itself a vital, living force; that it is self perpetuating. Elsewhere it is taken for granted that Obeah men are to be found solely among "salt-water" Negroes; that with the abolition of the slave trade, Obeah must of necessity die a natural death, as the race of imported Obeah men become extinct.

Even in Jamaica, up to the rebellion of 1760, Obeah occasioned nothing more than scornful mirth at the absurd superstitions of the blacks, and yet for more than a century, a terrible menace had been gathering force and threatening to obliterate the civilization and the morality of the island.

Mary H. Kingsley, in reference to that part of West Africa which had been described by Colonel Ellis, remarks: "From this one district we have two distinct cults of fetish in the West Indies, Voudou and Obeah (Tchanga and Wanga). Voudou itself is divided into two sects, the white and the red—the first a comparatively harmless one, requiring only the sacrifice of, at the most, a white cock or a white goat, whereas the red cult only uses the human sacrifice—the goat, without horns. Obeah on the other hand kills only by poison— does not show the blood at all. And there is another important difference between Voudou and Obeah, and that is that Voudou requires for the celebration of its rites a priestess and a priest. Obeah can be worked by either alone, and is Dot tied to the presence of the snake. Both these cults have sprung from slaves imported from Ellis's district, Obeah from slaves bought at Koromantin mainly, and Voudou from those bought at Dahomey. Nevertheless it seems to me these good people have differentiated their religion in the West Indies consider-ably; for example, in Obeah the spider (anansi) has a position given it equal to that of the snake in Voudou. Now the spider is all very well in West Africa; round him there has grown a series of most amusing stories, always to be told through the nose, and while you crawl about; but to put him on a plane with the snake in Dahomey is absurd, his equivalent there is the turtle, also a focus for many tales, only more improper tales, and not half so amusing."[4]

Here Miss Kingsley is as much in error when she associates Obeah with serpent worship, as she is when she ascribes to the Anansi of Jamaica any rôle at variance with his established place in Ashanti folklore.[5]

W. P. Livingston has well said "Obeahism runs like a black

thread of mischief through the known history of the race. It is the result of two conditions, an ignorant and superstitious receptivity on the one hand, and on the other, sufficient intelligence and cunning to take advantage of this quality. The Obeah Man is any Negro who gauges the situation and makes it his business to work on the fears of his fellows. He claims the possession of occult authority, and professes to have the power of taking or saving life, of causing or curing disease, of bringing ruin or creating prosperity, of discovering evil- doers; or vindicating the innocent. His implements are a few odd scraps, such as cock's feathers, rags, bones, bits of earth from graves, and so on. The incantations with which he accompanies his operations are merely a mumble of improvised jargon. His real advantage in the days of slavery lay in his knowledge and use of poisonous plants. Poisoning does not now enter his practices to any extent, but the fear he inspires among the ignorant is intense, and the fact that he has turned his attention to particular persons is often sufficient to deprive them of reason. Obeahism is a superstition at once simple, foolish, and terrible, still vigorous, but in former times as powerful an agent as slavery itself in keeping the nature debased."[6]

The Jamaica term Obeah is unquestionably derived from the Ashanti word Obayifo, which according to Captain Rattray signifies "a wizard, or more generally a witch."[7] As noted else where:[8] "An Ashanti legend runs as follows. When Big Massa was busy with the work of creation, it happened that the little monkey Efo was making himself generally useful, and when the task was accomplished, he asked Big Massa that, in return for the help rendered, all creatures should bear his name. To this Big Massa acceded to such an extent that henceforth certain classes of creatures added to their proper names the suffix FO, in acknowledgment of the little monkey's part in the work.[9] Such is the Ashanti fable, and hence we find the suffix FO in the names of peoples, nation and occupations. Dropping the suffix, then, from Obayifo, the resulting Obayi, as heard from the lips of the Koromantin slaves (shown to be Ashanti, at least as regards their leading spirits), was variously rendered by the Jamaican whites as obeah, obia, etc. For even now there is no agreement as to the correct spelling of the word. . . . Both with the Ashanti themselves and their descendants in Jamaica the word is commonly shortened into Obi. Thus we find the Obi country referred to in the history of the Ashanti Fetish Priest, Okomfo-Anotchi, that is Anotchi the priest. About the year 1700 after committing a capital offence, as Captain Rattray tells us, he 'fled for his life to the Obi country. Here he had made a study of fetish medicine and became the greatest fetish-man the Ashanti have ever had.' Referring to the Obi country, Rattray notes: 'I have so far been unable to trace this place, but to this day in Ashanti any big fetish priest is called Obi Okomfo, that is, Obi Priest.' So also in Jamaica, in the practice of Obeah, the natives 'make obi' even today."

Captain Rattray, whose scholarly works on the Ashanti really led the way to a complete revolution in the study and evaluation of West Africa customs, fearlessly abandoned the trodden path of narrow prejudice and *a priori* reasoning of the Spencerian School, and literally reconstructed the entire system of scientific research among the Negro tribes. We cannot do better then, than to study in some detail the Ashanti prototype of the Jamaica Obeah as described by so discriminating a scholar, who knows nothing of the bearings his observations will have on Jamaica witchcraft, but is conscientiously setting down the facts as he sees them in his own chosen field where he is the undisputed master.[10]

Captain Rattray is unequivocally of the opinion that the Ashanti worship a Supreme Being, Onyame.[11] Furthermore he states: "I am convinced that the conception in the Ashanti mind, of a Supreme Being, has nothing whatever to do with missionary influence, nor is it to be ascribed to contact with Christians or even, I believe, with Mohammedans."[12]

Bosman had noticed at the beginning of the eighteenth century as regards certain West African tribes: "By reason God is invisible, they say it would be absurd to make any corporeal representation of him . . . wherefore they have such multitudes of images of their idol gods, which they take to be subordinate deities to the Supreme God. . . . and only believe these are mediators betwixt God and men, which they take to be their idols."[13]

This condition is verified by Rattray in regard to the Ashanti. He tells us: "In a sense, therefore, it is true that this great Supreme Being, the conception of whom has been innate in the minds of the Ashanti, is the Jehovah of the Israelites. As will be seen presently, every Ashanti temple is a pantheon in which repose the shrines of the gods, but the power or spirit, that on occasions enters into these shrines, is directly or indirectly derived from the one God of the Sky, whose intermediaries they are. Hence we have in Ashanti exactly that 'mixed religion' which we find among the Israelites of old. They worshipped Jehovah, but they worshipped other Gods as well."[14]

These intermediary deities engross the chief attention of the Ashanti and their religious system consists principally in their service and veneration. One by one they come into fashion and then pass out of vogue, only perhaps to bob up again if the right individual is found to espouse their cause. Listen to Captain Rattray's description of the origin of one such spiritual entity: "The word shrine is used in this particular context, to designate the potential abode of a superhuman spirit. It consists (generally) of a brass pan or bowl, which contains various ingredients. This pan upon certain definite occasions, becomes the temporary dwelling, or resting-place of a non-human spirit or spirits. . . .

"The following is an account, from a reliable source, checked and rechecked from many independent witnesses, of the making and consecration of a shrine for one of the Tano gods. . . .

"A spirit may take possession of a man and he may appear to have gone mad, and this state may last sometimes even for a year. Then the priest or some powerful god may be consulted and he may discover, through his god, that it is some spirit which has come upon the man (or woman). The one upon whom the spirit has come is now bidden to prepare a brass pan, and collect water, leaves, and 'medicine' of specific kinds. The possessed one will dance, for sometimes two days, with short intervals for rest, to the accompaniment of drums and singing. Quite suddenly he will leap into the air and catch something in both his hands (or he may plunge into the river and emerge holding something he has brought up). He will in either case hold this thing to his breast, and water will be at once sprinkled upon it to cool it, when it will be thrust into the brass pan and quickly covered tip. The following ingredients are now prepared: clay from one of the more sacred rivers, like the Tano, and the following medicinal plants and other objects; afema (*Justicia flavia*), Damabo (*Abras precatorius*), the bark of the odum, a creeper called hamakyerehene, any root that crosses a path, a projecting stump from under water, the leaves of a tree called aya—these are chosen which are seen to be quivering on the tree even though no wind is shaking them—the leaves, bark and roots of a tree called Bonsam dua (lit. the wizard's tree), a nugget of virgin gold (a gold that has been in use or circulation must not be used), a bodom (so-called ag-grey bead), and a long white bead called gyanie. The whole of these are pounded and placed in the pan, along with the original object already inside, while the following incantation or prayer is repeated: 'Supreme Being, upon whom men lean and do not fall, (whose day of observance is a Saturday), Earth Goddess (whose day of worship is Thursday), Leopard, and all beasts and plants of the forest, today is a sacred Friday; and you, Ta Kwesi (the particular god for whom in this case the shrine was being prepared), we are installing you, we are setting you (here), that we may have long life; do not let us get

"Death"; do not let us become impotent; life to the head of the village; life to the young men of this village; life to those who bear children, and life to the children of this village. O tree, we call Odum Abena (to whom belongs the silk-cotton tree), we are calling upon you that you may come, one and all, just now, that we may place in this shrine the thoughts that are in our heads. When we call upon you in the darkness, when we call upon you in sunlight, and say, "Do such a thing for us" you will do so. And the laws that we are decreeing for you, this god of ours, are these—if in our time, or in our children's and our grandchildren's time a king should arise from somewhere, and come to us, and say he is going to war, when he tells you, and you well know that should he go to fight he will not gain the victory, you must tell us so; and should you know that he will go and conquer, then also state that truth. And yet again, if a man be ill in the night, or in the daytime, and we raise you aloft and place you upon the head, and we inquire of you saying, "Is So- and-so about to die?" let the cause of the misfortune which you tell him has come upon him be the real cause of the evil and not lies. Today, we all in this town, all our elders, and all our children, have consulted together and agreed without dissent among us, we have all united and with one accord decided to establish your shrine, you, Ta Kwesi, upon this a sacred Friday. We have taken a sheep, and a fowl, we have taken wine, we are about to give them to you that you may reside in this town and preserve its life.

From this clay, and so on to any future day, you must not fly and leave us. From this day, to any future day, you, O Tano's fire, in anything that you tell us, do not let it be a lie. Do not put water in your mouth and speak to us. Today you become a god for the chief, today you have become a god for our spirit ancestors. Perhaps upon some tomorrow the Ashanti King may conic and say, "My child So-and-so (or it may be an elder) is sick," and ask you to go with him, or maybe he will send a messenger here for you; in such a case you may go and we will not think that you are fleeing from us. And these words are a voice from the mouth of us all.

"The various sacrifices are then made, and in each case the blood is allowed to fall upon the contents in the brass pan.

"I have had many similar accounts of the consecration of a new shrine as the temporary home of a new manifestation of a spirit universal and always present, but not subject to control.

"It will be noted that other minor spirits or powers of nature are not wholly ignored or neglected, and that all are considered as able in some manner to help the greater spirit that is called upon to guide and assist mankind.

"The priests tell me that at times, when the greater emanation of God is not present, that the spirits of some of the lesser ones will flash forth for a moment and disclose their presence. For example, a priest will suddenly burst forth, singing, odomae, die odo me omera ('I am the odoma tree, let him who loves me come hither'). It seems that the priest and priestess, when in the ecstatic condition, are subject to many spirit influences. I have heard a priestess begin to talk in a different dialect from her own. This did not at all surprise the onlookers, who merely said, 'Oh that is the spirit of So-and-so'—a dead priestess of the same god, who had come from another district, and had used that dialect. . . .

"Once the ingredients described have been put into the shrine, that is apparently an end of them. They are not directly mentioned, and it is only when the spirit of one of the ingredients the shrine takes charge, as it were, for a moment, that they even considered,"[15]

In connection with the Ashanti religious practices there is a strong veneration for ancestors as shown especially in the functions connected with the stools which are supposed to be closely associated with the vital spirit of these forebears.

So also we encounter animism in its broadest sense. This is well illustrated in the use of the protective charm or suman which really forms an integral part of the Ashanti religious practice. In describing some "proverb" weights, Rattray calls attention to the fact that they really represent a medicine man sacrificing a fowl to one of the best known charms in Ashanti, the "nkabere charm" and adds, "I once witnessed the making of one of these charms, and the following short account may be of interest. That this charm should have been represented shows how generally the rite is seen.

"The object upon the ground, over which the offering is being held . . . is known throughout the Ashanti as a charm (suman) called nkabere, and the ceremony the medicine man is here seen performing is the sacrifice of a fowl preparatory to or after the ceremony known as Kyekyere nkabere, lit. to tie or bind the nkabere. The nkabere consists of three sticks:

(a) A stick from the tree called bonsam dua, lit. the wizard's tree.

(b) A piece of the root of a tree called akwamea, taken where it crosses a path.

(c) A stick from the tree called adwin.

These three sticks are placed upon the ground, or sometimes upon an inverted pot, along with some pieces out of a sweeping broom. A piece of string is placed on top of all.

"The medicine man or priest now retires a few paces and then advances towards the charm with his hands behind his back, crossing one leg over the other as he walks.

When he reaches the charm he stands with legs crossed, with his hands still behind his back, and stooping down sprays pepper and guinea grain—which he has in his mouth—over the charm, saying: 'My entwining charm Nkadomako (Note: "A title of Tano. The priest whom I saw performing this rite informed me that he gave his suman all these high-sounding titles to please and flatter it, as if it were really a god."), who seizes strong men, mosquito that trips up (Note: "The word used literally signifies to trip in wrestling.")

the great silk-cotton tree, shooting stars that live with the Supreme Being, I have to tell you that So-and-so are coming here about some matter.' Here he takes his hands from behind his back and, stooping down, picks up the sticks and twine. Making a little bundle of the sticks, saying as he does so: 'I bind up their mouths. I bind up their souls, and their gods. I begin with Sunday, Monday, Tuesday, Wednesday, Thursday, Friday, Saturday.' As he repeats each day he gives a twist of the string round the sticks till he has bound them all together, when he knots the string to keep it from unravelling, ending by saying: 'Whoever comes may this be a match for them.' From time to time a fowl will be offered to this suman. The medicine man or priest will advance upon it with crossed legs and hands held behind the back and perhaps with a whistle in his mouth, to call up the spirits, and will stand over the charm with legs crossed. He then holds the fowl by the neck and blows the whistle. This is what is shown in the weight." [16]

Thus far we have briefly outlined what might be called the religious atmosphere of the Ashanti. Concomitant with this and essentially antagonistic to it, we have another condition of affairs which may be summed up as witchcraft. Of this phase of life, Rattray says: "Witchcraft was essentially the employment of antisocial magic. The belief in its general prevalence was largely due to the fact that certain forms of illness resulting in death could not otherwise be accounted for. There appears to be considerable logic in regarding killing by witchcraft as akin to murder, even if its classification as such by the Ashanti was not directly due to an acknowledgment of a fact which was in many cases true, *i. e.* that poison in some form or other was often an important stock-in-trade of the professed witch."[17]

As already stated, the Ashanti word for witch was Obayifo, and they have the proverb, "Obayifo oreko e! obayifo oreko e! na wonye obayifo a, wuntwa wo ani.—A witch is passing! a witch is passing! (someone cries), but if you are not a witch you do not turn your eyes to look."[18] This mysterious being is thus described by Rattray: "Obayifo, Deriv. bayi, sorcery (synonymous term ayen), a wizard, or more generally witch. A kind of human vampire, whose chief delight is to suck the blood of children whereby the latter pine and die.

"Men and women possessed of this black magic are credited with volitant powers, being able to quit their bodies and travel great distances in the night. Besides sucking the blood of victims, they are supposed to be able to extract the sap and juices of crops. (Cases of coco blight are ascribed to the work of the obayifo.) These witches are supposed to be very common and a man never knows but that his friend or even his wife may be one. When prowling at night they are supposed to emit a phosphorescent light from the armpits and anus. An obayifo in everyday life is supposed to be known by having sharp shifty eyes, that are never at rest, also by showing an undue interest in food, and always talking about it, especially meat, and hanging about when cooking is going on, all of which habits are therefore purposely avoided. A man will seldom deny another, even a stranger, a morsel of what he may be eating, or a hunter a little bit of raw meat to anyone asking it, hoping thereby to avoid the displeasure of anyone who, for all he can tell, is a witch or wizard.

"The obayifo can also enter animals, etc., *e. g.* buffalo, elephant, snakes, and cause them to kill people. The obayifo is discovered by a process analogous to the 'smelling out' of witches among the Zulu, *i. e.* the 'carrying of the corpse'. Witches and wizards are guarded against by a suman, and a little raw meat or other food is frequently placed at the entrance to a village for them to partake of. This offering also frequently takes the form of a bunch of palm nuts pinned down to the ground with a stick."[19]

Hence the proverb: "Obayifo kum wadi-wamma-me, na onkum wama me-na-esua.—The sorcerer kills (by magic) the one who eats and gives him nothing, but he does not kill him who eats and gives him (even) a little piece."[20]

Another Ashanti proverb runs: "Sasabonsam ko ayi a, osoe obayifo fi.—When a sasabonsam (devil) goes to attend a funeral, he lodges at a witch's house. [21] "This Sasabonsam will be met with again in Jamaica. Rattray here remarks well to our purpose: "Sasabonsam, Deriv. bonsam, a devil, or evil spirit (not the disembodied soul of any particular person, just as the fetish is not a human spirit). Its power is purely for evil and witchcraft. The obayifo is perhaps its servant as the terms are sometimes synonymous. Sasa or sesa is the word used for a person being possessed of a spirit or devil (oye no sesa)."[22] And again: "The Sasabonsam of the Gold Coast and Ashanti is a monster which is said to inhabit parts of the dense virgin forests. It is covered with long hair, has large blood-shot eyes, long legs, and feet pointing both ways. It sits on high branches of an odum or onyina tree and dangles its legs, with which at times it hooks up the unwary hunter. It is hostile to man, and is supposed to be essentially at enmity with the real priestly class. Hunters who go to the forest and are never heard of again—as sometimes happens—are supposed to have been caught by Sasabonsam. All of them are in league with abayifo (witches), and with the mmotia, in other words, with the workers in black magic. As we have seen, however, and will see again farther on, their power is sometimes solicited to add power to the suman (fetish), not necessarily with a view to employing that power for purposes of witchcraft, but rather the reverse. I cannot help thinking that the original Sasabonsam may possibly have been a gorilla. Under the heading of Witchcraft we shall see how the Sasabonsam's aid is solicited to defeat and to detect the very evil with which he is thought to be associated indirectly."[23]

That the Ashanti clearly distinguished between religious practices and witchcraft is evidenced by the following observation of Rattray: "From the information at our disposal, we now know that the Ashanti makes a distinction between the following: the okomfo (priest) the sumankwafo or dunseni (the medicine man); and the Bonsam komfo (witch doctor). The word okomfo, without any further qualification, refers to a priest of one of the orthodox abosom (gods). We see, however, that a witch doctor is allowed the same name as a kind of honorary title or degree, being known as a Bayi komfo (a priest of witchcraft). Again, the ordinary medical practitioners are never termed okomfo, they are sumankwafo, dealers in suman; or dunsefo, workers in roots; or odu'yefo, workers in medicine."[24]

Clearly defined Ashanti witchcraft, then, as a practice of black magic, is in theory at least essentially antagonistic to religion in any form, and as clearly dissociated from the making of a suman, which may be regarded as white magic, as its practitioner, the Obayifo, is distinguished from the medicine man Sumankwafo. Nevertheless, the title Bayi komfo, a priest of witchcraft, would indicate that even in Ashanti, there has developed a phase of what might be called devil-worship in as much as the Sasabonsam, or devil, is so closely associated with witches.[25]

In all this, however, we do not find any real evidence of Ophiolatry, either as regards the religion or the witchcraft of the Ashanti.[26]

No doubt the Obayifo affected at times the rôle of medicine man. He might remain respectable before the community at large as a Sumankwafo, while in secret he plied his trade as a wizard. So, too, he must naturally have borrowed occasionally from the suman-maker's technique to effectually disguise his own incantations. If in the making of a suman the real Sumankwafo actually invaded his realm by soliciting the aid of Sasabonsam, why should he not return the compliment in kind?

Practically, in a general way, the differentiation was in the specific object of the rite which determined whether the magic was to be regarded as white or black.[27] But over and above all this, there was also a wide divergence in the ingredients employed, just as the knowledge of vegetable qualities, good and evil, was used for curative or destructive purposes, according to the profession of the herbalist.

In fact, it would be natural to suspect that the really skilful Obayifo would play the double rôle from motives of self-protection if not from any mercenary reasons.[28]

D. Amaury Talbot, wife of the District Commissioner of the Nigerian Political Service, in her book, *Woman's Mysteries of a Primitive People*, devotes a chapter to "Love Philtres and Magic" wherein she tells us: "The principal ingredients in these philtres are the hearts of chickens pounded up to a smooth paste, together with leaves thought to contain magical qualities. It is not without significance, that among the Ibibios, save when administered in 'medicine,' intended to weaken the will and destroy the courage of the recipient, the hearts and livers of chickens are carefully avoided as food, since it is thought that those who partake will become 'chicken-hearted' in consequence. In order to render the charm efficacious it is necessary to draw forth the soul of some person and imprison it amid fresh-plucked herbs in an earthen pot never before used. The vessel is then hung above a slow fire, and, as the leaves dry up, the body of the man or woman chosen for the purpose is said to wither away."[29] Of course a little poison judiciously administered will supplement the efficacy of this sympathetic magic.

Père Baudin, in turn, speaking of fetish beliefs in general, tells us: "The great or chief fetish priests have a secret doctrine, which differs greatly from the popular doctrine. In this secret doctrine they gradually initiate the priests of the lower ranks." Among these secrets he includes: "the medicinal receipts, especially those for poisons," and immediately adds: "I do not believe that there exists in the world more skilful poisoners. They preserve these receipts with great care."[30]

Moreau de Saint-Méry assures us: "It is unfortunately too certain that some of the old Africans profess at San Domingo the odious art of poisoning. I say profess, for there are those who have a school where hate and vengeance has sent more than one disciple."[31]

Louis p. Bowler, who urges as his credentials for presenting his little volume: "Eight years' experience in the jungle of the Gold Coast Colony,"[32] recounts a number of cases of poisoning which came under his personal observation. From his narrative we may quote the following instances:

"Another case was brought to my notice where a European unwisely parted with money to a chief for consideration on a concession. After obtaining the chief's promise to accompany him to the coast town to sign the usual declarations before a District Commissioner, it appeared that he had previously sold the same concession and obtained money thereon. The European dies mysteriously the night before his projected departure. He was fond of pineapples, and the chief sent him a couple as a present, which he unfortunately partook of. It seems that the chief, or his medicine man, had inserted a deadly poison into the pineapple with a piece of thin wire."[33]

It may be objected that this is not Obeah, but cold-blooded murder. Yes, and the same may be said of Obeah wherever the end is produced in this way. No doubt the natives ascribed the untimely death to the workings of Obeah, and it is equally probable that the agent employed was himself an Obeah man.

The second instance which we are about to relate is, in a way, even more characteristic. Bowler writes: "I remember an instance of very fine powdered glass being placed in some soup on the table of a European, which fortunately was discovered in time.

Powdered glass is a favourite Fantee[34] means of injuring or killing those they have a grudge against. It is broken up fairly fine, put into kankee or fufu (native food), and when swallowed lacerates the bowels, setting up internal hemorrhage. Another of their methods is to rub the sticky latex of the rubber vine on the latch of the doors, rails of beds, on the loin cloths, or anything their victim is likely to touch. They then shake the poisoned broken glass on the sticky rubber, and any person taking hold of these things and receiving a prick in the hands is inoculated with the poison. There are many deaths of Europeans in West Africa that are put down to fever, black-water, typhoid, and stomach complaints, that if their true cause were investigated, would be found to arise from irritants and other poisons that the natives are adepts at using."[35]

It is with good reason, then, that Norman Eustace Cameron, Principal of the Guianese Academy, insists: "I believe that African medicines should be taken more seriously, even though we in British Guiana and the West Indies are accustomed to think of African medicine in terms of Obeah practice. It is true that the native doctors (called medicine men or witch doctors by those who will not regard them with dignity) were acquainted with many deadly poisons; as, for instance, those which were used for poisoning their arrows in war; and it is also true that the Kings of Benin and Zimbabwe took precautions against death by poisoning. But we ought to bear in mind that poisoning any member of an African community was and is considered by the community as murder, and if a person was suspected of having been killed by poison, elaborate inquiries were made to detect the murderer who would be tried and executed, sometimes cruelly, if found guilty."[36]

This is in keeping with the practice of the Jamaica Myalist to "dig up Obeah." And as we shall see in the next chapter, it was precisely with the suppression of the Myal dance in Jamaica that Obeah began to gain an ascendancy and develop into a quasi-religion with hatred of the white man and the ultimate overthrow of the white masters as an object.

In view of all this, it is hard to understand how Sir Harry Johnston could have written: "Obia (misspelt Obeah) seems to be a variant or a corruption of an Efik or Ibo word from the northeast or east of the Niger delta, which simply means 'Doctor.' . . . Obia is like Hudu or Vudu a part of the fetishistic belief which prevails over nearly all Africa, much of Asia, and a good deal of America. . . . In its 'well-meaning' forms, it is medical treatment by drugs or suggestion combined with a worship of the powers of Nature and a propitiation of evil spirits; in its bad types it is an attempt to frighten, obsess, and hypnotize, and failing the production of results by this hocus-pocus, by poison."[37]

Far more accurate is the definition of *The Encyclopedic Dictionary*:[38] "Obi (Obeah), A system of sorcery prevalent, though not to so great an extent as formerly among the Negro population of the West Indian Colonies. It appears to have been brought from Africa by Negroes who bad been enslaved, and to these obeah-men (or women) the blacks used to resort for the cure of disorders, obtaining revenge, conciliating favour, the discovery of a thief or an adulterer, and the prediction of future events. The practice of Obi had become general towards the close of the last century, both in the West Indies and the United States, and there is little doubt that the Obeah man exercised vast influence, and that they carried on a system of secret slow poisonings, the effects of which were attributed by their more ignorant fellows to Obi. The system resembles other superstitions of savage peoples. It may have originated in ancient religious practices, in which sorcery bore a large part."

Hesketh J. Bell who spent many years in the British Colonial

Service in the West Indies and was subsequently Governor of the Island Mauritius, has written at length on the subject of Obeah and incidentally contributed valuable data gathered either from personal observation or through reliable eye-witnesses.

Writing of Granada, an English island in the Windward Group, Bell says: "Before the emancipation, the practice of Obeah was as rampant in all the West Indian colonies, and laws and ordinances had to be framed to put it down, and combat its baneful influences. There were few of the large estates having African slaves, which had not one or more Obeah men in the number. They were usually the oldest and most crafty of the blacks, those whose hoary heads and somewhat harsh and forbidding aspect, together with some skill in plants of the medicinal and poisonous species, qualified them for successful imposition on the weak and credulous. In these days, an Obeah man wouldbe hard to distinguish from other blacks, and might only be known by wearing his hair long, or some other peculiarity, or else by possessing a good substantial house, built out of the money obtained from his credulous countrymen, in exchange for rubbishing simples or worthless love-spells. The trade which these impostors carry on is extremely lucrative. A Negro would not hesitate to give an Obeah man four or five dollars for a love-spell, when he would grudge three shillings for a bottle of medicine, to relieve some painful sickness. A veil of mystery is cast over their incantations which generally take place at the midnight hour, and every precaution is taken to conceal these ceremonies from the knowledge of the whites. The deluded Negroes who thoroughly believe in the supernatural power of these sorcerers, screen them as much as possible and the bravest among them tremble at the very sight of the ragged bundle, the eggshells or Obeah bottle stuck in the thatch of a hut, or in the branches of a plantain tree to deter thieves.

"The darker and more dangerous side of Obeah is that portion under cover of which poison is used to a fearful extent,, and the dangerous and often fatal effects of many a magic draught are simply set down, by the superstitious black, to the workings of the spells of Obeah, and never to the more simple effects of the scores of poisonous herbs growing in every pasture, and which may have formed the ingredients of the Obeah mixture. Owing to the defective state of the laws relating to declaration of deaths and inquests, it is to be feared that very many deaths occur from poisoning, which are set down to a cold or other simple malady."[39]

Bell recounts the following narrative as he received it from the lips of a French priest in Granada: "I was riding to see a sick person living on the other side of the parish, when I happened to pass a small wooden house, before which a number of people were congregated, all talking together and evidently much exercised in their minds about something inexplicable. On asking what was the matter, I was told that the owner of the house was lying dead, and that he was an Obeah man who had lived quite alone in the place for many years, and that there was consequently no one willing to undertake the job of looking after the corpse and burying it. In fact no one would go inside the hut at all, as it was affirmed that his

Satanic Majesty was there in person looking after the body of the Obeah man, which now undoubtedly belonged to him. To allay their alarms, I got off my horse, and with the assistance of a couple of men broke open the door and entered the hut. Lying on a wooden stretcher was the body of the unfortunate individual, whose death must have occurred a good many hours before, and the body was in urgent need of burial, so after scolding the people for their cowardice I prevailed on them to see about a coffin and other details as quickly as possible, It was, however, only in evident fear and trembling that any of them would enter the room, and the slightest noise would make them start and look towards the door, in the expectation of seeing *le diable en personne* coming to claim his property.

"The dirty little room was littered with the Obeah man's stock-in-trade." Then after the catalogue of gruesome finds, he continues: "In a little tin canister I found the most valuable of the sorcerer's stock, namely, seven bones belonging to a rattlesnake's tail—these I have known sell for five dollars each, so highly valued are they as amulets or charms—in the same box was about a yard of rope, no doubt intended to be sold for hangman's cord, which is highly prized by the Negroes, the owner of a piece being supposed to be able to defy bad luck.

"Rummaging further, I pulled out from under the thatch of the roof an old preserved- salmon tin, the contents of which showed how profitable was the trade of Obeah. It was stuffed full of five-dollar bank-notes, besides a number of handsome twenty-dollar gold pieces, the whole amounting to a considerable sum, which I confess I felt very reluctant to seal up and hand over to the Government, the Obeah man not being known to have heirs. I then ordered the people to gather up all the rubbish, which was soon kindled and blazing away merrily in front of the hut, to the evident satisfaction of the bystanders, who could hardly be persuaded to handle the mysterious tools of Obeah.

The man, I heard, had a great reputation for sorcery, and I was assured that even persons who would never be suspected of encouraging witchcraft had been known to consult him or purchase some love-spell."[40]

Another incident related by the same French priest in Granada to Mr. Bell, must close this chapter. The incident runs as follows: I will give you an instance which happened to me, and which I have never been able to explain satisfactorily.

"Some years ago I was in Trinidad and had been sent by the Archbishop to take charge of a parish far in the interior of the island, and at that time but very little known and developed. There being no presbytery, I had to make shift, until I could build one, with part of a small wooden house, of which one room was occupied by an old coloured woman, who lived there with a little girl. This woman was looked on with a good deal of dread by the people, being supposed to possess a knowledge of a good many unholy tricks, and it was confidently hoped that my near neighbourhood would do her good, and at all events induce her to be seen now and then at church, which is here a great sign of respectability. When taking possession of my part of the house, I was shown her room, and noticed particularly that it contained some really handsome pieces of the massive furniture so much esteemed by Creoles. A tremendous family four-poster, with heavy, handsomely turned pillars, stood in one corner near a ponderous mahogany wardrobe, and various other bits of furniture pretty well filled the little room. The door of her apartment opened on to my room, which she had to pass through every time she went out of the house. This was an unpleasant arrangement, but was shortly to be remedied by having another door made in her room leading outside. However, the night after my taking possession, I heard a monotonous sound through the partition, as if someone crooning a sing-song chant. This continued for over an hour, and more than once I felt inclined to rap at the partition and beg the old dame to shut up her incantations, but it finally acted as a lullaby and I soon dropped asleep. The next morning having got up and dressed, I noticed that all was perfectly silent next door, and on listening attentively failed to hear a sound. I feared something had gone wrong, but noticed that the door leading outside had not been opened, as a chair I had placed against it was in precisely the same position as I had left it. I then knocked at her door several times, but obtained no answer; fearing an accident had happened, I opened the door, and as it swung back on its hinges I was astonished to see the room perfectly empty and evidently swept clean. On examining the room carefully I found it only had two small windows besides the door leading into my room. From that day to this neither I nor anyone living in that district have ever seen or heard anything of that woman or of her little girl. How she moved all her heavy furniture out of that little room, has ever remained an inexplicable mystery. I would have defied any man to move the wardrobe alone, and even if the old woman had had strength enough to carry the furniture away, she never could have dragged it through my room without disturbing me. However, these are the facts of the case, and I have never been able to explain them."[41]

CHAPTER V
Development of Obeah in Jamaica

AS SHOWN ELSEWHERE it was the Ashanti in Jamaica who, during the days of slavery, maintained a commanding influence over all the other types of slaves, even imposing on them their peculiar superstitions and religious practices, and who have left their impress on the general population of the Island to such an extent that they may undoubtedly be declared the dominant influence in evolving our Jamaica peasant of the present day.[1] Thus, to briefly summarize a few of the principal facts, in Jamaica folklore, or Anancy stories, we find the spider, anancy, as the central figure and his son Tacoma as next in importance, with both names and characters derived directly from the Ashanti. Here also the Ashanti name of Odum is perserved {sic} for the silk-cotton tree. These stories are passed along by the Nana or Granny, and again the function and title are both Ashanti. The funeral custom of raising and lowering the coffin three times, seemingly as a courtesy to the Earth Goddess before starting for the grave, while peculiar to the Ashanti in West Africa, is still prevalent in the Jamaica "bush" where they know nothing of its origin or significance, and where they give as the sole reason for doing so, that it is always done that way. Again, the fowl with ruffled feathers, and half- naked neck and which the Jamaica "picknies" call peal-neck, *i. e.* bald-neck, is technically known as sensey fowl in Jamaica and asense in Ashanti. So, too, the staple food of the Ashanti is fufu, consisting usually of mashed yarn, and sometimes of mashed plantain.

The term is the reduplicated form of fu, meaning white. In the Jamaica "bush" there is a particularly fine grade of white yam that is known as fufu yam, and it has lately been brought to my attention that mashed yam in Jamaica still goes by the name of fufu. Many other details of identity in words and customs might be adduced but these must suffice for the present.

True it is, the Ashanti are not always expressly named as such in the rôle they occupied in Jamaica. It is as Koromantins that they figure so prominently in the history of the island, especially as regards the various slave-uprisings that so often threatened the white supremacy. But, as has been shown, the Koromantin, while generically Gold Coast slaves, were specifically, at least as applies to their leading spirits, Ashanti.[2]

Gardner declares: "Little can be said with confidence as to the religious beliefs of these people. The influence of the Koromantins seemed to have modified, if not entirely obliterated, whatever was introduced by other tribes. They recognized, in a being called Accompong, the creator and preserver of mankind; to him praise, but never sacrifice, was offered. . . . The tutelary deities included the departed heads of families, and the worship of such was almost the only one observed to any great extent by Africans or their descendants in Jamaica."[3]

The Supreme Being among the Ashanti, as we have seen, was Nyame, and his primary title was Nyankopon, meaning Nyame, alone, great one. Accompong, then, was the white man's attempt to transliterate the Nyankopon which he so often heard on the lips of the expatriated Ashanti.

As previously noted: Bryan Edwards, in his brief outline of the religious beliefs of the Koromantin slaves, asserts: "They believe that Accompong, the God of heavens, is the creator of all things; a Deity of Infinite goodness. In fact we have in Jamaica today, in the parish of St. Elizabeth, a Maroon town called Accompong, which according to Cundall, the Island Historian, was so called after an Ashanti chief who figured in one of the early rebellions of the Island. One's first impression would be that this chief had abrogated to himself the title of Deity. But we are assured by J. G. Christaller that among the Ashanti the Divine Name was frequently given to a slave in acknowledgment of the help of God enabling the owner to buy the slave."[4]

Herbert G. De Lisser, a native Jamaican whose facile pen has won for him well-merited distinction, writes: "The West African natives and particularly those from the Gold Coast (from which the larger number of Jamaica slaves were brought) believe in a number of gods of different classes and unequal power. All these gods have their priest and priestesses, but there is one particular malignant spirit, which on the Gold Coast has no priesthood. He is called Sasabonsum, and any individual may put himself in communication with him. Sasabonsum's favorite residence is the ceiba, the giant silk-cotton tree. He is resorted to in the dead of night, his votary going to the spot where he is supposed to live, and collecting there a little earth, or a few twigs, or a stone, he prays to the god that his power may enter this receptacle. If he believes that his prayer has been heard he returns home with his shuman, as the thing is now named, and henceforth, he has a power which is formidable for injurious purposes, to which he offers sacrifice, and to the worship of which he dedicates a special day in the week. By the aid of this shuman he can bewitch a man to death. He can also sell charms that will cause death or bodily injury. His charms may also be put to other and less pernicious uses. Thus the shuman charm in the shape of a bundle of twigs, if hung up where it can be seen, is very efficacious for keeping thieves away from a house or provision-ground. Any-one may go out and get a shuman if he likes, but few there are who dare to do so, through fear of Sasabonsum, the witch's god, and public opinion which looks down upon a man with a shuman. The legitimate priests whose office it is to approach the gods also sell charms both for good and injurious purposes, but the main func-tions are to propitiate the gods and bewitch the people. They were called upon to undo the injury caused by the wizard and his shuman. Both witches and wizards, priests and priestesses were brought to Jamaica in the days of the slave trade, and the slaves recognized the distinction between the former and the latter. Even the masters saw that the two classes were not identical, and so they called the latter 'Myal men' and 'Myal women'-the people who cured those whom the Obeah man had injured. Of the present-day descendants of these priests or Myal men more will be said later on. It is probable that many of the African priests became simple Obeah men after coming to Jamaica, for the simple reason that they could not openly practice their legitimate profession. But when known as Obeah men, however much they might be treated with respect, they still were hated and feared. Every evil was attributed to them. The very name of them spread dread."[5]

Myalism, then, was the old tribal religion of the Ashanti which we have studied in detail in the preceding chapter, with some modifications due to conditions and circumstances. It drew its name from the Myal dance that featured it, particularly in the veneration of the minor deities who were subordinate to Accompong, and in the commemoration or intercession of ancestors.

The old antagonism to Obeah or witchcraft on the part of the priesthood becomes accentuated, and gradually takes on a rôle of major importance, so that it actually forms a part of the religious practice. In Ashanti, the Okomfo openly combated the Obayifo as a matter of principle, and he had the whole force of Ashanti religious traditions and public sentiment to support him, until he eventually looked down with more or less disdain on the benighted disciple of Sasabonsam. In Jamaica, on the other hand, native religious assemblies were proscribed by law, as we shall see shortly, which greatly hampered the Okomfo in his sphere of influence, even his title being changed to Myal man, while the Obayifo or Obeah man, who had always worked in secret, flourished in his trade. For the very status and restrictions of slave life put his fellows more and more at his mercy and filled them with a growing fear of his spiteful incantations, backed up as they were with active poisonings. Their gods had abandoned them; why not cultivate the favour of the triumphant Sasabonsam, or at least assuage his enmity and placate his vengeance?

It was natural, too, for the Okomfo to adapt his practice to the new state of affairs. His hated rival, the Obayifo, must be conquered at any price. Personal interests demanded this as strongly as religious zeal. Since public service of the deities was no longer possible, he in turn was forced to work in secret, and it is not surprising that he met fire with fire, incantation with incantation. His religion had aimed primarily at the welfare of the community, even as the object in life of the Obayifo was the harm of the individual.

Open intercession for tribal success and prosperity necessarily gives way to secret machinations to break the chains of bondage. A fanatic zeal takes hold of the Myalist Okomfo and he devises the most impressive ritual he can, to arouse the dormant spirits of his fellow-slaves.

Thus it came to pass that it was the Okomfo and not the Obayifo, as is generally assumed, who administered the terrible fetish oath. It was he who mixed the gunpowder with the rum and added grave dirt and human blood to the concoction that was to seal upon the conspirators' lips the awful nature of the plot for liberty, and steel their hearts for the dangerous undertaking. It was he, no less, who devised the mystic powder that was to make their bodies invulnerable, and enable them to meet unscathed the white man's bullets. Finally, it was the Okomfo and not the Obayifo who, taking advantage of herbal knowledge, induced a state of torpor on subservient tools, that he might seem to raise the dead to life.

Yet, through it all, while he frequently substitutes for his own religious ceremonial the dark and secret rites of his rival practitioner, his aim at least is still within the triballaw, as he works white magic for the welfare of the community, no less than he continues to combat the black magic of his adversary.

It is not surprising, then, that the rôle of the Myalist Okomfo has been so little understood, and that his most effective work was ascribed by the whites of Jamaica to the agency of Obeah and that Myalism itself should become confused with witchcraft and even regarded by some as an offshoot of Obeah and nothing more.

Gardner is only partially correct when he states: "Of late years Myalism has generally been regarded as an art by which that of the Obeah man could be counteracted. Its first mode of development was as a branch of Obeah practice. The Obeah man introduced a dance called Myal dance, and formed a secret society, the members of which were to be made invulnerable, or if they died, life was to be restored. Belief in this miracle was secured by trick. A mixture was given in rum, of a character which presently induced sleep so profound, as, by the uninitiated and alarmed, to be mistaken for death. After this had been administered to someone chosen for the purpose, the Myal dance began, and presently the victim staggered and fell, to all appearance dead. Mystic charms were then used; the body was rubbed with some infusion; and in process of time, the narcotic having lost its power, the subject of the experiment rose up as one restored to life, a fact for which the Obeah man claimed all the merit. The plant said to be used was the branched calalue, or solanum. If so, it can only be the cold infusion which has the narcotic power, and which is stated to belong to the European variety; for when boiled it is harmless. It is commonly used in Jamaica as a substitute for spinach, and enters largely into the composition of the famous pepper-pot."[6]

Matthew Gregory Lewis records in his diary under date of February 25, 1817: "The Obeah ceremonies always commence with what is called, by the Negroes, 'the Myal dance.'[7] This is intended to remove any doubt of the chief Obeah man's supernatural powers; and in the course of which, he undertakes to show his art by killing one of the persons present, whom he pitches upon for that purpose. He sprinkles various powders over the devoted victim, blows upon him, and dances round him, obliges him to drink a liquor prepared for the occasion, and finally the sorcerer and his assistants seize him and whirl him rapidly round and round till the man loses his senses, and falls to the ground to all appearances and the belief of the spectators a perfect corpse. The chief Myal man then utters loud shrieks, rushes out of the house with wild and frantic gestures, and conceals himself in a neighbouring wood. At the end of two or three hours he returns with a large bundle of herbs, from some of which he squeezes the juice into the mouth of the dead person; with others he anoints his eyes and stains the tips of his fingers, accompanying the ceremony with a great variety of grotesque actions, and chanting all the while something between a song and a howl, while the assistants hand in hand dance slowly round them in a circle, stamping the ground loudly with their feet to keep time with this chant. A considerable time elapses before the desired effect is produced, but at length the corpse gradually recovers animation, rises from the ground perfectly recovered, and the Myal dance concludes."[8]

With the decline of Myalism from its early religious standards, it took on more and more a character of antagonism to Obeah until eventually to "dig up Obeah" became its principal differentiation from witchcraft, at least as far as the uninitiated were concerned. The spirit of fanaticism, however, held apace and after the abolition of slavery, when the restrictions on assemblies were removed, there was a recrudescence of the cult, sometimes referred to as "Revivalism" that has disturbed at times the peace of more than one Jamaica community. Thus for example, Gardner tells us: "In 1842 several Negroes residing on an estate near Montego Bay gave themselves out to be Myal men; and in St. James, Westmoreland, and Trelawney, thousands of deluded people became their followers. They were accustomed to meet together after nightfall, generally beneath the shadow of a cotton tree. Fowls were sacrificed, and wild songs sung, in the chorus of which the multitude joined. Dancing then began, becoming more and more weirdlike in character, until one and another fell exhausted to the ground, when their incoherent utterances were listened to as divine revelations. Half-demented creatures sat among the branches or in the hollow trunks of trees, singing; while others with their heads bound in fantastic fashion, ran about with arms outstretched, and declared that they were flying. It became necessary at last to swear in several hundreds of special constables, and to punish numbers of these deluded people for disturbing the peace. . . . Some six years later a Myal man, called Dr. Taylor, gave much trouble in Manchester and Clarendon, drawing great crowds after him. He was sent to the penitentiary, where he was accidentally killed. In 1852, the delusion again appeared: some now gave themselves out to be prophets, and saw visions, but the firmness of the missionaries soon put an end to these practices."[9]

There are some interesting details of the Myalistic outbreak of 1842 given by the Reverend R. Thomas Banbury, a native Jamaican, in a little volume which he published at Kingston, in 1895 on *Jamaica Superstitions*. He tells us: "It took its rise at Newman Hall estate in St. James and went through that parish, Westmoreland and Hanover, increasing as it went until it consisted of hundreds of deluded fanatics. They went by the name of 'Myal people'; they were also called 'angel men.' They declared that the world was to come to an end; Christ was coming, and God had sent them to pull all the Obeahs, and catch all the shadows that were spell-bound at the cotton trees. In preparation for these events they affected to be very strict in their conduct. They would neither drink nor smoke. Persons who were known to be notorious for their bad lives were excluded from their society. They went from place to place pulling out Obeahs and catching shadows and uttered fearful threats against sinners. About the time mentioned there was a very extraordinary comet, which continued in the heavens for several weeks. It was in the west, and the shape of it was like a 'salt fish' (a cod fish split in two, with the head cut off), the head square and the body tapering off to a point. It was remarkably brilliant. These people made reference to it in their songs and pointed to it as an illustration of their divine mission, and the people were not a little alarmed at its appearance. . . . Many songs were used when taking up Obeahs, which they did openly in the daytime, in the presence of a large concourse of people who flocked from all parts to see it. The overseers and bookkeepers on the sugar estates all were present. There were present an attorney and a proprietor. An Englishman and a member of the House of Assembly, who took them on his estate gave them room and encouraged them in every way. They publicly dug out of his yard a lot of Obeahs for him. . . . The amber was a talisman by which they pretended to divine. Both Myal men and Obeah men use it.

Anything through which they look at the Obeah, either in the ground or skin is called an amber, the name not being strictly confined to the substance properly so-called.

"Four shillings was the price for pulling an Obeah and six shillings for catching a shadow, and they did make money. They accompanied their operations with violent singing and dancing. They worked themselves into violent animal excitement and fanaticism, jumping about, yelling like so many demoniacs. It was frightful to hear them. Sometimes one would bolt out of the ring and run into the bush and then the others would go after him, declaring that the spirits had taken him away. They had vials filled with the juice of bad-smelling bushes which they called 'their weed.' It was said that it had the effect of causing those upon whom it was sprinkled to become Myal people. Not a little injury was done to the churches by this Myal procession. A number of young people, especially females, were drawn away. They followed them all about and fell into immorality with the men, notwithstanding the affected piety of the latter. They went into the churches on Sundays and interrupted divine services by pulling out persons whom they suspected of dealing in Obeah, or who were so reported to them. Old men who looked suspicious were beaten, rolled in cotton bush and half killed.

"In a Baptist church at Slater's Hill an attack of this kind was made on a man whom these people considered notorious for Obeah. Afterwards the authorities had to take cognizance of their outrages and sent some of them to prison. In returning from prison their song was:

> Myal nigga, we come oh,
> We go da jail, we come out.
> Myal nigga, we come oh,
> We work again, we come back,
> Myal man we come oh.

And according to the song they did begin their revelries again.

"There is no doubt that these people laboured under a delusion from the devil. The Myalism of these people also put on a somewhat different feature from that which existed before. They professed to take up Obeahs, which the regular Myal man never did, for the work of the latter was confined to shadows, recovering persons who were struck by duppies and bringing home those who were carried away into the woods by the spirits."[10]

In this last statement, we fear, Mr. Banbury is a little confused, since "digging up Obeah" was the distinctive characteristic of the Myalist, while we have here for the first time any reference to "catching shadows," and their connection with "duppies." But what, it may be asked were these shadows and duppies?

Captain Rattray calls our attention to the fact that "The Ashanti use a number of names translated in to English by the words 'soul' or 'spirit' or 'ghost'." He then proceeds to define these various terms. Thus Saman "is a ghost, an apparition, a spectre; this term is never applied to a living person or to anything inherent in a living person. It is objective and is the form the dead are sometimes seen to take, when visible on earth. . . . The word 'has no connection whatever with any kind of soul."[11] This is the Jamaica "duppy," in every detail.

Again, he tells us: "The sasa is the invisible spiritual power of a person or animal which disturbs the mind of the living, or works a spell or mischief upon them, so that they suffer in various ways... The sasa is essentially the bad, revengeful, and hurtful element in a spirit; it is that part which at all costs must be 'laid' or rendered innocuous, the funeral rites . . . are really, I believe the placating, appeasing, and the final speeding of a soul which may contain this very dangerous element in its composition."[12] This is the "shadow" of Jamaica, where, however, both "duppy" and "shadow" have gradually assumed a material element in the general acceptation of the "bush."

Thus for example, on the occasion of deaths in the neighbour-hood, especially if by violence, the superstitious will plug up every crack and crevice of their hovels at night, "to keep the duppies out," an entirely useless precaution if the expected visitants were purely spiritual and so impassible. After the hurricane in Montego Bay in November, 1912, when about a hundred were drowned, I wanted to send a messenger on the following day on an errand that would keep him out after dark. It was with the greatest difficulty that I found one—the usual form of excuse being: "Everybody stay home a night. Too many det (dead) round, Sah!"

So, too, at a "bush" funeral, the most important circumstance is frequently the catching of the "shadow." I have more than once watched the process from a very short distance, near enough, in fact, to be able to hear all that was said, and to watch carefully most that was done, as the actors, for such I must call them, scrambled and grasped at empty nothingness, with such realism of pretence, that I found myself actually rubbing my eyes, almost convinced against myself that there must be an elusive something that escaped my vision.

When sufficient rum had been imbibed, and the singing led by a "selfish" voice had keyed up the assembly to the proper pitch, someone would excitedly cry out: "See 'im yere!" Immediately two or three or even more rival hunters would start after that "shadow" at one and the same time. From outside where I stood, it looked as if a general scramble had started in the hovel and I could see forms falling over one another and hear the imprecations and exclamations. After a time, one more "forward" than the rest would claim to have caught the prey, only to be greeted with cries of scorn: " 'Im get away! See 'im dah!" Whereupon the scuffle would start anew.

Eventually when all of them were breathless, dripping with perspiration, their clothes soiled or at times actually torn, and eyes almost popping out of their heads with excitement, while a general condition of hysteria had taken possession of the entire gathering, the feat would be accomplished by some belligerent individual, who would clasp his hands and let out a veritable Scream of defiance: "Me got 'im! Me got 'im!" with such vehemence that he would literally shout down all protests to the contrary, with perhaps just a little hint of possible physical violence that might follow as a support to the power of his vociferation. Then a box or at times a small coffin would be produced and with much ado, not perhaps without a final effort to escape, the poor "shadow" would be securely fastened in and properly "laid" to be buried later at the funeral.

I have further listened to two disputants on the following morning, while the rum fumes were still assertive, almost coming to blows as to which one of them had actually accomplished the feat of catching the shadow, and yet when I questioned them individually a few days later, despite the fact that I knew them intimately, both of them in perfect scorn, asserted, almost in the same identical words: "Me no belieb in 'shadow,' Sah! 'Im all nonsense, Sah!"

As far as I could form any judgment from my own observations, it seemed to me that one of the supposed avocations of the Obeah man was to catch the shadows of the living and nail them to a cotton tree, while the Myal man, to undo the damage, was busying himself by "pulling" the shadows from their imprisonment in the tree. Again as the shadow may be harmful to the family of the deceased, it is the function of the Myal man and not the Obeah man to catch them at the funeral—for this is a beneficial act.

Reverend A. J. Emerick, who devoted more than a decade to mission work in Jamaica, in a privately printed article gives us valuable information about Myalism as it existed at the beginning of the present century. He writes: "To attempt to describe Jamaica Mialism, a superstition imported from Africa, is like trying to describe the intricacies of the most cunningly devised Chinese puzzle. Mialism is so mixed up with Obeahism, Duppyism and other cults of African warp, together with whatever in Protestantism or Catholic ritual that may appeal to the bizarre African imagination, that it is hard to tell which is which and what is what. But for all that it is a most interesting study for the student of folklore. . . .

"But whatever may have been its origin, Mialism, properly so-called in Jamaica, is a species of Spiritualism, mixed with a peculiar form of animism. Mialism with its Mial men and Mial women, has been just as prevalent in Jamaica as Obeahism with its Obi men and Obi women. At present you do not often hear the words, 'Mialism and Mial people,' but they are still there in large forces, masquerading under other names.

"The mysterious operations of Mialism consist in communications with spirits or deaths ('dets' as the Jamaican terms it). The persons who are favoured with communications with spirits are called 'mial' people. They are said to be 'fo-eyed,' that is four-eyed, by which is meant that they can see spirits and converse with them. Both sexes make pretention to this power; hence you have mial men and mial women. They are believed to be able to kill or injure anyone by aid of spirits. A mial man and obi man are equally dreaded. The mial man harms by depriving persons of their shadows, or setting deaths upon them.[13] It is believed that after a person's shadow is taken he is never healthy and if it be not caught, he must pine away until he dies. It is said that the word for shadow in the language of some African tribes is the word for soul. Obi men and mial people sometimes carry little coffins to catch and keep shadows, which shadows they are supposed to nail to the cotton tree. This cotton tree in the days of slavery, like the oak in the days of Druidism was worshipped and sacrifices were offered at its roots. This tree was held in veneration and it was hard to get Negroes to cut it down because they were afraid that if they did so the deaths which took up their abode at its roots would injure them. There are many interesting superstitions connected with the cotton trees, one curious belief about them was that they had the power of transporting themselves at night to hold conferences together. . . .

"In connection with shadow taking is shadow catching, that is, -the restoring of the shadow to the person who had been -deprived of it. The performance is rather strange. Shadow catching is invariably done in the night. The person suspected of having lost his shadow is taken to the cotton tree, where his shadow is, as the Jamaica people say, 'pell bound,' that is spellbound, or to which it was nailed. The mial men and mial women are accompanied by a large concourse of people. The victim is dressed all in white, with a white handkerchief about his head. Eggs and fowls are taken together with cooked food, to the cotton tree. The mial men and mial women parade up and down before the cotton tree with white cloths over their shoulders, singing and dancing, and all the people join in the chorus. The cotton tree is pelted with eggs, and the necks of fowls are wrung off and the bodies are cast at it. This is done to propitiate the deaths or duppies that had their shadows enthralled at the tree. The singing and dancing proceed more vigorously as the shadow begins to make signs of leaving the tree. A white basin of water to receive it is held up. After they have sung and danced to their heart's content, they suddenly catch up the person and run home with him, affirming that his shadow is caught and covered up in the basin. When the patient has reached his home, a wet cloth is applied to his head and his shadow is said to be restored to him."[14]

The narrative may here be interrupted to remark that Fr. Emerick fails to make the clear distinction between Obeah man and Myal man, since at times the two functions are so confused and even exercised by the same individual under a dual rôle. In general, however, Obeah is secretive and malicious; Myalism is open and benevolent. When the "shadow" is "pulled" at the cotton tree, or "caught" at the funeral, just as when Obeah is "dug up," the larger the body of witnesses the greater is the satisfaction of the Myal man in this good deed which he performs. The Obeah man, on the contrary, seeks to avoid all publicity, as his purpose is evil. And even if, as occasionally does happen, the same individual is today an Obeah man and tomorrow a Myal man, to the best of my knowledge, he observes perhaps unconsciously the technique of the rite which he is performing, and his entire manner and method will change overnight.

Bringing the subject up to date, Fr. Emerick states: "Bedwardism has all the ear-marks of mialism, and in its fetish origin is fundamentally the same. Its founder was a lunatic, named Bedward, who was suffering from religious monomania. He claimed that he had visions from God, and that the spirit of God had descended upon him and that in him the prophets were reincarnated, at one time Jonas, at another Moses, then John the Baptist. He declared that in a vision God had made known to him that the water of Hope River cleansed from diseases and sin. It was rumoured that a sick woman was cured by partaking of this water. Belief in Bedward's miraculous powers gradually grew until persons from all over the island carne to get the healing waters from him and stories of wondrous cures by him were spread about. The craze grew until as many as twenty and thirty thousand Negroes used to gather every Wednesday morning along the river bank at a place called August Town, on the Hope River. In the great throng were hundreds of the crippled, the deformed, lepers, the blind, consumptives and sufferers from every form of disease. At a few moments of nine the so-called prophet would appear in flowing white robes, and with a wand in his hand, with elaborate and majestic ceremonies, he would bless the water, whereupon, these thousands of men, women and children of all ages would strip naked and jump into the water. An indescribable scene followed. . . . I only introduce this short account of it here as a help to my study of Mialism and because Bedwardism seemed to have a parental affinity to Revivalism[15] which is now rampant it, Jamaica and which is nothing but Mialism pure and simple under a new name. . . .

"The Revivalists masquerade as a Christian sect and cover themselves with a glamour of Christianity, by such practices as exclaiming in the mialistic songs. . . . such expressions as 'Lord have mercy on us,' 'Christ have mercy on us,' words evidently taken from the Catholic Mass. But despite all this they are but pagan mialists, and their service is pagan. The mialists as a body as well as individually, believed and especially *FELT* themselves called by the spirit for their work. Their supreme effort in their demoniacal, frenzied worship was to get a plenitude of the spirit. So also the Revivalists believe and feel an excited call to perform some work or give some message. Sometimes individuals, getting the spirit during the night, arise and in a frenzied condition go over the hills and along the roads, stopping sometimes before houses and shouting at the top of their voices, quoting Holy Scripture, giving warning, and announcing what they consider their God-given message. They will sometimes give warning by shouting 'Hammer and nails!' This is intended to be a death warning. During the day you will sometimes see them making curious marking on the road before certain houses. One night while I was going along a mountain path I met a woman who was under this peculiar spell. She seemed to me like one of the frenzied Eumenides whirling by me. You see again from the name of 'Angel people,' as they call themselves, where they get their idea of being messengers from heaven." At one place in the mountains, I have myself heard one of these unfortunate creatures, half-crazed with emotionalism, as night after night for weeks on end, she stood up against a flat wall of rock which served as a sounding board and sent her voice booming out over the valley in a seemingly interminable repetition of "Fire and brimstone {sic}, Fire and brimstone, judgment on men, judgment on men!"

After stating: "The original mial dance is said to be an old West African priest dance," Fr. Emerick continues: "The Mialists robed themselves in white and affected the power of divination. The Revivalists do all this. There was a band of Revivalists who met every Thursday at a place called Retirement, in the Dry Harbour Mountains. I often heard them, for it was one perpetual howl from morning till night, like the rise and fall of tidal waves on the sea beach. I have gone to see them and any account of demoniac possession that I ever read seemed tame in comparison with the demoniacal contortions, the hysterical singing and moaning, the frenzied gyrating, swaying, dancing and the abominable jerkings, of these people in the heat of their wild African, weird fetish worship to become possessed by the spirit. They form a compact circle, or rather wheel, of men and women. The whole living, squirming wheel circles and swirls in a body and each individual gyrates at the same time with many a curious bow and bend and dip and twist. Alternately they sing and moan and shout and scream. Every now and then by spells they go through abdominal contortions, just as if some infernal spirit of wondrous strength gripped them and threw into convulsions every fibre of their being. Their eyes and faces with the demon of possession looking from them made a horrible sight to see, and once you have seen it you will never forget it. They all do not do the same thing at the same time, some are doing one thing and others are doing different things, but all together they make a harmonious inharmonious whole. Each one held in his hand a green piece of bush or twig. I asked the reason for this, but got no satisfactory answer. . . . There is always one man who is called the leader, or band master. He stands still not performing any of the gyrations, but directs the performance like the director of an orchestra or band, and announces the revelations which those possessed by the spirit receive."[16]

Describing. a similar open-air meeting of Revivalists, De Lisser says: "Each of the white-robed women had a bit of withe twisted round her left wrist, and each carried a short cane. Noticing this, remembered that when the priests and priestesses of the African Gold Coast were about to dance in honour of their gods and to become possessed by them, they bound their wrists with addor and carried bundles of canes in their hands.

Here then, clearly, was the survival of an African custom masquerading as a native Christian revivalist demonstration."[17]

Whatever, then, may be thought of the present-day decadent Myalism as seen in Bedwardism and other revivalist outbreaks, it is certain that in its inception, as the offshoot of the old Ashanti tribal religion, it was of so potent a religious force, that it ha survived a century and a half of legal proscription and still a further century of an undisguised death-struggle with the powers of Obeah, and still is able to vitalize each recurrent upheaval against formal Christianity, even as it inspired the futile efforts to break the chains of slavery and cast off the white man's rule, before constitutional methods had found a way to right the crying wrong of humanity.

It is not surprising, then, that from the earliest days of legislation in Jamaica, a serious source of danger to the peace of the Colony was recognized to be ever present in the assemblies of slaves where the old religious tribal dances were openly accompanied by drumming which aroused the fanaticism of Africans to such a pitch as to endanger a general uprising. Before long it was discovered that a second cause of danger, this time a personal one to master and slave alike, was to be traced to the secret poisonings that were ever becoming more common. And yet many years passed before it was even suspected that there could be any connection between this state of affairs and Obeah, which was looked upon with amused toleration as foolish superstition and nothing more. But even when the rebellion of 1760, disclosed the connection of Obeah and poisoning, and there was a set determination to crush the dread menace at any cost, it was not suspected that they were not dealing with witchcraft alone but a recrudescence of the old religious spirit in a new and more dangerous guise.

In early legislation we find accentuated the danger from fanaticism aroused by religious assemblies and nothing more. Then appears due provision against the menace of poisonings and finally formal condemnation of Obeah. But through it all the secret phase of Myalism and its confederation with its archenemy Obeah against the oppressor of both, never seems to have been suspected. We may be pardoned, if we review somewhat in detail the legal development of this phase in the Law of Jamaica.

Appended to the *Laws of Jamaica passed by the assembly and confirmed by His Majesty in Council, April 17, 1684*[18] immediately following the Royal Confirmation and consequently disallowed, we have "An Act for the better ordering of slaves," wherein we find the words: "And it is further enacted by the authority aforesaid, that every master or mistress or overseer of a family in this island shall cause all slaves houses to be diligently and effectively searched once every fourteen days, for clubs wooden swords, and mischievous weapons, and finding any, shall take them away and cause them to be burnt."[19] This would indicate that even at this early date there was danger from a slave uprising.

Among the Acts passed in 1696 is one entitled: "An Act for the better order and government of slaves." Herein we read under Clause XIII the very same words as in the above Act which was disallowed in 1684.[20] Clause XXXII of this new Act runs as follows: "And whereas divers slaves have of late attempted to destroy several people, as well white as black, by poison; the consequences of which secret way of murdering may prove fatal, if not timely prevented: Be it enacted by the authority aforesaid, That if any Negro, or any slave or slaves, before the making of this Act, have maliciously given or attempted to give, or shall hereafter maliciously give, attempt or cause to be given to any person whatsoever, free or slave, any manner of poison, although the same was never taken, or if taken, death did not or shall not ensue upon the taking thereof; the said slave or slaves, together with their accessories, as well before as after the fact, being slaves, and convicted thereof . . . shall be adjudged guilty of murder, as if the party or parties that took or shall take the same had died; and shall be condemned to suffer death, by hanging, burning, or such other way or means as to the said justices and freeholders shall seem most convenient."[21] Moreover Clause XXXIV of the same Act prescribes: "And for the prevention of the meeting of slaves in great numbers on Sundays and Holidays, whereby they have taken liberty to contrive and bring to pass many of their bloody and inhuman transactions: Be it enacted by the aforesaid authority, That no master, or mistress, or overseer, shall suffer any drumming or meeting of any slaves, not belonging to their own plantations, to rendezvous, feast, revel, beat drum, or cause any disturbance, but forthwith endeavour to disperse them, by him, or herself, overseer or servants; or if not capacitated to do the same, that he presently give notice to the next commission-officers to raise such number of men as may be sufficient to reduce the said slaves."[22] Failure in duty on this point, the commission-officers included, carries a penalty of "forty shillings for every offence." This Act was confirmed, January 5, 1699, [23] and thus became the first approved *Code Noir* of Jamaica.

We have, then, in the very foundation of the Jamaica Slave Law, and that before the close of the seventeenth century, a clear distinction between danger from the rebellion of slaves and danger from poisoning.

In 1717 there was passed "An Act for the more effective punishing of crimes committed by slaves,"[24] of which Clause VIII thus accentuates the danger of slave uprisings: "And whereas the permitting or allowing of any number of strange Negroes to assemble on any Plantation, or settlement, or any other place, may prove of fatal consequences to this your Majesty's Island, if not timely prevented: and forasmuch as Negroes can, by beating on drums, and blowing horns, or other such like instruments of noise, give signals to each other at a considerable distance of their evil and wicked intentions: Be it further enacted, That in one month's time after the passing of this Act, no proprietor, attorney, or overseer, presume to suffer any number of strange Negroes, exceeding five, to assemble on his plantation or settlement, or on the plantation or settlement under the care of such attorney or overseer; nor shall any proprietor, attorney, or overseer, suffer any beating on drums, barrels, gourds, boards, or other such like instruments of noise on the plantations and settlements aforesaid." The penalty for each offence is to be ten pounds in the case of proprietor or attorney, and half that sum for overseers. This was an early recognition of the power of the "talking drums" which so long mystified African travellers.

In this Act of 1717, there is no mention of the danger of poisoning. However, in 1744, in consequence of a frustrated rebellion of the slaves, wherein "a general massacre of the white people was intended," there was passed: "An Act to explain and amend an Act, entitled, 'An Act for the better order and government of slaves,'" in which it is explained: "That it was the true intent and meaning of the said Act, that the crime of compassing and imagining the death of any white person by any slave or slaves, should be deemed and adjudged a crime of as high a nature as the crime of murder, and should be punished as such,"[25] and again reiterates "although the bloody purposes of such slave or slaves be prevented before any murder hath been or shall be committed."[26]

Thus what was originally applicable to the case of poisoning alone, is now by extension applied generally to any attempt whatsoever at the taking of the life of any white person. Again, before this last Act, the danger from rebellion had been clearly dissociated from the danger of poisoning. Henceforth, while the two groups of prohibitions will be preserved, the danger of rebellion is recognized in both. However, the second group of Clauses are now formally connected with Obeah, while the prohibition against assemblies becomes more detailed and specific in purpose. Gardner tells us: "The safety of the island was again imperilled by the Koromantins. Several of the leaders met in St. Mary's in July 1765, when the solemn fetish oath was administered. Into a quantity of rum, with which some gun-powder and dirt taken from a grave had been mingled, blood was put, drawn in succession from the arm of each confederate. With certain horrid ceremonies this cup was drunk from by each person, and then came the council. It was agreed that during the ensuing Christmas holidays the rising should take place, and in the meantime all were to obtain companions."[27] The impetuosity of one of their number frustrated the plans of his associates who were acting not under the influence of Obeah but of Myalism, as the "solemn fetish oath" makes clear.

On Dec. 21, 1781, there was passed "An Act to repeal several Acts and Clauses of Acts, respecting slaves, and for the better order and government of slaves, and for other purposes."[28] The purpose of this consolidated Act was to rewrite the Code Noir in its entirety, and being passed for three years only, it was to expire with December 31, 1784. Clauses XII to XIV renew the former prohibitions about assemblies of slaves but the penalties are greatly increased. The master, owner, guardian or attorney is now liable in the sum of one hundred pounds, while overseers and bookkeepers may be punished with six months' imprisonment for violations of the code. As regards amusements which are permissible among their own slaves, the use of "drums, horns and such other unlawful instruments of noise" are of course prohibited.

Clause XLIX takes direct cognizance of Obeah. It runs as follows: "And in order to prevent the many mischiefs that may hereafter arise from the wicked art of Negroes going under the the {sic} appellation of Obeah men and women, pretending to have communication with the devil and other evil spirits, whereby the weak and superstitious are deluded into a belief of their having full power to exempt them whilst under protection from any evils that might otherwise happen: Be it therefore enacted by the authority aforesaid, That from and after the first day of January, aforesaid, any Negro or other slave who shall pretend to any supernatural power, and be detected in making use of any blood, feathers, parrots-beaks, dogs-teeth, alligators-teeth, broken bottles, grave-dirt, rum, eggshells, or any other materials relative to the practice of Obeah or witchcraft, in order to delude and impose on the minds of others, shall upon conviction before two magistrates and three freeholders, suffer death or transportation; anything in this or any other act to the contrary in any wise notwithstanding."[29]

This Act never received the Royal Assent and at its expiration the matter was allowed to rest for a couple of years, but the action of the Assembly in Jamaica during the years 1787 and 1788 resulted in what was commonly called "The New Consolidated Act,"[30] to which Stephen Fuller refers as "being the present Code Noir of that Island." Clauses XIX to XXI prohibit the meetings of slaves, etc. along the general lines of previous Acts.

Clause XL represents the restrictions on Obeah without enumerating the paraphernalia, but specifies as the purpose of the deed: "In order to affect the health of lives of others, or promote the purposes of rebellion."[31] In Clause XLI, we find repeated the old penalty against poisoning, which had been overlooked in the Act of 1781, where it was supposed to be contained under the general decree against Obeah.[32]

December 14, 1808, there was passed "An Act for the protection, subsisting, clothing, and for the better order, regulation, and government of slaves, and for other purposes," which was replaced on December 19, 1816, by "An Act for the subsistence, clothing, and the better regulation and government of slaves, for enlarging the powers of the council of protection; for preventing the improper transfer of slaves; and for other purposes."[33]

In the latter Act, Clauses XXXIV to XXXVI prohibit the assemblies of slaves in the usual form, but under the section permitting, amusements on the properties to which they belong, "so as they do not make use of military drums, horns and shells" we find the further restriction, "Provided that such amusements are put an end to by ten o'clock at night." [34]

Clause XLIX (p. 123 f.) deals with Obeah and Clauses LII and LIII[35] repeat the former penalties for poisoning and having poisons in one's possession. By Clause L, placed immediately between Obeah and poisonings, slaves are forbidden to preach or teach "without a permission from the owner and the quarter sessions," and by Clause LI nightly[36] and other private meetings of slaves are declared unlawful. And as there is no mention of outside slaves or drumming or dancing we may safely conclude that these two new Clauses are associated with Myalism in its new form, the true nature of which even here escapes detection.[37] This surmise is strengthened by the fact that the whole matter is thus placed immediately after Obeah to which the legislators evidently thought it was connected. Clause LIII proceeds to extend the scope of previous legislation against the danger from poisonings and further identifies the process with Obeah. It runs as follows: "And be it further enacted, That if there shall be found in the possession of any slave any poisonous drugs, pounded glass, parrot's beaks, dog's teeth, alligator's teeth, or other materials notoriously used in the practice of Obeah or witchcraft, such slave upon conviction, shall be liable to suffer transportation from this island, or such other punishment, not extending to life, as the court shall think proper to direct."[38] The Act of 1781 had made the use of such instruments unlawful, the present Clause is directed against even having them in possession.

The prevalence of poisonings in Jamaica about this period is evidenced by a visitor to the island in 1823, as follows:[39] "A Negro man, named Schweppes or Swipes, to which his comrades had added the appellation of Saint, took it into his head to poison a preacher at Montego Bay. He but half killed the poor creature, who discovered the nature of the poison in time to prevent its fatal effects, though it is more than probable he will never recover his former health. The maniac did not escape, but argued that the spirit moved him to kill Massa Parson. He affirmed that the preacher always said 'he longed to lay down his burden; to quit this mortal life; to go to Abraham's bosom, to the bosom of his Saviour, to glory' and so forth—and he Swipes (whose brain was turned topsy-turvy) out of good-will and love, wished to help him to Heaven and glory, for which he was anxious." Again while visiting an estate on Morant River, we are told: "The cook a few days before, had endeavoured to poison Mr. G. and his family, by mixing, I think he said, ground glass in some soup, which was, however, fortunately detected in time to prevent mischief."[40] Finally, just before sailing from Port Antonio, he thus describes the contents of the "cutacoo" of a vagrant Obeah man who was apprehended: "There was an old snuff-box, several phials, some filled with liquids and some with powders, one with pounded glass; some dried herbs, teeth, beads, hair, and other trash; in short the whole farrago of an Obeah man."[41]

On December 22, 1826, was passed "An Act to alter and amend the Slave Laws of this Island." Clause LX to LXIV cover unlawful assemblies of slaves. The time for "innocent amusements" on their own properties is extended to midnight.[42] Clause LXXXII deals with Obeah and the following Clause repeats the prohibition against slaves preaching and teaching without permission, another evidence of rejuvenated Myalism.[43] In Clause LXXXIV there is a further extension of the general safeguard against the formation of "plots and conspiracies"[44] whereby meetings of sectarians between sunset and sunrise are prohibited: "Provided always, that nothing herein contained shall be deemed or taken to prevent any minister of the Presbyterian kirk, or licensed minister, from performing divine worship at any time before the hour of eight o'clock in the evening at any licensed place of worship, or to interfere with the celebration of divine worship according to the rites and ceremonies of the Jewish and Roman Catholic religions." Then follows an article for the punishment of designing teachers for laying contributions on slaves[45] and the usual prohibition against nightly meetings of slaves and the Clauses on poisoning.[46]

Clause LXXXIV prohibiting meetings of sectarians between sunset and sunrise aroused strong opposition, especially on the part of the Methodists who claimed that the instruction of the slaves was thereby practically restricted to the Established Church of England,[47] and the Act was accordingly disallowed. The despatch thereupon sent by W. Huskisson, His Majesty's Principal Secretary of State for the Colonies, addressed to the Governor of Jamaica, Sir John Keane, under date of September 22, 1827, states, in part: "Among the various subjects which this Act presents for consideration, none is more important in itself, nor more interesting to every class of society in this kingdom, than the regulations on the subject of religious instruction. The eighty-third and the two following clauses must be considered as an invasion of that toleration, to which all His Majesty's subjects, whatever may be their civil condition, are alike entitled. The prohibition of persons in a state of slavery assuming the office of religious teachers might seem a very mild restraint, or rather a fit precaution against indecorous proceedings; but amongst some of the religious bodies who employ missionaries in Jamaica, the practice of mutual instruction is stated to be an established part of their discipline. So long as the practice is carried on in an inoffensive and peaceable manner, the distress produced by the prevention of it will be compensated by no public advantage.

"The prohibition of meetings for religious worship between sunset and sunrise will, in many cases, operate as a total prohibition, and will be felt with peculiar severity by domestic slaves, inhabiting large towns, whose ordinary engagements on Sunday will not afford leisure for attendance on public worship before the evening. It is impossible to pass over without remark the invidious distinction which is made not only between Protestant dissenters and Roman Catholics, but even between Protestant dissenters and Jews. I have indeed no reason to suppose that the Jewish teachers have made any converts to their religion among the slaves, and probably, therefore, the distinction in their favour is merely nominal; still it is a preference, which, in principle, ought not to be given by the Legislature of a Christian country."[48]

Again he says further on:[49] "It may be doubtful whether the restrictions upon private meetings among the slaves, without the knowledge of the owner, was intentionally pointed at the meetings for religious worship. No objection, of course, could exist to requiring that notice should be given to the owner or manager whenever the slaves attended any such meetings; but, on the other hand, due security should be taken that the owner's authority is not improperly exerted to prevent the attendance of the slaves.

"I cannot too distinctly impress upon you that it is the settled purpose of His Majesty's government to sanction no colonial law, which needlessly infringes on the religious liberty of any class of His Majesty's subjects, and you will understand that you are riot to assent to any bill imposing any restraint of that nature, unless a clause be inserted for suspending its operation until His Majesty's pleasure shall be known."

Later, taking up the question of Obeah, he writes: "The definition of the offence of Obeah will be found to embrace many acts, against which it could not have been really intended to denounce the punishment of death. The definition of the crime of preparing to administer poison is also so extensive as to include many innocent and even some meritorious acts. Thus also the offence of possessing materials used in the practice of Obeah is imperfectly described, since no reference is made to the wicked intention in which alone the crime consists."[50]

The acknowledgment, to the Governor, of the receipt of this communication, on the part of the House of Assembly, on December 4, 1827, contains these significant words: "In enacting the eighty-third, eighty-fourth, and eighty-fifth clauses, which are particularly objected to, the House had before them the example of Demerara, and they deemed the restrictions necessary, as well for the peace of the colony as for the well-being of the slaves; that opinion the House still retains, and consequently are unable to present to your Honour any modified law on this subject."[51]

In the formal answer to the letter, passed unanimously[52] by the Jamaica House of Assembly on December 14th we read: "The eighty-third clause prohibits the preaching and teaching of slaves, not because mischief might possibly accrue, but because it has been found by experience, as the preamble in the clause declares, 'to be attended with the most pernicious consequences, and even with the loss of life.' So long as the slave subsists at the cost of the master, so long must that master's right be admitted to watch over his actions, on which depend his health and his life. Neither health nor life can be secure, if slaves are allowed to unsettle the understanding of each other, by mutually inculcating their crude notions of religion, and have free license to meet under the pretence of preaching at unseasonable hours and in improper places. The House duly appreciate the pious motives of the King's ministers, who would extend the blessings of religion all over the world, but nevertheless it is their opinion, that no persons are competent to judge of regulations intended to restrain the malpractices of 'ignorant, superstitious, and designing slaves,' unless they have made themselves acquainted with the African character by a long residence among them. These remarks equally apply to the eighty-fourth clause. Meetings for religious worship between sunrise and sunset, are prohibited only to unlicensed preachers; and it is believed that in no well organized society are persons, without character or of doubtful or secret views, suffered to go at large, under shelter of the night, amongst an ignorant peasantry, and make upon their minds an impression that may be dictated by political or religious fanaticism. . ..

Although the slaves of Jamaica have advanced rapidly in civilization within a very few years, yet it is not pretended that their progress has been so great that all those guards can be dispensed with which were thought essential by our predecessors. The eighty-third and eighty-fourth clauses are not innovations, as Mr. Huskisson seems to suppose; they are taken from the old slave law, and come again into operation on the disallowance of the new law, with this difference, that the new law provides against any misconception of the law in respect to Catholics and Jews, and permits licensed ministers to perform divine worship at any licensed place of worship to the hour of eight; and when it is remembered that in Jamaica the setting sun varies from half-past five to half-past six, it will appear that time enough is afforded for the night worship of slaves. . ..

"The remarks of Mr. Huskisson, on the clause for the punishment of Obeah, naturally offer themselves to one ignorant of the extent of African superstition, and the horrible crimes Negroes will perpetrate sometimes to gratify revenge, and often to acquire influence that may enable them to levy contributions on the fears of their more timid fellows. Negroes are seen to pine away to death under the pretended sorceries of the Obeah man; and, where the imagination does not perform the work of death with sufficient celerity, the more certain aid of poison is called in, to hasten the fate of the victim. Mr. Huskisson considers, that under the next clause, many innocent and some meritorious acts are exposed to punishment. But it is submitted, that the possession of poisonous drugs by Negroes cannot be innocent, unless confided to them by their masters; which fact can readily be proven."[53]

Both sides to this controversy were right in part, and yet they both failed to discern the real point at issue. To the home government, there was actual need of suppressing what appealed to them as an outburst of religious bigotry against the non-conformists; to the planters in Jamaica it was clear that there was growing up among the slaves a religious fanaticism and unrest that could augur nothing but another upheaval of the social order with attempted massacre and destruction of property. What neither side of the argument even suspected was that under guise of Methodist Revivalism, the long persecuted and seemingly forgotten Myalism was taking a new lease of life and imbuing the slaves in general with its own peculiar religious mania in preparation for the day when the solemn fetish oath might be administered for the general overthrow of the white regime. And the Methodist authorities, on their part, could only see a consoling outpouring of the spirit, and countless brands saved from the burning, when in reality the consequence of misguided zeal was a dangerous recrudescence of pagan practices with a veneer of Christianity, cloaked and disguised as a Methodist Revival.[54]

Similar excesses were experienced later by another group who surpassed even the Methodists in the unbridled spirit of Revivalism.

Gardner thus describes the facts. "With a few exceptions, native Baptist churches became associations of men and women who, in too many cases, mingled the belief and even practice of Myalism with religious observances, and who perverted and corrupted what they retained of these; among them sensuality was almost unrestrained. Their leaders or 'daddies,' as a class were overbearing, tyrannical, and lascivious, and united the authority of the slave-driver with the darkest forms of spiritual despotism. Of scriptural teaching there was little. Simple facts were so perverted, that they would have been ridiculous had they not been blasphemous."[55] It was this condition of affairs that led up to the final slave-rebellion just before emancipation went into effect.

As recently as October 12, 1932, a letter appeared in THE DAILY GLEANER of Kingston, Jamaica, entitled "An Open Letter to Ministers of Religion" and signed by R. H. Ferguson, wherein the latest form of Myalistic Revivalism, known as Pocomanism, is thus described. "I see a house yonder. Those within are singing. Come stealing sweet cadences the notes of that well-known hymn

'Day is dying in the West,
Heaven is touching earth with rest.'

"The hymn ceases and ah! They strike up some lively tune as 'Bright soul, wha' mek you tun' back?' Bodies are swaying, and, oh soul of Bacchus! Are they drunk?

Pandemonium!—a religious frenzy. I am minded of the Berserkers—a little madness as men and women jumping like kangaroos, to a well-timed rhythm place their hands to their mouths, grunting (is it grunting?) for all they are worth, like wild boars sounding their war-cries as they resist the onslaught of the charging hounds.

"That exercise over, a stalward Negro man, wearing a red and white bandana, steps forth and makes an oration. Listen. 'I come here to take off ghosts and if the Devil himself come with you, him must go!' Can it be possible in law-abiding Jamaica? Sick folks are washed and anointed with evil-smelling oils, presumably, 'oil a tun' back,' 'oil a carry-away,' 'oil a keep him down,' 'oil a bamba,' 'dead man drops.' Oh shade of Æsculapius! Songs, songs, sacred songs.

"Does the law punish the man who practices Obeah? Are these practices a form of Obeah? If so, are they carried on in the guise of Christianity? Do such meetings contribute to the uplift of the people, and make of the children the ideal citizens of the days to come? . . .

"My humble opinion is that that sect should not be allowed to broadcast such demoralizing influences. The island can safely do without Pocomanism. . . .

"With the greatest alarm I once listened to a man haranguing a crowd in New Town. Said he, 'Your ministers tell you when you die, you gwine a heaven go drink milk and honey. Who tell dem say God have cow-pen a heaven? etc.' . . . And now I am asking potently, should such people be allowed to carry on and broadcast heresies, pernicious, destructive, damning? . . .

"I respectfully beg your fraternity to get together and represent this matter to the legislators to the end that our fair island may be saved the disaster of a religious upheaval brought about by whom? An ignorant set of dancing, prancing, steppers, a set of howling windbags—men too lazy to work, and so elect to collect toll while preying on the credulity of the simple—self-styled 'shepherds' determined to make a mess of Christianity."

This letter evoked the following editorial in THE DAILY GLEANER Of the following day. "POCOMANISM. Mr. R. H. Ferguson cries aloud in his Open Letter to Ministers of Religion (published in this paper yesterday) that Pocomanism is 'tearing at the vitals of the Church.' He is aware that this 'Pocomanism,' which he says is the result of Pocomania, will strike the average reader as being something strange and weird; therefore in this letter to the ministers of religion he explains what Pocomanism is, and it turns out to be neither more nor less than our old friend Myalism, which is much better known in these days as Revivalism. Pocomania, then, is a frenzy brought about by men and women exciting themselves—'jumping like kangaroos,' as Mr. Ferguson expresses it—singing hymns calculated to stimulate the emotions, deliberately surrendering their minds and bodies to superstitious influences. The leaders of these revivalists or pocomaniacs claim to be able to exercise ghosts that are haunting afflicted persons, and also to cure the sick by anointing them with special mixtures, usually of an evil-smelling description. These men are nothing but a survival of the 'Myal men' of a hundred years ago, and of West African priests who practiced the same rites in their native country. And they seem to thrive on their deceptions.

"It is a pity that Mr. Ferguson writes in a manner that suggests a sort of long, loud scream of the pen, varied by spasmodic jumps, for the evil to which he calls attention is one that should certainly not be overlooked. His application to it of the term 'Pocomanism' is very effective in directing notice to the thing to which it refers.

Religious revivals are of all sorts and descriptions; to speak of a revival merely, therefore, is not to evoke in the mind of the average hearer any startling picture of physical obscenity or moral degradation; which perhaps is why, when a protest is voiced against 'Revivalism' of the ghost-catching or 'balm' healing type, not much notice is taken of it. Yet those who have seen the ceremonies by which ghosts are supposed to be laid and sickness to be cured, recognize that even the ejaculatory manner adopted by Mr. Ferguson in describing- them does not exaggerate the facts. The thing itself is worse than any picture of it could be, and it is no wonder that he wants to know whether these practices are not a form of Obeah, even if carried on under the guise of Christianity. He suggests that legislation should be brought to bear on this Pocomanism and that the ministers of the island should unite to crush the Pocomaniacs, 'an ignorant set of dancing, prancing, steppers, a set of howling windbags, men too lazy to work, self-styled "shepherds" determined to make a mess of Christianity.'

"The language is strong, but not too strong; the denunciation is fully merited. We agree entirely that this sort of Revivalism, or Pocomanism, must have a bad effect upon the minds and morals of the younger people who witness it and that it deliberately encourages the basest forms of superstition. But it is no use appealing to the ministers of religion; they cannot put a stop to it. preaching and teaching will doubtless have a salutary effect in the long run, but that long run means years and years, a couple of generations, perhaps a century. We ought to have quicker and more effective action to deal with the evil; such action means legislation, and that in its turn will demand a comprehensive description and definition of the practices to be suppressed. That may not be easy, but we should hope that it will not be impossible. The claim to 'take off ghosts,' to heal diseases by anointing with oil, and incantations, is really a form of fraud such as Obeah is defined to be in our laws. A disguise is thrown over these thing by the use of terms current in the Christian religion, but the fraud, the superstition, the vileness of the dancing and the sexual excitation that follows are patent to everyone except the willingly deluded. It will have to be the lawyers, however, who must try their hands at framing legislation to suppress the practices complained of. We hope these lawyers will be equal to the task, for these orgiastic revival dances—this Pocomanism which seems to be more common than should be possible at this date of our history—undoubtedly do much to frustrate the efforts made by educationists and the religious organizations in this country."

But even if they do legislate against this latest Myalistic outbreak, it is to be feared that they will at best abolish for a time the public expression of the real spirit which we must expect merely to retire once more to secret functions in preparation for the day when it will ultimately break out anew under another guise in which it will not be immediately recognized. It is not always easy to analyze the Negro's purpose in a dance.

In quite recent times, I have personally known well-meaning Ecclesiastics, comparatively new to Jamaica and its ways, commenting with approval regarding the Minto dance, that it was graceful and free from the objectional embraces of most modern dances. In their innocence, or rather ignorance, they never suspected the entire purpose of the dance which consists in the arousing of the passions, being derived from the same source as the Haitian Calenda already described. When told of its true import they blushed at the memory of the interest they had shown in watching the dance. An interest that had probably made the participants chuckle shamelessly at Parson's lack of understanding,—"Im ignorant fee true, Sah!"—For they who dance the Minto know full well its evil purpose.

William Wilberforce asserted: "The Jamaica planters long imputed the most injurious effects on the health and even lives of their slaves, to the African practice of Obeah, or witchcraft. The Agents for Jamaica declared to the Privy Council, in 1788, that they 'ascribed a very considerable portion of the annual mortality among the Negroes in that island to that fascinating mischief.' I know that of late, ashamed of being supposed to have punished witchcraft with such severity, it had been alleged, that the professors of Obeah used to prepare and administer poison to the subjects of their spells; but anyone who will only examine the laws of Jamaica against these practices, or read the evidence of the agents, will see plainly that this was not the view that was taken of the proceedings of the Obeah men, but that they were considered as impostors, who preyed on their ignorant countrymen by the pretended intercourse with evil spirits, or by some other pretences to supernatural powers."[56] And remarks on the very next page: "No sooner did a Negro become a Christian, then the Obeah men despaired of bringing him into subjection."[57]

This statement of Wilberforce brought almost immediately from the Reverend George Wilson Bridges, an Anglican Clergyman in Jamaica the following caustic retort: "You speak of the African practice of witchcraft, called Obeah; and referring to the laws which make the dreadful effects of that superstition punishable by death, you call it 'folly' to attempt 'rooting out pagan superstition by severity of punishment.' Are you then so ignorant, Sir, of the manners and customs of the people whose cause you profess to advocate, as not to know that Obeah, and death, are synonymous: that the latter is the invariable end and object of the former, and that this imported African superstition is widely different from the harmless tales of witches and broomsticks, which once frightened you in the arms of your nursery maid? Your feelings have probably been shocked by stories of burning old women for bewitching pigs, and swimming them for assuming the shape of a hare; but are you not to be told that

Obeah is a superstition dreadfully different from these fantasies; that it is, in fear, the practice of occult poisons: by which thousands have suffered in these islands, and which, though gradually giving way beneath the spreading influence of Christianity, must nevertheless, in every proved case, be punished by human laws, as severe as those which attach to the convicted murderer in every land."[58]

And yet, as we have seen, Wilberforce was not far astray in his estimates, not only of the Laws of Jamaica, but also of the general attitude of amused toleration with which Obeah was usually regarded by the planters of the island, until the rebellion of, 1760 opened the eyes of all to the connection between Obeah and poisonings, and led the Assembly to legislate directly against the practice of this black art.

Still, despite the fact that chroniclers made no specific mention of the dangerous pest as such, there are many indications that it exacted an awful toll of human lives from the earliest days of Jamaica as an English Colony.

In an appendix to his *Reports of the Jamaica Assembly on the subject of the slave trade*, Stephen Fuller gave a summary of the Negroes from Africa who were sold in Jamaica between 1764 and 1788. During this period some 50,000 slaves were imported by the five principal agents and of these nearly 15% came from the Gold Coast and about 10% from Whydah. One firm, Messrs Cappells, who seemingly specialized in Gold Coast Negroes, reports between November, 1782, and January, 1788, out of a total of 10,380 importations, 5,924, or nearly 60% as from the Gold Coast and only 444 from Whydah.[59]

But it is not only numerically but also by his dominant spirit, as we have seen, that the Gold Coast or Ashanti slave asserted an ascendancy over the rest of the slaves and firmly established in Jamaica his own form of witchcraft, Obeah, with its concomitant poisonings.

Robert Hammill Nassau states: "The slaves exported from Africa to the British possessions in the West Indies brought with them some of the seeds of African plants, especially those they regarded as 'medicinal,' or they found among the fauna and flora of the tropical West Indies some of the same plants and animals held by them as sacred to fetich in their tropical Africa. The ceiba, or silk-cotton tree, at whose base I find in Africa so many votive offerings of fetich worship, they found flourishing in Jamaica.

They had established on their plantations the fetich doctor, their dance, their charm, their lore, before they had learned English at all. And when the British missionaries came among them with school and church, while many of the converts were sincere, there were those of the doctor class who, like Simon Magus, entered into the church-fold for sake of whatever gain they could make by the white man's new influence, the white man's Holy Spirit. Outwardly everything was serene and Christian. Within was working an element of diabolism, fetichism, there known by the name of Obeah, under whose leaven some of the churches were wrecked. And the same diabolism, known as Voodoo worship in the Negro communities of the Southern United States has emasculated the spiritual life of many professed Christians."[60] Again he says, "There are native poisons.

It is known that sometimes they are secretly used in revenge, or to put out of the way a relative whose wealth is desired to be inherited. . . . The distinction between a fetich and a poison is vague in the thought of many natives. What I call a 'poison' is to them only another material form of a fetich power, both poison and fetich being supposed to be made efficient by the presence of an adju-vant spirit. Not all deaths of foreigners in Africa are due to malaria. Some of them have been doubtless due to poison administered by a revengeful employee."[61]

Sir Hans Sloane, who accompanied the Duke of Albermarle to Jamaica in 1687, in capacity of physician to the Governor, remarks of the slaves: "They formerly on their festivals were allowed the use of trumpets after their fashion, and drums made of a piece of a hollow tree, covered on one end with any green skin, and stretched with thouls or pins. But making use of these in their wars at home in Africa, it was thought too much inciting them to rebellion, and so they were prohibited by the customs of the island."[62] Again he says: "The Indians and Negroes have no manner of religion by what I could observe of them. 'Tis true they have several ceremonies, as dances, playing, &c. but these for the most part are so far from being acts of adoration of a God, that they are for the most part mixed with a great deal of bawdry and lewdness."[63] With the suppression of drumming and assemblies, the Myal dance (and in a disguised form) was all that was left of their religious practices that could be produced in public. In passing Sloane remarks a couple of cases of poisoning, but makes no mention of Obeah as such.[64]

Charles Leslie, writing in 1740, states: "When anything about a plantation is missing, they have a solemn kind of oath, which the eldest Negro always administers, and which by them is accounted so sacred, that except they have the express command of their master or overseer, they never set about it, and then they go very solemnly to work.

They range themselves in that spot of ground which is appropriated for the Negro burying place, and one of them opens a grave. He who acts the priest, takes a little of the earth, and puts it into every one of their mouths; they say, that if any has been guilty, their belly swells, and occasions death. I never saw any instance of this but once; and it was certainly a fact that a boy did swell, and acknowledged the theft when be was dying: But I am far from thinking there was any connection betwixt the cause and the effect, for a thousand accidents might have occasioned it, without accounting for it by that foolish ceremony."[65] While this passage is frequently quoted as an example of Obeah, it is really a religious ordeal, similar to so many practiced in Africa. It is employed publicly and for the general good. Consequently we must ascribe it to Myalism and not to Obeah.[66]

Edward Long, the first historian to refer to Obeah by name is writing after the revelation caused by the rebellion of 1760. As yet his views are not as set as we find them fifteen years later in the document studied in an earlier chapter, and he quite naturally confuses Obeah and Myalism. He says of the slaves: "They firmly believe in the apparition of spectres. Those of deceased friends are duppies; others, of more hostile and tremendous aspect, like our raw-head-and-bloody bones, are called bugaboos. The most sensible among them fear the supernatural powers of the African Obeah men, or pretended conjurers; often ascribing those mortal effects to magic, which are only the natural operation of some poisonous juice, or preparation, dexterously administered by these villains. But the creoles imagine, that the virtues of baptism, or making them Christians, render their art wholly ineffectual; and for this reason only, many of them have desired to be baptized, that they might be secured from Obeah.

"Not long since, some of these execrable wretches in Jamaica introduced what they called the Myal dance[67] and established a kind of society, into which they invited all they could. The lure hung out was, that every Negro, initiated into the Myal society, would be invulnerable by the white man; and although they might in appearance be slain, the Obeah man could, at his pleasure, restore the body to life. The method, by which this trick was carried on, was by a cold infusion of the herb branched calalue; which, after the agitation of dancing, threw the party into a profound sleep. In this state he continued, to all appearances lifeless, no pulse, nor motion of the heart, being perceptible; till on being rubbed with another infusion (as yet unknown to the whites), the effects of the calalue gradually went off, the body resumed its motions, and the party on whom the experiment had been tried, awoke as from a trance, entirely ignorant of anything that had passed since he left off dancing."[68] A few pages later, Long adds: "Bits of red rag, cats teeth, parrots feathers, eggshells and fish-bones are frequently stuck up at the doors of their houses when they go from home leaving anything of value within, (sometimes they hang them on fruit trees, and place them in cornfields), to deter thieves. Upon conversing with some of the Creoles upon this custom, they laugh at the supposed virtue of the charm, and said they practiced it only to frighten away the salt- water Negroes, of whose depredations they are most apprehensive."[69]

Long seems too easily satisfied with the explanation of this Creole. Even today, every Negro in Jamaica has a superstitious fear of anything that is referred to, even in joke, as preternatural. On more than one occasion I have seen a gentleman throw a piece of ordinary paper on the floor and say to the housemaid, a married woman of exemplary character and a regular church-member: "Look out Aida, duppy there." To which Aida would invariably reply with a laugh: "Me no belieb duppy, Sah! All nonsense, Sah!" And yet she would give that piece of paper a wide berth, and if told to bring something that would necessitate her passing the suspicious object, she would walk all the way around the room to avoid it. When asked why she did not go direct, she would explain: "Me prefar walk dis way, Sah!" And that paper would remain there untouched until a friendly breeze blew it out of the house.

During the last quarter of the eighteenth century, there lived one of the most desperate characters in Jamaica history. His depredations accomplished single handed and over a wide area left the impression that he was the head of a numerous and well-organized band of robbers and his very name became synonymous with terror throughout the country districts. Owing to the loss of two fingers in an early encounter with a Maroon, he was generally known as Three-finger Jack. Concerning this desperado, many accounts have come down to us, all of which show that his chief reliance was the machinations of a notorious Obeah man. Thus we are told: "Dr. Moseley in his Treatise on Sugar, says, 'I saw the Obi of this famous Negro robber, Three-finger Jack, this terror of Jamaica in 1780. The Maroon who slew him brought it to me. It consisted of a goat's horn, filled with a compound of grave dirt, ashes, the blood of a black cat, and human fat, all mixed into a kind of paste. A cat's foot, a dried toad, a pig's tail, a flip of virginal parchment, of kid's skin, with characters marked in blood on it, were also in his Obeah bag."[70] Burdett thus describes the Obeah man who bestowed this grewsome gift on Mansong: "Amalkir, the Obeah practitioner, dwelt in a loathsome cave, far removed from the inquiring eye of the suspicious whites, in the Blue Mountains; he was old and shrivelled; a disorder had contracted all his nerves, and he could hardly crawl. His cave was the dwelling-place, or refuge of robbers; he encouraged them in their depredations; and gave them Obi, that they might fearlously rush where danger stood. This Obi was supposed to make them invulnerable to the attacks of the white men, and they placed implicit belief in its Virtues."[71] He evidently played the rôle of Myalist as well as Obeah man.

Coming now to the nineteenth century, as would be expected, every writer in Jamaica has something to say about Obeah which still remains, however, a great enigma to be explained according to each individual's point of view. Thus Stewart writing in 1808, and expressing the opinion that was commonly maintained by the missionaries: "There is one good effect which the simple persuasion of his being a Christian produces on the mind of the Negro; it is an effectual antidote against the spells and charms of his native superstition. One Negro who desires to be revenged on another, if he fears a more open and manly attack on his adversary, has usually recourse to Obeah. This is considered as a potent and irresistible spell, withering and palsying, by undescribable terrors, and unwonted sensations, the unhappy victim. Like the witches' cauldron in *Macbeth*, it is a combination of all that is hateful and disgusting; a toad's foot, a lizard's tail, a snake's tooth, the plumage of the carrion crow, or vulture, a broken eggshell, a piece of wood fashioned into the shape of a coffin, with many other nameless ingredients, compose the fatal mixture. It will of course be conceived that the practice of Obeah can have little effect, without a Negro is conscious that it is practiced upon him, or thinks so: for as the sole evil lies in the terrors of a perturbed fancy, it is of little consequence whether it is really practiced or not, if he only imagines that it is. An Obeah man or woman upon an estate, is therefore a very dangerous person; and the practice of it for evil purposes is made felony by the law. But numbers may be swept off by its infatuation before the practice is detected; for, strange as it may appear, so much do the Negroes stand in awe of these wretches, so much do they dread their malice and their power, that, though knowing the havoc they have made, and are still making, many of them are afraid to discover them to the whites; and others, perhaps, are in league with them for sinister purposes of mischief and revenge. A Negro under this infatuation can only be cured of his terrors by being made a Christian; refuse him this indulgence, and he soon sinks a martyr to imagine evils. The author knew an instance of a Negro, who, being reduced by the fatal influence of Obeah to the lowest state of dejection and debility, from which there were little hopes of his recovery, was surprisingly and rapidly restored to health and to spirits, by being baptized a Christian; so wonderful are the workings of a weak and superstitious imagination. But, though so liable to be perverted into an instrument of malice and revenge, Obeah, at least a sort of it, may be said to have its uses. When placed in the gardens and grounds of the Negroes, it becomes an excellent guard or watchman, scaring away the predatory runaway, and midnight plunderer, with more effective terror than gins and spring guns. It loses its effect, however, when put to protect the gardens and plantain walks of the Buckras."[72]

Matthew Gregory Lewis, who was already quoted on Myalism, records in his diary, in his own delightful way, an accusation of Obeah brought by one of his own servants, Pickle, against a fellow-servant Edward, as follows: "He had accused Edward of breaking open his house, and had begged him to help him to Ills goods again; and 'Edward had gone at midnight into the bush' (*i. e.* the wood), and had gathered the plant whangra, which he had boiled in an iron pot, by a fire of leaves, over which he went puff, puffie: 'and said the sautee-sautee; and then had cut the whangra root into four pieces, three to bury at the plantation gates, and one to burn; and to each of these three pieces he gave the name of a Christian, one of which was Daniel; and Edward had said, that this would help him to find his goods; but instead of that, he had immediately felt this pain in his side, and therefore he was sure that, instead of using Obeah to find his goods, Edward had used it to kill himself.'"[73] Even in my time in Jamaica, it was enough to threaten to "burn whangra" within the hearing of some petty thief, to have the goods returned at once. I understood that failure to do so, would cause the body of the thief to break out into the most terrible sores, in case the threat had been carried into execution.

Another entry in Lewis' diary is worth repeating here. Under date of January 28, 1816, we find it recorded: "There are certainly many excellent qualities in the negro character; their worst faults appear to be this prejudice respecting Obeah, and the facility with which they are frequently induced to poison to the right hand and to the left. A neighbouring gentleman, as I hear, has now three negroes in prison, all domestics, and one of them grown grey in his service, for poisoning him with corrosive sublimate; his brother was actually killed by similar means; yet I am assured that both of them were reckoned men of great humanity. Another agent, who appears to be in high favour with the negroes whom he now governs, was obliged to quit an estate, from the frequent attempts to poison him; and a person against whom there is no sort of charge alleged for tyranny, after being brought to the doors of death by a cup of coffee, only escaped a second time by his civility, in giving the beverage, prepared for himself, to two young bookkeepers, to both of whom it proved fatal. It, indeed came out, afterwards, that this crime was also effected by the abominable belief in Obeah, the woman who mixed the draught, had no idea of its being poison, but she had received the deleterious ingredients from an Obeah man, as 'a charm to make her massa good to her!' by which the negroes mean, the compelling a person to give another everything for which that other may ask him."[74]

James Stephen, on the other hand, writing in 1824, in defence of the slaves, still clings to the old estimate of Obeah as being for the most part fanciful. Thus he argues: "Obeah also is a practice, which has, by laws of Jamaica and Dominica, all of a modern date, been constituted a capital offence: and many negroes have of late years been executed for it in the former island, though in many of our other islands it has never been considered as worthy of having a place in the copious and comprehensive catalogues of crimes furnished by their penal slave laws. Obeah and poison are deserving of a particular consideration, because they were: once seriously alleged by the Agent of Jamaica and other colonists, as great causes of the dreadful mortality which prevails among the slaves in our islands. The subjects also are curious in their nature, and I was prepared to offer much authoritative information upon them, tending to prove that they are for the most part the grounds only of fanciful, though fatal imputations on the unfortunate slaves."[75]

This passage drew a sharp reply from Alexander Barclay who had just returned from a twenty-one years' residence in Jamaica: "Another part of the slave law which Mr. Stephen disapproves of is the punishment of Obeah with death but he has not assigned his reasons for thinking that 'it has been, for the most part, the ground of a fanciful though fatal imputation on the poor slaves.' The deaths which the Obeah man occasioned by working on the imaginations of their superstitious countrymen, and by poison, certainly were not 'fanciful,' whatever their pretended supernatural powers might be.

"I was present some years ago, at a trial of a notorious Obeah man, driver on an estate in the parish of St. David, who, by the over-whelming influence he had acquired over the minds of his deluded victims, and the more potent means he had at command to accom-plish his ends, had done great injury among the slaves on the proper-ty before it was discovered. One of the witnesses, a negro belonging to the same estate, was asked—"Do you know the prisoner to be an Obeah man?' 'Ess, massa, shadow-catcher, true.' 'What do you mean by shadow-catcher?' 'Him ha coffin, (a little coffin produced),him set for catch dem shadow.' 'What shadow do you mean?' 'When him set obeah for summary (somebody), him catch dem shadow, and dem go dead'; and too surely they were soon dead, when he pretended to have caught their shadows, by whatever means it was effected. Two other causes, besides the law, have contributed to make this now a crime of much less frequent occurrence,—the influence of Christianity, and the end put by the abolition to the importation of more African superstition."[76]

George Wilson Bridges, in his *Annals of Jamaica*, is also outspoken. In explaining African Fetishism he observes: "The Obeah, with which we are so fatally familiar in Jamaica, is no other than this doctrine of the fetish."[77] He had previously said: "The dexterity with which the Negroes make use of poison to gratify their human propensities, surpasses the utmost refinements of Asiatic cruelty . . . it is concentrated in so small a compass, that the immersion in any liquor of the finger in whose nail it lies concealed, causes the immediate death of the drinker."[78]

In the closing days of slavery, on the very eve of Emancipation, we have the testimony of Dr. R. R. Madden, who, as he tells us himself was one of six stipendary magistrates who in October 1833, were sent out to Jamaica.[79] In a letter dated Kingston, September 8, 1834, Madden writes: "An Obeah man was lately committed to the Spanish Town prison for practicing on the life of a Negro child. It appeared in evidence that he went to a Negro hut, and asked for some fire to light his pipe; that he was seen to put some bush (herb) into the pipe, and then placing himself to windward of the child, commenced smoking, so that the fumes were directed by the wind towards the child. Immediately after he went away, the child was taken alarmingly sick; the father pursued the man suspected of Obeahing, and brought him back. He was accused of being an Obeah man, of having injured the child; and being threatened with violence if he did not take off the Obeah he consented to do so, and accordingly performed certain ceremonies for that purpose; the child improved and he was suffered to depart. The improvement however was only temporary; he was again sent for and with a similar result.

"I have copied the account of his examination by the attorney-general, from the original document. He confessed that he was a practicer of Obeah, that he did it not for gain or vengeance, but solely because the devil put it into his head to be bad. He had learned the use of the bush from an old Negro man on . . . estate, where master had been poisoned by old man. It was a small plant which grew in the mountains, but did not know the name of it; (he gave some of the dried leaves to the attorney, who showed them to me for examination; but they were so broken that nothing was to be made of them). He said it did him no hurt to smoke this plant; but whoever breathed the smoke was injured by it; he had no spite against the father or mother of the child, nor wish to injure them. He saw the child, and he could not resist the instigation of the devil to Obeah it, but be hoped he would never do it any more; he would pray to God to put it out of his head to do it. Such was the singular statement made to the attorney-general by the prisoner; and the attorney-general informed me, made with an appearance of frankness and truth which gave a favourable impression of its veracity."[80] This looks like smoking whangra or wanga which has become very common of recent years. The effect on the smoker, however, is similar to that of Indian hemp, and renders many of the devotees veritable maniacs.

Dr. Madden also records: "There are two descriptions of Obeah; one that is practiced by means of incantations; and the other by the administering of medicated potions in former times, it is said of poisons, and these practitioners were called Myal men."[81] He is here mixing up the two, Obeah and Myalism, as might be expected from one insufficiently acquainted with the island to discriminate. The whole subject interests him nevertheless, as he takes note: "In the criminal record-book of the parish of St. Andrews, I find the following obeah cases:

"1773. Sarah, tried 'for having in her possession cats' teeth, cats' claws, cats' jaws, hair, beads, knotted cords, and other materials, relative to the practice of Obeah, to delude and impose on the mind of the Negroes.'—Sentenced to be transported.

"1776. Solomon, 'for having materials in his possession for the practice of Obeah.'—To be transported.

"1777. Tony, 'for practicing Obeah, or witchcraft, on a slave named Fortune, by means of which, said slave became dangerously ill.'—Not Guilty.

"1782. Neptune, 'for making use of rum, hair, chalk, stones, and other materials, relative to the practice of Obeah, or witchcraft.'—To be transported."[82]

Immediately after Jamaican emancipation, and during the trying days of reconstruction of the entire social order, with a readjustment to conditions that were so vastly different from the accepted status of nearly two hundred years when the word of the master usually stood against the world, free rein was given to the religious frenzy that brought again into vogue the Myalistic spirit so long repressed. A spirit of exultation naturally drove the slave of yesterday to take advantage of his freedom and sate himself with long-forbidden joys and the outbursts of religious fanaticism became so intermingled with nocturnal saturnalia, that for a time it was difficult to distinguish the one from the other. The old objective of Myalism quickly reasserted itself. Now that the shackles had been stricken from their bodies, why not strike the chains from their souls as well? To "dig up Obeah" consequently became widespread and persistent.

This gave witchcraft a set-back for a time, or rather made it even more secretive and vindictive. As a consequence, there was no abatement in the general fear and terror in which it was held by Negroes without exception. And it cannot be surprising if occasionally the practitioner of Obeah, perhaps for self-protection, assumed the rôle of Myalist, and "dug up" perhaps the Obeah that he himself had planted. In public, too, he might became a Myalist Doctor, while in secret he was still the Obeah man. He could apply the healing properties of herbs to counteract the very poisons he had occultly administered. Finally, together with the vile concoction devised at the midnight hour for harm and ruin, he might fashion the protective fetish as a counter-irritant. And the Myal man in turn! Is it entirely improbable that he may have on occasion stooped to unprofessional practices, and with his knowledge of vegetable poisons played the rôle of his rival in herbal lore? In any case, from this time on, we find an ever increasing confusion of Obeah and Myalism in the accounts that have come down to us.

Thus John Joseph Gurney, in a letter addressed to Henry Clay of Kentucky and dated Flushing, L. I., June 8, 1840, writes as the tourist and not as a scientific investigator. He is describing his visit to Jamaica a few month earlier, and remarks: "Under the guidance of our friends J. and M. Candler, we drove several miles into the country, to breakfast at Papine, the estate of J. B. Wildman, late member of parliament for Colchester. There we were entertained by William Manning, a catechist of the Church Missionary Society, who like other agents of that institution in the island, is very valuable and useful. . . .

"We were disappointed, on visiting the sugar works of Papine, to find them stopped; and we saw young men, doing nothing, in some of the comfortable cottages which have been built on the property. The reason assigned was, that there was 'a matter to settle.' The said matter turned out to be the trial of a 'Myalist,' or 'black doctor,' one of those persons who hold communion, as is imagined, with departed spirits, and practice medicine, under their direction, for the cure of the living-the diseases themselves, being ascribed to Obeah, or evil witchcraft. These superstitions, although not nearly as prevalent as formerly, still prevail in some places, and deprived as the Negroes now are of regular medical attendance, some of them have recourse to these magical quack doctors, to the great danger of their lives. The whole day was now given up by the people to this strange concern; but under a promise of their working for their master two of their usual spare days, in lieu of it. The Myalist, a young fellow of eighteen or twenty, dressed in the height of fashion and jet black, was brought up before our friend Manning to be examined—several men, and a crowd of women, being in attendance. He openly confessed his necromancy, and as a proof of its success, showed us two miserable women, one sick of fever, the other mutilated with leprosy, whom he pretended to have cured. The evidence was regarded by the people as resistless, and our plain declaration of disbelief in Myalism, were very unwelcome to them, They said it was 'no good.' We were sorry to observe the obstinacy of their delusions, but such things will be gradually corrected by Christian instruction."[83] If Mr. Gurney could only have looked well into the future, he might have revised his prophecy!

The same fatuous hopefulness inspired the Reverend James M. Phillippo of Spanish Town, who spent twenty years as a Baptist Missionary in Jamaica. Writing of this same period, he says: "It may be remarked that the spell of Obeism and its kindred abominations is broken. In some districts, it is true, Myalism has recently revived; but it has been owing to the absence of a law since the abrogation of the Slave Act, by which the perpetrators could be punished, together with the difficulties and expensiveness, in many districts, of procuring proper medical advice and aid. Thus the Myal men having most of them been employed in attendance of the sick in the hospitals of estates, and thereby acquiring some knowledge of medicine, have, since the abolition of slavery, set up as medical men; and, in order to increase their influence, and, consequently, their gains, have called to their aid the mysteries of this abominable superstition, in many cases accomplishing their purposes by violence as well as by terror. The more effectually to delude the multitude, the priests of this deadly art, now that religion has become general, have incorporated with it a religious phraseology, together with some of the religious observances of the most popular denominations, and thus have in some instances succeeded in imposing on the credulity and fears of many of whom better things had been expected."[84]

We will find our next witness more discriminating. From long experience and close contact with every class of Jamaicans, he had learned to recognize the fundamental elements that made up their natural religious and superstitious tendencies, so commonly confused and intermingled in practice, but nevertheless, even then actually distinguishable in their principles.

In consequence of the rebellion that started at Morant Bay in October, 1865, and which led to the trial and execution of George William Gordon, a Royal Commission was appointed "to inquire respecting certain disturbances in the Island of Jamaica." Oil February 26, 1866, Beckford Davis, Clerk of the Peace of St. George's, now a part of the Parish of Portland, appeared before the Commission and was examined under oath. One point on which he was questioned in detail was the prevalence and influence of Obeah. His evidence, in part, was as follows: "It is a twofold art; it is the art of poisoning, combined with the art of imposing upon the credulity of ignorant people, by a pretence of witchcraft. Its effects are produced by poisoning. The Obeah men are parties who are acquainted with many of the simples of this country, which are not known, and they administer them with a very pernicious effect. . . . I can only imagine what they

are from the effects which I have seen produced on individuals. . . .
I did not see the poison administered. I know that the general belief
is that Obeah men are acquainted with the venomous plants of this
country; their habit of practice in it is by imposing on the Negroes by
means of charms and things of that kind, such as dried fowl's head,
a lizard's bones, old eggshells, tufts of hair, cats' claws, ducks' skulls,
and things of that kind. I have seen a good deal of it."

Asked: "Are these Obeah men still much consulted?" he answered: "Very much indeed; and their influence is so great that nothing that can be said to the black population can induce the more
ignorant of them to question the power of the Obeah man. . . . They
have no fixed residence. They wander about the country wherever
they can pick up dupes. . . . The people have many superstitions
about them, but they are mortally afraid of them."

He testifies about one particular Obeah man who was apprehended in his district but was sent to Port Antonio for trial, and
describes the contents of his chest "and a book full of strange characters." Among the Obeah articles noted in the chest was a white
powder, which was identified by Dr. Robert Edward Gayle of St.
George's as being arsenic.

Being asked: "Did you ever see an Obeah stick?" he replies:
"Oh yes, plenty of them." "With twisted serpents round them?" "Yes,
some; and some with the likeness of a man's head, only of a very
deformed cast. They have different kinds of things on them. The
Negroes are in great dread of them; they consider if an Obeah man

touches you with one of these sticks, some great misfortune will happen, if not death itself."

Questioned further if he had ever seen an Obeah man with "a globe of glass into which persons look to see the future?" he asserts: "They have not arrived at that stage of superstition yet. Grave dirt is a favourable article with the Obeah man. . . . It is the grave dirt taken from whence the corpse is buried. It is supposed that if an Obeah man throws that at a person, he will die."

To the inquiry: "Are the Obeah men solitary persons or have they wives and families?" he answers: "Those that I have seen have always been single men." "Has he any distinct mark by which he is known?" "None in particular, that I know of, except that he is generally possessed of a very bad countenance. . . . There is generally a peculiarity about them."

Finally asked: "Do not they possess the art of curing as well as poisoning?" he declared: "No; it is another class that do that, called 'Myal men'; they profess to undo the work of the Obeah man." "They are the antidote, not the bane?" "Just So."[85]

The real sinister element of Obeah now began to assert itself. As the entire tone of the Royal Commission had been from the start antagonistic to Governor Eyre and its every move was sympathetic towards the restless masses who had been implicated in the Morant Bay uprising where Obeah had played its evil part, many an Obeah man boasted of the influence he had exercised throughout the conduct of the investigation and consequently applied his trade with new energy and the general terrorization of the island.

Seven years after the publication of the *Report of the Jamaica Royal Commission*, Charles Rampini writes: "Of all the motive powers which influence the Negro character, by far the most potent, as it is also the most dangerous, is that of Obeah. . . . The Obeah man or woman is one of the great guild or fraternity of crime. Hardly a criminal trial occurs in the colony in which he is not implicated in one way or another. His influence over the country people is unbounded. He is the prophet, priest, and king of the district. Does a maiden want a charm to make her lover 'good' to her? does a woman desire a safe delivery in child-birth? does a man wish to be avenged of his enemy, or to know the secrets of futurity?—the Obeah man is at hand to supply the means and to proffer his advice. Under the style and title of a 'bush doctor' he wanders from place to place, exacting 'coshery' from his dupes on all hands; supplied with food by one, with shelter by another, with money by a third, denied naught from the mysterious terror with which he is regarded, and refused nothing from fear of the terrible retribution which might be the consequences of such a rash act. His pretensions are high; but he has means at hand to enforce them. He can cure all diseases, he can protect a man from the consequences of his crimes; he can even reanimate the dead. His knowledge of simples is immense. Every bush and every tree furnishes weapons for his armoury.

Unfortunately in too many instances more potent agents are not wanting to his hand. His stock in trade consists of lizard's bones, old eggshells, tufts of hair, cats' claws, ducks' skulls, an old pack of cards, rusty nails, and things of that description. 'Grave dirt,' that is earth taken from where a corpse has been buried, is also largely used. . . . But ground glass, arsenic and other poisons, are not infrequently found among the contents of the Obeah man's 'puss-skin' wallet, and it is not difficult to conjecture for what purposes these are employed.

"As an outward and visible sign of his power, the Obeah man sometimes carries about with him a long staff or wand, with twisted serpents or the rude likeness of a human head carved round the handle. He has his cabalistic book, too, full of strange characters, which he pretends to consult in the exercise of his calling. One of these is now in my possession. It is an old child's copy-book, well thumbed and very dirty. Each page is covered with rude delineations of the human figure, and roughly traced diagrams and devices. Between each line there runs a rugged scrawl, intended to imitate writing. . ...

"There is something indescribably sinister about the appearance of an Obeah man, which is readily observed by persons who have mixed much with the Negroes. With a dirty handkerchief bound tightly round his forehead, and his small, bright cunning eyes peering out from beneath it, he sometimes visits the courts of. petty sessions throughout the island, if some unfortunate client of his who has got into trouble requires his aid to defend him. . ...

"Serpent or devil worship is by no means rare in the country districts; and of its heathen rites the Obeah man is invariably the priest. Many of them keep a stuffed snake in their huts as a domestic god-a practice still common in Africa, from which of course the custom has been derived."[86]

This is evidently an element of decadent Voodoo that temporarily impinged itself on Obeah. I have found many references to this in recent writers but never came across any indication of it in my own investigations. As regards the cabalistic book, referred to by both Beckford Davis and Rampini, we have possibly a residue of Mohammedanism. In the *Report of 1789*, answering the question about the religion of those among the slaves who were not Christian, Stephen Fuller replied, "They are either Pagans or Mohammedans, but principally Pagans. The Mohammedans are those that come from the Mandongo Country chiefly." Père Labat had already stated: "Nearly all the Negroes are idolators. There are only those from the neighbourhood of Cape Verde, of whom some are Mohammedans. When they bring these last to the Islands, it is necessary to be on one's guard in assuming charge of them. For besides the fact that they will never embrace Christianity they are extremely subject to the abominable sin which caused the destruction of the four ill-famed towns: and it is of the greatest importance that this vice be not introduced among the Negroes nor in the country."[87] He is writing in the year 1698. Much of the sensuous in Voodoo is probably due to this influence of these Mohammedans, and possibly Obeah, too, may owe to a like source some of the more repulsive features of its later practice.[88]

Rampini gives some of the results of his own investigations concerning Obeah and incidentally mentions in passing: "I have before me the records of the slave courts held in the parish of Portland between the years 1805 and 1816. They are full of cases of Obeah. One woman attempts to murder her master by putting arsenic into his noyeau; another by mixing pounded glass with his coffee; a third is charged with practicing upon the credulity of his fellow-slaves by pretending to cure another of a sore in his leg, and 'taking from thence sundry trifles,—a hawk's toe, a bit of wire, and a piece of flesh.'

"On 22d February, 183 l, William Jones was tried and sentenced to death 'for conspiring and contriving to destroy William Ogilvie, overseer of Fairy Hill estate in the Parish of Portland.' The notes of the evidence taken at the trial state: 'This prosecution arises out of the confession of Thomas Lindsey, who was shot to death pursuant to the sentence of a court-martial, on the 31st day of January, 1832. The part of the confession which inculpates Williams Jones is as follows: About three weeks before Christmas me and David Anderson; and William Rainey, and Alexander Simpson being together, the devil took hold of us, tell us we must destroy the overseer; and we agreed to go to a man named William Jones, belonging to Providence Mountain, an Obeah man, to give us something to kill the busha, so that his horse may throw him down and break his neck in a hole. Jones said as this was a great thing he could not do it for less than a doubloon, and we had only five shillings to give him. But we agreed to carry him a barrow (hog) with five dollars, and a three-gallon jug of rum, and three dollars in cash. He then gave us something and told us to give it to the waiting-boy to throw it in the water, and that would kill him. The waiting-boy, James Oliver, did throw it into the water, but it did the busha no harm and the waiting-boy said the Obeah man was only laughing at us. We then went to the Obeah man, and he said the waiting-boy could not have put the things into the water. And then he came himself one day, took the bag of an ant's house, etc. etc. etc.' 'Here,' says the report, 'follows an account of Obeah tricks practiced.'"[89]

Finally Rampini warns us: "The Obeah man must not be confounded with the Myal man, who is to the former what the antidote is to the poison. He professes to undo what the other has done; to cure where the other has injured, but it must be confessed that, both in its operation and its results, the cure is often worse than the disease. In truth, the boundary line between the two classes of professors is oftentimes but a shadowy one."[90]

We have already seen that the Ashanti Obayifo is in league with Sasabonsam, the forest monster or evil spirit.[91] Now, Bryan Edwards, in his day recognized as a result of his direct inquiries among the Gold Coast slaves that besides their belief in Accompong, the Nyankopon of the Ashanti, the God of the Heavens and the Creator of all things, they lived in fear of a malicious deity, the author of all evil, whom he calls Obboney.[92] The very title, which is Edwards' attempt to transliterate the name as he heard it from the slaves, is suggestive of the deity's connection with the Obayifo, or witch, and in many respects this evil spirit corresponds with the Sasabonsam of the Ashanti. Hence it isthat we find modern Obeah classified at times as devil worship, in which guise it poses more and more as a religion.

It would seem that during the days of slavery, with the drastic suppression of Myalistic meetings, the need was felt more imperative of placating the other deity. And so it came to pass that Obeah did in a sense develop more and more as a religion in which, of course, the object of worship was not the Divine Being but rather the evil spirit whether we refer to him as Sasabonsam or Obboney, and whom we must regard either as the Evil One, or perhaps more properly one of his satellites. The act of worship, however, is not really one of adoration, but pacification or propitiation, wherein an effort is made to assuage his enmity and restrain his vindictiveness.

It is not surprising then to find the Reverend R. Thomas Banbury, writing towards the close of the last century, thus describing the Obeah man: "He is the agent incarnate of Satan, the Simon Magus of these good gospel days, the embodiment of all that is wicked, immoral and deceitful. You may easily at times distinguish him by his sinister looks and slouching gait. An Obeah man seldom looks you in the face. Generally he is a dirty- looking fellow with a sore foot. But some few are known to be decent in appearance and well clad. He never goes without a wallet or bag in which he carries his things. He is a professional man that is as well paid as the lawyer or doctor, and sometimes better. It is a well known fact that in cases of lawsuits the Obeah man is retained as well as the lawyer, and at times he not only works at home on the case but goes to the court with his client for the purpose of stopping the mouth of the prosecutor and his witnesses and of influencing the judge and jury."[93]

A more recent writer remarks: "Obeah! What's in an imposing name? Evidently a good deal; for, though owing to the attitude taken by the law in Jamaica with regard to these esoteric principles, the high priests and high priestesses of the cult efface themselves as much as possible, it would appear from what can be ascertained that their system is rudimentary compared with the complicated forms of devil worship that obtain in India and elsewhere.

"Obeah is an ignorant, superstitious foreigner, but owing to 'man's eternal sense of awe,' to the indestructible desire deep down in the breast of most human beings to connect themselves with the unseen world, and to that most powerful of all reasons, the thirst of revenge, it has not died out. There are outward and visible signs of this mangrove- rooted curse well known to the police. A white cock, it would seem, plays a similar rôle to that personated by the black cat of the witch in medieval times. Whether the prime movers in this money-making business really believe in all the accessories of their trade, or whether their by-play resembles merely the conjurer's arts, when he attempts to divert the attention of the onlookers while he performs his tricks, I have not heard, but this is sure: that the strength of their influence lies in one word—poisons."[94]

A few pages later Miss Cook thus describes a part of a conversation which was held at the home of a resident magistrate in Jamaica, just after his return from Court where he had tried a case of Obeah: "'Oh! Obeah!' said the winter tourist, 'I have heard of that, I think, a ridiculous superstitious idea. How very stupid all these people must be!' 'I beg your pardon,' objected the pen-keeper's wife, 'that only states half the case. These Obeah men and women (whom you can so seldom catch) do, no doubt, pretend to cure diseases which they know little or nothing of, shamelessly extracting money from a too credulous public, though it is a fact that they well understand the preparation of simples; but the dread of Obeah, which is another name for witchcraft, is not altogether caused by superstitious fear. Obeah often means poison. When anyone wishes to be revenged on his enemy he puts Obeah on him: that is, he first consults the Obeah man as to the best mode of procedure, with the result that poison is administered in such a cunning manner that it is almost impossible to find it out. The strange thing is thatthose who give the poison hardly realize what they are doing, but attribute the result to supernatural agency.' 'That is true ' corroborated the hostess."[95]

We cannot close this chapter without quoting again from the experienced missionary who threw so much light on the question of Myalism. Father Emerick is speaking from eleven years of experience and close study in some of the most pronounced Obeah districts of Jamaica. Space, however, restricts us to a few of the more striking passages taken from his valuable and careful study. Thus he says: "The West Indies are like so many little Africas or African colonies, with many of the customs, ideas, words, observances and superstitions of their home country, Africa, still clinging to them. Since a nation's religion exerts the strongest influence upon its people, for they cling with greater tenacity to it than to anything else, it is natural to suppose that the last thing that they would give up, and that only after a great struggle, would be what to them was their religion, their fetish worship and superstitious practices. Thus it is that the Africans brought with them their African superstitions, which soon became prevalent in all the West Indies, and I can assure you that Jamaica has its share of them.

"There was a saying in vogue that the African Obeah man carried his Obeah magic under the, hair of his head when he was imported; for this reason the heads of Africans were shaved before landing. It was also said that before leaving Africa he swallowed his magical instrument. These imported superstitious practices flourished in the island, in spite of the fact that these people have been under the civilizing influence of a christian nation for 400 years, and in spite of the fact that slavery in Jamaica has been abolished since August 1, 1824, Obeah flourishes in Jamaica although the most drastic laws have been passed against it. . . . and in spite of the fact that twelve months' hard labour and the lashes of the cat-o'-nine-tails are inflicted upon those found guilty of practicing it.

Obeah may be defined in general to be a superstitious belief that certain men and women, known as Obeah men and Obeah women, can exercise certain preternatural power over places, persons and things and produce effects beyond the natural powers of man, by agencies other than divine. It seems to be a combination of magic and witchcraft. Magic, we are told, is an attempt to work miracles by the use of hidden forces beyond man's control, so it is in Obi; it is an attempt to produce by some undetermined, invisible power, effects out of proportion to and beyond the capabilities of the things and activities employed. In witchcraft, we are told, . . . there is involved the idea of a diabolical pact, or at least an appeal to the intervention of the spirits. In the history and make up and practice of Obi there is involved the idea of association with the devil. . . .

"His Satanic majesty is the invisible head of Obeah. The visible agent, head and front of Obeah is the Obeah man or Obeah woman, more often and more characteristically the Obeah man. Who and what is the Obeah man? In general the Obi man or woman is any man or woman who is supposed to have communication with some invisible agent through which he or she can exert preternatural power over animate and inanimate beings. You have Obi men of all sorts, just as you have professional doctors and quack-doctors. As Obeahism is so common among the people and is a form of religion, it comes natural for any individual to practice it as he would practice any religious rite. From this you can easily understand how any rascal who wants to gratify his revenge, avarice or lust, can work upon the superstitious, practice Obi and get a following as an Obi man. Hence Obi-working is very common. . . .

"The Obi man's incantation is generally the muttering of strange sounds, often meaningless, the pronouncing of some word or words over the objects to be Obeahed, joined with some grotesque actions. It may consist in words or actions alone.

"The following lines which I find in my notes on Obeah, by a Jamaican poet describe an Obi man at work:

Crouched in a cave I saw thee and thy beard,
White against black, gleamed out; and thy gaunt hand Mixed lizard skins, rum, parrots' tongues and sand
Found where the sinking tombstone disappeared.
Sleek galli-wasps looked on thee; grimly peered Blood-christened John Crows with a hissed demand
Who art thou? then like ghouls to a dim land
Fled for they saw thee working and they feared.

"Compare this description of the Obi man making Obeah or an Obi charm with that given by Shakespeare in Macbeth of the witches making a charm through which they raised spirits and deceivingly foretold to Macbeth his future; and you will find that they have much in common. . . .

"If a gentleman in Jamaica find a rusty nail or knife hanging over his door he knows that it is an obeah, it has been placed there by one of his servants who has been offended or discharged. The idea of placing it there is that when the master passes under it he will meet with a violent death, or be afflicted with some misery, or that he will be compelled to reemploy the discharged servant. If you should happen to go to Jamaica and find under your pillow at night some grave dirt, or a bit of feather in your soup, or a few lizard bones in your coat pockets, you had better look out, someone is trying to work Obeah on you. It is the custom in Jamaica in the coloured Protestant Churches to expell members who are guilty of certain crimes, or as the Jamaica peasants says, 'Cratch der name off der church book.' If the minister, after one of these suspensions, finds when he opens the bible on the pulpit for his text, a quaint collection of cat claws, feathers, dried leaves, eggshells, etc., he is not puzzled as to the meaning of it all. He knows that is expresses 'Quashie's' desire to be received back into the membership of the church.

Teachers will sometimes scatter obeahs over the school floor to compel the government inspector of schools to give the school good marks. . . .

"The Obeah credulous entertain the greatest dread of anything supposed to be an Obeah, an egg seen on the road, or anywhere, supposed to be placed designedly, would not be touched; they would not walk near it. It would be accounted madness to step over an egg or any parcel wrapped up with a string, found in the yard or on the path.

They will not walk near it, but take a circuitous way to avoid it. Even money would not be picked up if there was a suspicion that it had been used by the Obi man in washing some diseased person and cast in the road to transfer the disease to the person picking it up. But of all things an egg is perhaps the most dreaded. The story is told of an old woman giving her parting advice to her son going far away from home; 'James, my bwoy, you do go wa fra mi, alla warra you da go, no li, no tief, no swa, but if you do even tief, my bwoy, no tief fole egg; because if you do tek people's fole egg, my bwoy, dem tek narra fole egg go trowa same ina sea, same fassion de sea rowl as so you belly bottom da rowl.' That is: 'James my boy, you are going far away from me; but wherever you go, do not lie, do not steal, do not swear, but if you do even so forget yourself as to steal, do not steal a fowl egg, because if you do the person from whom you steal the fowl egg will take another fowl's egg and throw it in the sea, and as the sea waves roll so will the bottom of your belly roll' . . .

"Very frequently Obeah is used to bring about an influence over the mind of another, in order to gain some advantage from or over the person. It is a sort of hypnotism. This they call, 'Turn him yeye,' that is "Turn his eye,' the eye in the phrase meaning his mind or will, or the controlling of his actions. This frequently happens in law-suits. The Obi man at times is retained as well as the lawyer and the former is considered as indispensable, if not more so, than the later. The Obi man sometimes not only works on the case at home but also goes to the court with his client for the purpose, as, they call it, of 'Topping de mouts'—stopping the mouths, of the prosecutor and his witnesses and influencing the judge and jury. This is understood to be 'turning dem yeyes.'

"There is a 'Turn him yeye' Obeah, which is the equivalent of the 'Love Potion' in witchcraft: the Jamaicans call it 'De tempting powder.' Men and women use this 'Turn him yeye' Obeah in fits of jealousy. A Lady Clara de Vere must be very careful about breaking the heart of some country swain. He might get a 'Tempting powder' from the Obi man and put it in her tea and then she will fall madly in love with the broken- hearted swain. It is said that the making of this love potion is unspeakably filthy and disgusting. . . .

"Here is a case of an Obi man undertaking to force an undesirable lodger to leave a man's house: 'An old Obi man heard a respectable Negro proprietor say that he wished he could make a lodger leave his house as he was a nuisance. The Obi man offered to manage it for a price. The proprietor must get two white fowls, a white shirt, a pint of rum, some black thread, a bundle of wood, two nails and a hammer. It was then arranged that they meet at the proprietor's house. The proprietor pretending to agree, went and told the police. At the appointed time he concealed two policemen in some coffee bushes where they could see all that went on. After some weird incantations, the Obi man drove one nail into the front door and another into the back door of the house, tying the black thread from nail to nail. He then produced a flask filled with a mixture of oil, rum and fowl's blood and lubricated the string, at the same time monotonously chanting. The remnants of the liquid he threw into the fire. The next part of the ceremony was to kill the two white fowls and sprinkle their blood on the floor. The Obi man then demanded seventeen shillings and three bangles, remarking at the same time, "I gib dat fellow one day fe clear out, if him don't go, I catch bin, shadow and him go fe tru." The detectives then stepped in and arrested him.'"[96]

In rejecting the Slave Act of 1826, one reason assigned was, as we have seen, the restriction placed on preaching and teaching on the part of the slaves, as it was claimed that "amongst some of the religious bodies who employ missionaries in Jamaica, the practice of mutual instruction is stated to be an established part of their discipline."[97] The deleterious effect of such practice is shown in an earlier protest of the Jamaica Assembly against the rejection of the Slave Act of 1807, as we find it in the Report of the Committee of the Assembly dated November 16, 1809,[98] how two dissenting ministers while making application for a license before the Magistrates of Kingston in August, 1809, admitted freely: "That they had been informed that their predecessors did, upon many occasions, conduct themselves improperly, and did inculcate improper notions in the minds of the slaves."[99] Too frequently well-meaning ministers of the gospel, especially in the first days among the slaves, easily were misled to believe that what was in reality nothing but fanatical emotionalism consequent on the arousing of the spirit of the old African religions, was to them an awakening of the spirit. Even for the experienced it is hard at times to distinguish between the hysterical dementia of an old- time camp-meeting and the obsession of Myalism in a degraded form.

"So late as 1861," as Gardner remarks, "during the revival, as it was termed, a party of young women, in a state of religious excitement, went to the house of a reputed Obeah man, residing in one of the suburbs of Kingston, and brought him, with all the implements of his art, to the parade. His box contained not only nearly all the abominations mentioned, but ... in the midst of all, sad to say, was a number of class tickets, indicating that he had been a member of a religious body for a good number of years."[100] Thus not only the persecuting Myalists but their victim the Obeah man as well, could be church members in good standing, during this weird stage of Revivalism.

And if the zealous, well-meaning Methodist missionaries were so easily deceived, why should we be surprised in our own day that such egregious blunders are made at times by chance visitors to Jamaica or even by the more experienced folklorist who spends a few hurried months in the island interviewing the very class of individuals who are least likely to furnish correct information, since they feel themselves called upon to deal with the whole question as a foolish superstition of the low and ignorant, and usually too, out of local pride, gloss over or deny the real workings of Obeah.[101]

CHAPTER VI
Conclusions

AS MOREAU DE SAINT-MÉRY remarks: San Domingo was the first place in America where African slaves were introduced. It was proposed to use them in place of the Indians who were dying off in consequence of the hard work in the mines to which they were ill- adapted.[1]

At that period, there were two sets of Negro tribes, one group back of the Gold Coast, the other further to the east across the Volta River, both in the formative stage and as yet unknown to the white man. These two groups, to be known later as the Ashanti and the Dahomans, were in time to become not only rivals for the supremacy of West Africa, but were destined to establish in the West Indies two distinct spheres of influence, as antagonistic in slave circles as their own political ambitions were to be at home.[2]

Among the Ashanti tribes, there was a strong religious organ-ization with well defined ritual, inspiring a coordination and spirit of nationalism that later drew from Lord Wolseley the encomium: "From the Ashantis I learned one important lesson, namely that any virile race can become paramount in its own region of the world, if it pos-sesses the courage, the constancy of purpose, and the self-sacrifice to resolve that it will live under a stern system of Spartan military discipline enforced by one lord, master or king." [3]

It was as a matter of fact, the exalted religious spirit that principally gave to the various tribal units the cohesive power that formed the Ashanti into a warlike people, and tended to crush down the antagonistic magic of the Obayifo.

Meanwhile at Sabee, the capital of the Kingdom of Whydah on the Slave Coast, well established Ophiolatry was extending its sway as a religious force of such proportions that the Dahomans themselves fell under its influence when once they had extended their domain to the sea through the conquest of Whydah.

It is clear, then, that in its inception, Voodoo, as the West Indian offshoot of the Ophiolatry of Sabee, must be considered technically as a form of religion. The serpent worship of its African prototype was ultimately addressed to the Supreme Being through the ancestral spirits supposedly indwelling in the sacred serpents. The same conditions undoubtedly marked the Haitian Voodoo when it was first established in its new field, but its ritual quickly suffered modifications through contacts with the other religious influences derived from every part of the dark continent through the influx of the heterogeneous masses of slaves that found their way to West Indian bondage.

Shortly before the outbreak of the Haitian Revolution, an offshoot of Voodoo developed into the more sanguinary Don Pédro rites, but Voodoo itself continued for a time, substantially unchanged. It was a secret religious function with its own peculiar dance unaccompanied by drums or other instruments.

Gradually it was found desirable to cloak the real Voodoo rites by holding in advance a public dance which was summoned and accompanied by the loud beating of the drums, presumably as an official excuse for the local authorities who secretly sanctioned all that was going on. This dance in turn developed into what came to be known as a Voodoo feast, since prolonged dancing without refreshments is scarcely compatible with the Negro temperament.

Meanwhile the religious element in Voodoo became somewhat decadent and superstitious practices associated themselves with its ceremonies at times. The Voodoo feast, in consequence, was more and more accentuated. It was developing into a social function, and amusement rather than worship frequently became the real objective.

Today it is difficult to believe, that, except in rare cases, do we find Voodoo in Haiti, strictly speaking, an act of worship. At least in the public estimation almost everything is classified as Voodoo and the very drums that were originally debarred from Voodoo by necessity if not by choice have actually come to be known by the name of Voodoo drums. Magic and even witchcraft have entered into an unholy alliance with Voodoo and the Papaloi and Mamaloi have somewhat assumed the rôle of medium if not that of witch and necromancer.

We are even told that the serpent has now been eliminated from the ritual. This may be true. We would not like to question the reliability of such an authority as Dr. Price-Mars in the matter. However, if so, the change must have been effected within the past few years, as I know from reliable witnesses that the practice was still in vogue well after the opening of the present century. In any case it seems inconsistent to have our friend Dr. Price-Mars insisting on this disappearance of the serpent from present-day Voodoo, and yet demanding that it still be classified as a religion. Let us quote his very words: "It is inconceivable that the Dahoman traditions should disappear without leaving traces in the Haitian beliefs. There remain as survival a few touches. We remark that the fear noticed among our peasants of killing adders (a species of water boa, *ungalia*) is the most pronounced manifestation of this survival. If, therefore, we omit the cult of the adder on which rests the whole economy of colonial Voodoo, probably because it approaches more closely to its Dahoman connection, what remains then of the original belief? Nothing except the dance and ecstasy, both strengthened by sacrifices. May we not be permitted to point out that these three elements: the dance, the ecstasy and the sacrifice, formed or form the permanent parts of religious rites and that one finds them connected or separated in the most exalted religions."[4] But if you eliminate the serpent from the cult, it should no longer be called Voodoo. Can you play Hamlet without the title part? It should at least be known by some other term, more generic and including all Negro cults, as did fetishism a generation ago. We can admit that much of the emotional religious manifestations of the Haitians today is not Voodoo in the strict sense of the word, but with all due respect to Dr. Price-Mars, we are not entirely convinced that the serpent cult, substantially the same as practiced in the last century is not still secretly in vogue in Haiti. The transition seems too sudden. Possibly, too, there is just a little verbal quibble in the repeated assertions that the serpent is no longer worshipped. Our contention, too, is that it was never worshipped. It was merely venerated as a depository of some spiritual entity, not even itself divine, but only an intermediary to the Divine Being, who is ultimately and alone worshipped.[5]

Arthur C. Millapaugh who was the Financial Adviser-General Receiver of Haiti, 1927- 1929, in depicting the condition of Haiti, in the eve of intervention in 1915, simply states: "In the interior the practice of Voodooism persisted but it was neither general nor open and tended to disappear."[6] But while he fails to define what he means by Voodooism, since his references are to Kilsey, St. John and Seabrook, we must conclude that he is taking it in its worst possible sense.

Certainly the wholesale confiscation of "Voodoo" drums by the American Marines shows that the popular form of Voodoo was still very much in evidence. As regards the conditions at the time of writing in 1931, Millapaugh has nothing to say about Voodoo beyond a passing remark in a footnote wherein he ascribes to the Medical Service the principal factors in the combating of ages of superstition and voodooistic beliefs.[7] Possibly the fact that he is writing for the World Peace Foundation makes him avoid whatever might offend the self-respect of the Haitians to the detriment of general peace and harmony.

Concerning human sacrifice, "the goat without horns" and cannibalism, despite theloud protests of the friends of Haiti, it is hard to believe that the practice is entirely extinct. It would, of course, be a grave mistake to suppose that it is a regular practice orconnived at by the present government authorities. Still it would be even more surprising if the sexual excitement of their various dances with the concomitant excessive use of stimulants, did not at times break down the nervous systems of individuals here and there, and induce a kind of paranoia with a recrudescence of all that is vilest and most degraded in fallen nature.

At all events, when such half-crazed outbreaks do occur, they are to be associated with the Don Pédro swinish rites where the ordinary victim is the pig, and where the human substitute would be more appropriately called not the "goat without horns" but the "long pig" as was done under similar circumstances in the distant islands of the Pacific.

As regards Obeah, we find at work a process directly opposite to that noticed in the case of Voodoo.

Obeah, no less than Myalism, as we have seen, derive their

origin from the Ashanti. The latter was the old religious dance modified somewhat by circumstances and surroundings in Jamaica, but substantially the same as practiced in West Africa. The former, on the other hand was Ashanti witchcraft, essentially antagonistic to Myalism which made one of its chief objects the "digging up" of Obeah.

The Ashanti warlike and indomitable spirit was not crushed by slavery, and the old religious practice easily stirred them up to a point of rebellion. Hence from the earliest days of legislation in Jamaica, the tribal religious dance remained inactive as assemblies were strictly prohibited.

During the long years of slavery, then, Myalism might be regarded as dormant. There was no opportunity of its development or branching out. It was preserved secretly and cherished as the fondest tradition of the past. No doubt the hours of amusement allowed to the slaves on their own cultivations, preserved in some degree the Myalistic rites, disguised as one of the social dances that were countenanced by the planters.

The native African is essentially religious in his own way and as formal ceremonies were debarred he found an outlet by associating with Obeah an element of worship, if not of Accompong, at least of Sasabonsam or Obboney. If he could not venerate the Supreme Being through the minor deities and ancestral spirits, he might at least placate the evil one, and bespeak his influence for purpose of revenge or to coerce his master to grant him something that he sought.

We find Obeah thus really becoming a form of devil worship in the Christian sense, and when at length Myalism entered into an alliance with it for the overthrow of the white regime it naturally gained in the popular estimation of the slaves, since its archenemy Myalism had come to recognize its power. And yet this public esteem was not one of devotion but of unholy fear, which the Obeah man naturally played up to his own advantage.

With Emancipation, Myalism made haste to assert itself in an endeavour to regain its pristine ascendancy and made open war on Obeah, at the expense be it said of the general peace of the community. Its new-found independence led to excesses of every kind and in course of years it became as great an evil as Obeah itself. Its old priestly class was dead, for a generation none had come from Africa, and there had been no opportunity of establishing a succession in the craft or of passing along the ritual in practice. The traditions and nothing more could have remained, and it is questionable whether the new leaders had any legitimate claim to the exercise of the rôle that they assumed. It is simple, then, to see that the decay of Myalism as a religious force was inevitable. And it would certainly soon have been entirely eliminated had not its spirit and much of its traditional ritual found new scope in the kindred spirit of the emotional Revivalism of the Methodists and even more so among the so-called native Baptist congregations. But perhaps it is more conspicuous of all among the Bedwardites, so characterized by the peculiar hip-movement that is clearly African, and which shows itself not only in their dance but also in their religious processions, and gives a peculiar lilt to all their hymns.

Here, strictly speaking, Myalism disappears as a separate entity, and its very name is dying out except as a mysterious something that has endured in its opposition to the Obeah man who more and more assumes the dual rôle of Myalist by day and Obeah man by night, using the title as a safeguard from the law in the prosecution of his real aims in life. As a further consequence, Obeah is taking on more and more of a religious aspect and it is now, not entirely undeservedly, classified by many as devil worship.

My first experience with an Obeah man in Jamaica was as follows. Accompanied by a native of the district I was returning late one night to my residence high up in the mountains, when suddenly my companion who was leading the way shrank back and pointing a trembling finger through an opening of the coffee walk where we happened to be passing, whispered almost inaudibly: "Obi, Sah!"

It was a bright moonlight night, and a short distance off the path might be seen a filthy- looking bedraggled fellow plying his art of Obeah for weal or woe. I drew my reluctant companion behind a shrub to watch the process which is so seldom vouchsafed to the eye of a white man.

The Obeah man had placed on the ground some sticks, feathers, eggshells and other objects that could not clearly be distinguished. A piece of string was placed on top of the little heap. He then retreated for a short distance and began a mumbling incantation which was accompanied by a rhythmic swaying of the body. With hands behind the back he next approached, crossing one leg over the other as he slowly advanced and drew near the incongruous ingredients of what was evidently intended for a fetish. With legs still stiffly crossed and swaying body he stooped and breathed upon and spat at it, and then gathered up the articles one by one, still mumbling some weird incantation as he placed the sticks together and crushed the eggshells and other ingredients within them and finally bound all together with the piece of string.

When the task was accomplished a cringing woman advanced from the shadow of a tree where her presence had not previously been noted. The Obeah man passed her the fetish charm and with fierce injunction charged her to hasten on her way without looking back or speaking to a living soul. She was especially warned to guard her fetish from every moisture. Should river or rain or dew, or even the perspiration of her own body chance to wet it, not only would all efficacy be lost but it would inevitably turn against herself. I could not follow all the words despite my knowledge of the language of the "bush," but I had been able to gather the general gist of the instructions which were almost in the form of an invocation or curse.[8]

Strictly speaking what I had been watching was not really the practice of Obeah but rather the making of a protective fetish or good luck charm, our friend was working in the rôle of Myal man and cared nothing if he was observed. Had he been really making Obi he would have been surer of his privacy and would have squatted on the ground surrounded by his paraphernalia and this would have been the scene with little variation:

Most of the ingredients to be used are concealed in a bag from which he draws them as he needs them. The special offering of his patron which must include a white fowl, two bottles of rum, and a silver offering are on the ground beside him. Before him is the inevitable empty bottle to receive the ingredients. The incantation opens with a prolonged mumbling which is supposed to be "an unknown tongue." This is accompanied by a swaying of the body.

Gradually ingredients are placed in the bottle, and a little rum is poured over them. The throat of the fowl is deftly slit and drops of blood are allowed to fall first on the silver offering, and then on the contents of the bottle to which is finally added a few feathers plucked from various parts of the fowl with a last libation of rum. During all this process the Obeah man has been drawing inspiration from frequent draughts of rum, reserving a substantial portion to be consumed later when he makes a meal off the flesh of the fowl.

When the bottle concoction has been completed and the last incantation has been said over it, the Obeah man entrusts it to his patron with minute instructions how it is to be buried on some path where the intended victim is sure to pass or as near his dwelling as possible.

In the days of slavery, the expert in Obeah was frequently distinguished by being physically or mentally defective or abnormal. So we find today that not a few of the pretenders to expertness in Obeah affect a disregard for cleanliness and hygiene, at strange variance with the Jamaican's characteristic love of bathing and neatness. If not actually disfigured, then, the Obeah man usually presents a disgusting and filthy appearance especially when actually making Obi. Again, he cannot as a rule meet your gaze, but shiftily moves his eyes around and nervously distorts his countenance, although on the other hand he will stare fixedly at the blazing tropical sun without blinking an eye. Possibly his very hang-dog look may be explained by injury to the optic nerve induced during his long preparation for his future avocation when as a little fellow he was forced to stand motionless by the hour with every muscle tense and set while he stared the sun out of countenance.

Another peculiarity of Jamaica Obeah should be noted here. Possibly through contact with missionaries at an early date in West Africa, Obeah in its various manifestations makes use of crosses to a great extent. In the making of a fetish, as we have seen, the Obeah man approaches his task, carefully crossing his legs at every step. So, too, while crouched over the bottle, in making real Obi, he is particular to keep his legs crossed under him. Many crosses are made during the ritual and sticks are crossed and re- crossed again and again. It is no uncommon thing to find a sickly child to whom the Obeah man has been called all marked up with crosses made with indigo or coloured clay. For "big obi" the wax drippings from altar candles and the refuse from the censer after benediction but especially the grains of unburnt incense, are particularly in demand. This last is probably explained by what follows.

The Obeah man has a wholesome fear of the priest and usually tries to avoid his presence. There is a conviction among them that the priest can exercise a more powerful influence than any Obeah man. This belief is expressed by the aphorism: "French obi, him strongest." The first priest to become well known through the Jamaica "bush" was a Frenchman, and the Catholic Church in consequence has come to be known familiarly as the French Church. Hence "French obi, him strongest" really means that the Catholic Church exercises the strongest Obeah. It is also accepted as a fact by the devotees of the Obeah cult that the priest can give evidence of this dominant power by "lighting a candle on them." This process is thus described: "Fadder take pin and Fadder take candle; and him stick der pin in der candle; and him light der candle on you. Der candle him burn, and him burn, and him burn. And you waste, and you waste, and you waste. And when der flame touch dat pin—you die." So that it is only necessary for a priest to make the playful remark to some black fellow in the "bush," "I think I'll have to light a candle on you," to bring him to his knees with: "O Fadder, don't."

The Ashanti Mmoatia, or little folks, are associated with the forest monster Sasabonsam and the Obayifo or witch in imparting power to the suman or fetish.[9] According to A. W. Cardinall they are "Preeminently mischief-workers, and are said to 'throw stones at one as one passes through the bush."[10] Captain Rattray calls them "fairies," and also tells us that in the Ashanti belief they are "Of three distinct varieties: black, red and white, and they converse by means of whistling. The black fairies are more or less innocuous, but the white and the red mmoatia are up to all kinds of mischief."[11] For this latter group perhaps imps would be a more appropriate name than fairies. Be that as it may, the Jamaica duppies or ghosts are notorious for their stone-throwing propensities, and this poltergeist, as it is technically called, is associated in the popular mind with evil agencies.

In this connection it is interesting to note the testimony of no less an authority than Lord Olivier, a former Governor of Jamaica, who recently wrote to me: "The occasional outbursts of this 'poltergeist' phenomenon in Jamaica is remarkable. I investigated with some care the evidence as to one case which occurred when I was in Jamaica and there have been very full reports in the local Press of another recent occurrence which seems to have been carefully investigated without detecting any possibility of corporeal agency."

The phenomenon itself is ascribed by the peasantry to duppies or ghosts who despite their intangible nature are extraordinarily good shots to all appearances. True, it is a frequent means of frightening or annoying an enemy to cast stones from a distance so that they will fall on the roof of his house and make him think that the duppies are after him. On the other hand there are undeniable instances of persons being stoned and that, too, by no determinable agency. The stones for example, simply came out of the trees with truly remarkable accuracy and no one can be found either in the trees or on the line of fire.

A Jamaica missionary already quoted on Myalism and Obeah, graphically describes some of his own experiences and gives many instances that he has investigated where the stones thus thrown seem to violate all the laws of science. For example, "Some of the stones which came from the bushy declivity, after smashing through a window, turned at a right angle and broke the teacher's clock, glasses, etc., on a side-board."[12] A man running from the stone-thrower turns and fires a gun in the direction from which the stones were coming, and as he does so another stone comes from the very opposite direction and hits him in the back of the neck.[13] "Some of them seem to come in the open door, turn around and fall at the teacher's feet."[14] A stone that has come flying into the house is marked by one of the occupants and thrown out again with the remark, "If him be a true duppy, him will throw this stone back," and back it came, "proving that the stone-thrower was a true duppy," in the common estimation.[15]

At times these duppies, imps, evil spirits, call them what you will, have other means of disturbing one's peace of mind.

On one occasion I was on the outskirts of a notorious Obeah district when a man, a non- Catholic, came to me and begged me to come and bless his house as his children were starving. "Why don't you give them something to eat?" was the obvious question. "Dem can't eat, Fadder," was the astonishing reply. "Someone put Obi on dem." He explained further that when they tried to eat, the food would fly up and hit them in the face, but that they could not get it into the mouth. Absolutely incredulous, I mounted my horse and followed him to his house. The entire village was assembled around the dwelling and a state of panicky hysteria had taken possession of all. While I did not actually witness the diabolic display myself, as I did not feel justified in provoking the evil one to an exhibition merely to satisfy my curiosity, all the men, women and children there present agreed in their testimony of what had happened. I blessed the house, but whether the blessing took or not, I cannot say, as I was shortly leaving Jamaica and never revisited the district.

To understand the rapid transition from Myalism to Revivalism in Jamaica, it is necessary to go into the question of the religious condition of the island in the closing days of slavery.

In his chapter on "Religion and Education" prior to 1782, Gardner writes: "It is no easy task to portray the religious history of the colony during the period now under review. With the exception of some letters written by the rector of Port Royal, immediately after the earthquake (preserved in GENTLEMAN'S MAGAZINE) there appears to be no document in existence which in any way illustrates the spiritual labours of the clergy.

From Mr. Bridges, as a clergyman, we might have expected

some account of the labours of his brethren; but though he devotes considerable space to the history of the established church, it is only so far as the emoluments and status of its clergy were concerned.

"Amidst the dearth of information, the letters of the Port Royal rector are of peculiar interest. Writing of the day of the earthquake, he says, 'On Wednesday, the 7th, I had been at prayers, which I did every day since I was rector of Port Royal, to keep up some show of religion amongst a most ungodly and debauched people.' This description of the general character of the population applies, it is to be feared, to the whole island, but it is questionable whether the incumbent of the doomed city was not almost singular in his zeal."[16]

Then after quoting further from the letter, Gardner adds: "For more than two generations we shall search in vain among the records of the colony for any further illustration of ministerial zeal and fidelity."[17]

Edward Long states: "The bishop of London claims this as a part of his diocese; but his jurisdiction is renounced and barred by the laws of the island, in every sense, except so far as relates or appertains to ecclesiastical regimen of the clergy; which imparts no higher power than that of granting orders, and giving pastoral admonitions."[18] On the following page he asserts: "The governor as supreme head of the provincial church, and in virtue of the royal instruments, is vested with a power of suspending a clergyman here, of lewd or disorderly life, *ab officio*, upon the petition of his parishioners; and I can remember one example of this sort. The governor inducts into the several rectories within the island and its dependencies, etc."[19] This power of patronage on the part of the governor naturally led to abuses as in the case of the Satirist "Peter Pindar" who was the last person one would expect to find gracing the pulpit of a church. And yet we read in Chambers's *Cyclopedia of English Literature*: "Dr. John Wolcot (1738-1819) was a coarse but lively satirist, who under the name of 'Peter Pindar,' published a variety of effusions on the topics and public men of his times, which were eagerly read and widely circulated. Many of them were in ridicule of the reigning sovereign, George III, who was a good subject for the poet; though the latter, as he himself acknowledged, was a bad subject to the king. . . . Wolcot was instructed in medicine, and 'walked the hospitals' in London, after which he proceeded to Jamaica with Sir William Trelawney, governor of the island, who had engaged him as his medical attendant. The social habits of the doctor rendered him a favourite in Jamaica; but his time being only partly employed by his professional avocations, he solicited and obtained from his patron the gift of a living in the church, which happened to be vacant. The bishop of London ordained the graceless neophyte and Wolcot entered upon his sacred duties. His congregation consisted mostly of Negroes, and Sunday being their principal holiday and market, the attendance at the church was very limited. Sometimes not a single person came, and Wolcot and his clerk—the latter being an excellent shot—used at such times, after waiting for ten minutes, to proceed to the sea-side, to enjoy the sport of shooting ring- tailed pigeons! The death of Sir William Trelawney cut off all further hopes of preferment, and every inducement to a longer residence in the island. Bidding adieu to Jamaica and the church, Wolcot accompanied Lady Trelawney to England, and established himself as a physician at Truro, in Cornwall."[20]

This prepares us for the startling testimony of Charles Leslie, written in 1840: "'Tis surprising that such worthless and abandoned men should be sent to such a place as this. The clergy here are of a character so vile, that I do not care to mention it; for except a few, they are generally the most finished of our debauchees.

Messrs. Galpin, Johnston and May, are indeed men whose unblemished lives dignify the character they bear. They generally preach either in their own churches, or to a few in some private houses every Sunday; but for others, their church doors are seldom opened. "[21]

With such an account of the clergy, it is not surprising to find Stephen Fuller, the Agent for Jamaica at London, addressing the Earl of Shelburne as regards the pressing military needs of the island, painting the free Negroes and mulattoes in sombre colours. Thus he writes on April 2, 1782. "The free Negroes and mulattoes have been reckoned about 900 fencible men, out of which number not above 500 can be employed to any useful purpose; the greatest part of them being the most idle, debauched, distempered, profligate wretches upon earth. Besides this, there is an insuperable objection to their being armed, as they are not to be trusted in Corps composed of themselves, and the incorporating them with the whites will not be endured."[22] What, then, the religious and moral condition of the slaves themselves must have been, can well be surmised.

William Wilberforce, writing in 1823, states: "It cannot be denied, I repeat, that the slaves, more especially the great body of the field Negroes, are practically strangers to the multiplied blessings of the Christian Revelation. What a consideration this! A nation, which, besides the invaluable benefit of an unequalled degree of true civil liberty, has been favoured with an unprecedented measure of religious light, with its long train of attendant blessings, has been for two centuries detaining in a state of slavery, beyond example rigorous, and in some particulars, worse than Pagan darkness and depravity, hundreds of thousands of their fellow-creatures, originally torn from their native land by fraud and violence. Generation after generation have been pining away; and in this same condition of ignorance and degradation they still, for the most part, remain."[23]

It was Wilberforce's *Appeal* that drew an answer from the Reverend George Wilson Bridges, Rector of the Parish of Manchester (1817-23) and later Rector of the Parish of St. Anns (1823-37) of whom Frank Cundall says, that he "as a rule displays more fertile imagination than Long without half his trustworthiness as a historian."[24] Cundall further observes in his regard: "In 1823 he published his *Voice from Jamaica*, written in defence of slave-owners, for which the Assembly two years later voted him 700 pounds."[25] This fact in itself renders Bridges' evidence of questionable value.

As regards the particular citation which we have given from Wilberforce, Bridges replies in part: "As to the 'pagan darkness' of the Negroes, though their progress certainly does not keep pace with our anxious wishes to see them in that state which would make it safe to confide ourselves to their estimation of a Christian oath, nor in that condition which would render it advantageous to themselves to be trusted with the liberty of self-control, yet the promises of Christianity are so far understood, and its preliminary rites so ardently desired by them, that during my residence in this parish, I have actually baptized 9,413 Negro slaves, many of them attend church; some have learned the Lord's prayer, and ten commandments, and a few have so far advanced, as to be now disseminating their little stock of religious knowledge on the estates to which they are attached. As I said before, I believe all my fellow-labourers here have been at least as assiduous as myself, and some more successful. I expect therefore that you, sitting by your own fireside, four thousand miles off, will not refuse credit to the unanswerable fact, advanced by one who is on the spot, an actor in the deeds he records, and who has certainly the better means of forming a correct judgment, on the point at issue."[26]

Here is a direct challenge, and it is taken up by a brother clergyman, also long resident in Jamaica. Reverend William James Gardner, Congregational Minister, who (11(2d in charge of the North Street Church, Kingston, in 1874, reviewing the whole question, takes Mr. Bridges to task in no uncertain manner. Thus he writes: "The Rev. G. W. Bridges, the annalist, stated in 1823, that he had baptized 9,413 slaves during two years, and that many of them attended church. The proportion must indeed have been small, for the church he refers to (Mandeville) could not at that time have held a twentieth part of that number. Most of these slaves paid half-a-crown each as a baptismal fee. Mr. Bridges, in happy oblivion of what he had said of the money given to missionaries being the result of a cruel and heartless imposition on their superstition and ignorance, observes of the fees received, that 'this laudable desire of exchanging worldly goods for celestial rewards,' evinces 'a measure of faith words cannot express.' By the end of another year this zealous baptizer was able to report that 12,000 out of 17,000 slaves in the parish had received the holy ordinance, and he adds 'happily there are no sectarians,'"[27] This last remark probably explains the bitterness of Mr. Gardner himself. However, the general estimate given is supported by the Reverend R. Bicknell, a contemporary of Mr. Bridges and like him a Minister of the Established Church, who was stationed at Kingston and Port Royal during the period that Mr. Bridges was at Manchester. He says: "In the parish church of Clarendon I have often been, and never saw a hundred of all colours there, latterly a much less number, and once in particular, about ten or twelve only; though within five or six miles of the church there were several thousands of inhabitants. The churches of St. John's, St. Thomas's in the Vale, St. Dorothy's, St. George's, St. Mary's, Hanover and Vere, are but little better attended, some of them even worse, as I can testify from my own knowledge, and the assurance of creditable persons; the remaining churches I believe to be but little better, with the exceptions of those in the parishes of Kingston, St. Thomas in the East,

St. Catherine, Port Royal, and St. Andrew."[28] Certainly if Mr. Bridges had been really accomplishing anything out of the ordinary some mention of it would be expected here.

The Reverend John Riland, Curate of Yoxall, Staffordshire, somewhat facetiously styles Mr. Bridges' claims of 9,413 baptisms of slaves: "A direct illustration of Obeah practice under the forms of Christianity." And adds: "If we assume these 9,413 to have been also actually converted from Paganism to Christianity, or even to have been taught enough of the fundamental truths of the Gospel to understand the engagements into which they entered, we have here a miracle as great as was exhibited on the Day of Pentecost. And if they were not converted to Christianity, of if they did not under-stand the nature of the solemn vow and covenant they were called to make, what a mockery of religion, and what a prostitution of the sacred initiatory rite of baptism, is here made the subject of boast."[29]

But let us return to Mr. Bicknell whom we have recently quoted. We find him advertised as: "A member of the University of Cambridge, late Naval Chaplain at Port Royal, sometime Curate of that Parish, and previously of the City of Kingston, in the aforesaid island." His description of conditions among the slaves is not a pleas-ant one. Thus he declares: "It is not enough that most of the slaves must work in their grounds a part of that Holy day, but to add to the abomination, a market must be kept also on the Sunday, for the sale of provisions, vegetables, fruit, &c. It is the only market-day, fellow- countrymen, and fellow-Christians, which the poor Negroes and coloured slaves have, and instead of worshipping their God, they are either cultivating their portions of land to preserve life, or trudging like mules with heavy loads, five, ten, or even twenty miles, to sell the little surplus of their provision grounds, or to barter it for a little salt fish to season their poor meals: or what is much worse, to spend, very often, the value in new destructive rum, which intoxicates them, and drowns for a time, the reflection that they are despised and burdened slaves. I shall never forget the horror and disgust which I felt on going on shore, for the first time, in Kingston, in the month of August, 1819; it was on a Sunday, and I had to pass by the Negro Market, where several thousands of human beings, of various nations and colours, but principally Negroes, instead of worshipping their Maker on this Holy day, were busily employed ill all kinds of traffic in the open streets."[30]

Again he tells us: "I have resided nearly five years in Jamaica, and have preached two or three sermons every Sunday; many other clergymen have also exerted themselves, but to very little purpose, as far as slaves are concerned, as those horrid and legalized scenes are just the same; for this Sunday market is a bait of Satan, to draw away the ignorant Negro; his temporal and pressing natural wants are set in opposition to his spiritual ones, and the former prevail to that degree, that most of the churches ill the island are nearly empty."[31]

He adds later: "I am aware that there is a law in Jamaica imposing a fine on proprietors or overseers for compelling the Negroes to do certain kinds of labour on the Sabbath; but it is notorious that this law is altogether a dead letter, and that in respect to their grounds, the Negroes not only go of their own accord to work there, as not having sufficient time allowed them otherwise; but if they are found inattentive, it is a custom to send one of the bookkeepers, on that Holy day, to see that all the slaves are at work, and to watch them a certain time, that there may not be a want of food. For putting the mill about (viz. for making sugar) on a Sunday, there is a fine of 50 pounds, one half of which, I believe goes to the informer; but though this is done in defiance of law in almost every, if not every parish in the island, I never heard of an information being laid for that. offence, as those planters who do not put their mills about, wink at it in others, and no clergyman or other religious person would venture, I think, to inform, as he would be sure to meet with insult, or some worse injury, for his conscientious interference."[32]

Mr. Bicknell's conclusion is: "Nearly the whole of the field Negroes (nine-tenths of the population) have not even the outward form of religion, and are just as great heathens as they were on the banks of the Gambia or Niger."[33]

The Reverend Peter Duncan, a Wesleyan-Methodist mission-ary, arrived in Jamaica early in 1821 and laboured there for over eleven years. In reference to Dr. Coke's visit to the island in 1789, he writes: "The island has been under British government for upwards of a century, yet scarcely anything had been done for the souls of the people. The habits of the whites had indeed become much more settled. They were friendly and hospitable in their intercourse with each other, and had improved in many of the external civilities of modern refinement, but the hallowed restraints of religion were as much unknown as ever. They were strangers to the enjoyments of the domestic circle, and throughout the whole country the standard of morals was deplorably low. It is true, emigrants from Great Britain were constantly arriving, but they left their profession of Christianity behind, and were soon assimilated to the corrupt mass by whom they were preceded.

The ordinances of religion in many parts were rarely administered. There was a famine of the bread of life. There was indeed a church in almost every parish, but many of the benefices were generally vacant; and excepting on the occasion of funerals, the churches in the country parishes were seldom open for divine service, even upon the Lord's Day. Numbers of the clergy were living openly in concubinage and were otherwise unblushingly immoral; and it may be fairly questioned whether before 1789 that Sabbath ever dawned upon Jamaica, which witnessed five hundred persons in all the places of worship put together out of a population of between four and five hundred thousand souls."[34]

The Reverend Claudius Buchanan while examining the "State of our Established Church in the West Indies, in regard to its efficiency as an instrument of instructing the people"[35] asserts: "In Jamaica there are twenty parishes. Supposing that there are also twenty Rectors (in some islands there are many pluralists) we shall then have twenty Clergymen in an island which is 150 miles long and 40 in a medium broad; which gives a district of 300 square miles for the labours of each Clergyman. The population of the island is stated by Mr. Edwards to amount to 30,000 whites, 10,000 free persons of colour and 210,894 slaves: which, when divided among twenty Clergymen, will give to each a cure of 12,554 souls. It will hardly be necessary to say more of the utter inadequacy of the public means of religious instruction in Jamaica. This island is a favourable specimen of the state of the Established Church in the old islands.

"On the whole it may be safely affirmed, that no human zeal could be equal to a tenth part of the duties of the parochial Clergy, were the slaves practically regarded as belonging to their flock. But the truth is, that this unfortunate mass of the population has, with very few exceptions, never been so regarded, either by the Government or the Clergy."[36]

The Reverend Peter Samuel reached Jamaica in January, 1832, where he was to labour as a Methodist missionary for over eleven years. In his account of the development of his denomination in the island, he stresses among the obstacles encountered at the start: "The pernicious influence of Obeahism and African superstitions"[37] and adds: "The immense influence possessed and exercised by West Indian proprietors in the Parliament of the mother country, as well as in the Colonial Assembly, gave a respectability, a consistency, an air of justice, and a degree of power sufficiently formidable to the apparently weak efforts of a few humble missionaries."[38]

We have indicated here the foundation of the bitterest religious controversy in the history of Jamaica. When Dr. Coke first visited the island in January 1789, he was deeply touched by the condition of religious abandonment that he found amongst the slaves.

He was not slow on his return to England to send out the Reverend William Hammett in that same year to establish the Wesleyan Missionary Society in Jamaica.

The emotional element in Methodism immediately appealed to the kindred Myalistic spirit among the Negroes, and as they found in the assemblies which the newly-arrived missionaries were convoking in open defiance of the authorities and in face of the opposition of the planters, an opportunity of renewing much of their own Pagan rites in connection with the Christian service, they were not slow to take advantage of the general confusion of ideas, and forthwith the "digging up" of Obeah again became much in evidence. And the missionaries, good, well meaning souls, derived comfort and consolation among their hardships and persecutions, in what they must have regarded as promising manifestations of faith. They watched with delight the zeal to stamp out this African superstition, which seemed to them the Negro's real religion, and which they rightly interpreted as a form of devil worship. And yet they were unconsciously fostering and abetting a movement among the slaves that was for the most part as Pagan as the Obeah that they were "digging up."

Space will not permit our going into this controversy in detail.

We can only touch on it as far as it has reference to our present study. The nucleus of the Wesleyan Mission in Jamaica was really formed of refugees from what is now the United States in consequence of the Revolutionary War, at least as regards the leading spirits. This in itself may have stirred up opposition.[39] On one occasion, Dr. Coke himself, while preaching in Kingston, was almost dragged from the hall by a party of whites who seriously threatened him with bodily harm.[40]

In November, 1790, the Grand Jury of Kingston presented to the Court of Quarter- Sessions a complaint against the Methodist Meeting in that city as a nuisance, on the grounds that it is "injurious to the general peace and quiet of the inhabitants of this town."[41]

Buchanan tells us: "After the Methodist Missionaries had been about ten years in the Island of Jamaica; and had built a chapel at Kingston, which was attended by some whites, and by many people of colour and Negroes; the Colonial Legislature passed an Act, on the 17th December, 1802, by which they prohibited, and made penal, 'preaching or teaching in a meeting of Negroes, or people of colour, by a person not duly qualified.' There had hitherto been no law in Jamaica for Dissenters to qualify at all; and the Legislature thought fit to determine, that a person regularly and legally qualified in England, under the Toleration Act, was not duly qualified for Jamaica. In consequence of this law, two of the Missionaries were thrown into prison. The penalty for first offence was 'one month's imprisonment, and hard labour in the common workhouse.' The penalty for the second offence was, 'imprisonment and hard labour for six months,' or such further punishment 'not extending to life, as the Court should see fit to inflict.'— Such a law, in relation to a white man, had never been heard of before in Jamaica; for the laws there are highly respectful to the privileged order. If again, a black man should 'teach or preach in a meeting of Negroes, not being duly qualified,' he was 'to be sentenced to receive, for the second offence, a public flogging, not exceeding thirty-nine lashes.'

"By the operation of this law, the places of worship of other denominations of Christians besides the Methodists, were shut up. The preachers were silenced; and among the rest, a regularly or-dained minister of the Church of Scotland. The missionaries, in the extremity of their sufferings, compared this legal opposition, and its effects, to the persecution of Diocletian; only that the punishments were not, as the law expressed it, 'to extend to life.'

"The alleged ground for passing this Edict in Jamaica, whatever the truth of the case might be, was certainly similar to that of the Edicts of Diocletian. It was stated in the preamble: That the Slaves, by being permitted to assemble at these meetings to hear Christian in-struction, were in danger of being 'perverted with fanatical notions; and that opportunity was afforded them of concerting schemes of much public and private mischief.'

"On an application made by the different religious societies in England whose missionaries had been silenced, the Committee of the Privy Council for matters of Trade, examined the merits of the new Act; and upon their Report, it was disallowed by his Majesty, and consequently ceased to have any force in Jamaica."[42]

While we cannot help admiring the energy and long-suffering manifested by the Methodist missionaries in their misguided zeal with the slaves, as we read their glowing reports of souls reclaimed, we must keep in mind the warning of Mr. Gardner: "With the exception of one or two denominations, copious accounts have been published by missionaries of the labours in which they have taken part in Jamaica. It may be asserted, without any violation of Christian charity, that the most glowing descriptions of the results which have followed such labours are the least trustworthy. Honest, well- meaning men have frequently described as fruit that which was only blossom; while vain, though pious men, too anxious for the praise of their fellow-creatures, and ambitious of the ephemeral fame of missionary chronicles or the applause of public meetings, have sometimes injured the cause they wished to serve by too highly- coloured descriptions of their success."[43]

In a Report of the committee of the whole house which had been appointed "to inquire into and take further into consideration the state of the island," presented to the House of Assembly of Jamaica on Dec. 20, 1815, we find the words:[44] "The subject of religion, and the best method of introducing genuine Christianity in the mild and beneficent spirit of its founder, is of so great importance that the committee decline going deeper into it at present; but recommend that early in the next session a. committee may be appointed, for the special purpose of discussing and considering the most eligible manner of diffusing religious information amongst that class of society.

"The Assembly has always been against communicating to them the dark and dangerous fanaticism of the Methodists, which, grafted on the African superstitions, and the general temperament of Negroes in a state of bondage, has produced, and must continue to produce, the most fatal consequences, equally inimical to their well being and comfort in this world, and to the practice of those virtues which we are led to believe ensure happiness in the next.

"But the representatives of the people have not displayed any of that aversion with which they have been charged, to encourage the propagation of Christianity in the form which they thought likely to be beneficial. . . .

"It shows further, however, that the representatives of the people have always been desirous to encourage the introduction of pastors, whose education gave security for the nature of the doctrines which they were to inculcate.

"They continue of that disposition, although equally satisfied, as in former times, that to communicate the lights of Christianity through Methodism would have consequences the most fatal to the temporal comforts of the slaves, and the safety of the community."

This Report was accepted unanimously, and on December 22, 1815, a resolution passed, also unanimously, to this effect: "That early in the next session, this house will take into consideration the state of religion amongst the slaves, and carefully investigate the means of diffusing the light of genuine Christianity, divested of the dark and dangerous fanaticism of the Methodists, which has been attempted to be propagated, and which, grafted on the African superstitions, and working on the uninstructed minds and ardent temperament of the Negroes, has produced the most pernicious consequences to individuals, and is pregnant with imminent danger to the community."[45]

As already noted, neither side of the controversy even suspected the real root difficulty. The Methodist Missionaries felt that they were the victims of the rankest bigotry and cried aloud in protest. If they had only realized that they were offering themselves as martyrs to revivify and extend absolute Paganism with a veneer of Christianity in the resuscitated Myalism that was parading as Revivalism, they might have been less outspoken in their denunciation of the entire House of Assembly. If the planters, on the other hand, who honestly recognized in the unrest, caused by the activities of the Methodists, among the slaves, the significant forerunners of serious disorders, if they had only been able to really analyze the situation, and distinguish between the strong Myalistic tendencies and the Methodistic emotional susceptibilities, they might have been able to direct the latter influence into less dangerous channels and have opened the eyes of its proponents to what was actually afoot. But each side of the controversy was deaf to the arguments of the other, just as they were both blind to the real nature of the terrific forces for harm that were accumulating among the mass of the blacks.

When the dreaded uprising actually began in St. James Parish on the night of December 28, 1831, the feeling of bitterness on both sides was intense. The Reverend David Jonathan East, writing on the West Indies in the *Centenary Volume of the Baptist Missionary Society*,[46] admits that the insurrection "broke out in the very district in which missionary labours had been most successful," and adds at once: "It is not perhaps surprising that the first thought of the planters was that missionaries were the authors of the rebellion."

Exaggerated as this view of the planters certainly was, it is no more extreme than the attitude of some of the missionaries themselves. Thus the Reverend Peter Duncan, who was a Methodist Minister in Jamaica at the very time of the slave-rebellion, fosters his own resentment, and writing eighteen years after the events, unhesitatingly insinuates, seemingly with absolutely no foundation in fact: "Time may yet show, whether, in some instances, the negroes were not directly instigated to violence for the purpose of casting odium upon the missionaries."[47] And in a note he explains: "This thought has been ridiculed, and it has been asked, whether it can be believed, that any man would instigate the negroes to destroy his own property: Perhaps not; but it never was pretended that the instigators of the negroes had property to destroy. The overseers, the parties alluded to, had no property. Such found it easier to kindle the fire than to put it out. It is not, however, suspected that many directly instigated the negroes to the work of destruction. "[48]

If both sides could only have understood the insidious workings of Myalism as we do today, how much different might have been the closing days of slavery in Jamaica.[49] In place of the mutual antagonism, and bitter recriminations, they might have worked harmoniously together for the peace and prosperity of the entire community." The years of apprenticeship might then have witnessed a gradual enlightenment of the masses of former slaves, spiritually as well as intellectually. And with their freedom from bondage, they might naturally have acquired a disillusionment as regards Myalism and Obeah alike. In that case the recrudescence of Paganism that blighted the early days of reconstruction might never have occurred.

In any case, the fact remains that actually the forces of Myalism and Obeah today have degenerated into a common form of witchcraft not unfrequently associated with devil worship, and even those of the blacks who belittle its general influence, in practice show a wholesome fear of the powers of the Obeah man. And here we must leave the question for the present, reserving for a future volume a detailed study of Duppyism and kindred subjects.

Footnotes

Introduction

1 Note:—*Magic Island* was unquestionably received with fulsome praise by reviewers generally. Thus THE BOOKMAN, February 1929, p. 68: "It has been a long time since a volume has
held my attention so completely as W. B. Seabrook's Magic Island. It is not a twice told tale
but a vivid record of things seen." The NEW YORK HERALD-TRIBUNE, January 8, 1929: "Here
in its own field is the book of the year." The NEW YORK EVENING POST, January 12, 1929,
calls it "a sensational vivid and immensely important book." To the OUTLOOK, January 9,
1929: "It is a prize among travel books." While the SATURDAY REVIEW, February 23, 1929,
declares: "Mr. Seabrook has done justice to this remarkable subject not only in investigating the system, but in presenting the results of his work." The more thoughtful reviews,
however, refuse to be entirely carried away by the general acclaim, and modify their
praise with almost hesitant reserve. Thus the YALE REVIEW, Autumn, 1929, p. 185, makes
the restriction: "He spoils much of his material by his exaggerated style and his dubious
psychology." The AMERICAN JOURNAL OF SOCIOLOGY, September, 1929, p. 316, insists:
"He has written as an artist, not as an ethnologist." And the NATION, February 13, 1929, p.
198, urges: "It is time for a tempered intelligent presentation on the manner in which they
live, one that staying close to facts, probing under the surface, and eschewing rumors, will
make quite as fascinating a tale."
We may be pardoned, then, if we seem to delay too long on Mr. Seabrook and his sensational book, but we must risk the criticism in the interest of fair play as regards Haiti and
the popular estimate of Voodoo.
2 February 23, 1929, p. 35 ff
3 Seabrook, *Magic Island*, New York, 1929, p. 61
4 Seabrook, l.c., p. 62
5 Ditto, p. 63
6 Ditto, p. 63 f
7 Ditto, p. 65
8 Ditto, p. 66
9 Note:—The author spells it with a final *e*, Simone. While in Jamaica, the family themselves
always spelt it simply Simon
10 Seabrook, l. c., p. 117
11 Note:—As one who knew the Simons in Jamaica, I can categorically deny both this
assertion as well as the plausibility of the pseudo-voodooistic murder which is shortly to
be described.
12 Seabrook, l. c., p. 121
13 Ditto, p. 122 f.
14 Ditto, p. 61 f
15 Ditto, p. 42

16 l. c., p. 48

17 l. c., p. 53

18 l. c., p. 118 f. Note:—For example, not only is the *Dies Irae* badly misplaced, but there can be no Credo in a funeral Mass

19 *En Haïti*, Paris, 1910, p. 46

20 P. Labat, *Nouveau Voyage aux Isles de L'Amérique*, La Haye 1724, Vol. II, p. 44

21 Seabrook, l. c., p. 318

22 Dr. Price-Mars, *Une-Étape de l'Évolution Haïtienne*, Port-au-Prince, 1929, p. 153.

23 Dr. Price-Mars, l. c., p. 154 f

24 Ditto, p. 54

25 Ditto, p. 172

26 Seabrook, l. c., p. 28 ff

27 Dr. Price-Mars, l. c., p. 161 f

28 Note:—It must not be supposed that what has been written is intended in any way to impeach the veracity of Mr. Seabrook. Personally I am convinced of his sincerity and straightforwardness and that in his really fascinating account he is no party to an imposition. Of course I can never agree with his extraordinary profession of faith, and I doubt if he really takes himself seriously in that regard. He was probably carried away by the spirit of his narrative.

As regards the story itself, I honestly believe that he has tried to stick to facts as he has seen them or in many cases as they have been told to him, with perhaps just a little of the personal element added for effect. But what I do fear is that he has been too credulous in accepting all that has been told to him.

The West Indian Negro, especially if paid by results, is a mine of "information." The workings of his imagination are extraordinary. A couple of years ago I was striving to collect all the various anansy stories, in connection with a folk-lore study of Jamaica. The teacher of a government "bush" school, seriously offered to invent for me all the stories, that I wanted if I gave him sufficient time and paid for the results. Fortunately for the value of my collection I was restricting the contributors to children of school age. I have no doubt that Mr. Seabrook must have encountered the same generous spirit, especially if he was paying by results.

Even the goat scene may have been a clever piece of acting. The histrionic powers of the West Indian are no wit inferior to his ability as a raconteur. But in any case, no matter how we are to explain away the objective inaccuracies of *Magic Island*, even if we must invoke hallucination or that subtle form of hypnotic influence, such as is at times ascribed to Voodoo worship, let there be no suspicion that there is any intention of questioning Mr. Seabrook's honesty of purpose.

Chapter I

1 Note:—Cfr. C. Staniland Wake, *Serpent-Worship and other Essays*, London, 1888, p. 105 f.:
"The facts brought together in the preceding pages far from exhaust the subject, but they appear to justify the following conclusions:—

"First. The serpent has been viewed with awe or veneration from primeval times, and almost universally as a re-embodiment of a deceased human being, and as such there were ascribed to it the attributes of life and wisdom, and the power of healing.

"Secondly the idea of a simple spirit re-incarnation of a deceased ancestor gave rise to the notion that mankind originally sprang from a serpent, and ultimately to a legend embodying that idea.

"Thirdly, This legend was connected with nature—or rather Sun-worship—and the Sun, was, therefore, looked upon as the divine serpent-father of man and nature.

"Fourthly, Serpent worship, as a developed religious system, originated in Central Asia, the home of the great Scythic stock, from whom all civilized races of the historical period sprang.

'Fifthly, These peoples are the Adamites, and their mythical ancestor was at one time regarded as the Great Serpent, his descendants being in a special sense serpent-worshippers." This of course, would presuppose that Adam was the founder of only a family and not of the human race that long antedated Adam.

Wundt, on the other hand, with equal assurance, suggests as a reason for the fact that spirits are so often depicted as assuming the shape of snakes, since the serpentine form naturally suggests itself to the primitive mind through the association of ideas with the maggots that commonly infest dead bodies during the process of decay.—Cfr. C. Meinhof, *Die Dichtung der Afrikaner*, Berlin, 1911, p. 18. This is perhaps about as reasonable as the claims of those who connect the snake with phallic worship

2 Edward B. Tylor, *Primitive Culture*, Boston, 1874, p. 239

3 London, 1905, p. 5

4 Ditto, p. 206 f. Note:—Dr. Oldham also states, p. 183: "It seems in the highest degree improbable that this close connection between the Sun and the serpent could have originated, independently, in countries so far apart as China and the west of Africa, or India and Peru. And it seems scarcely possible that, in addition to this, the same forms of worship of these deities, and the same ritual, could have arisen, spontaneously, amongst each of these far distant peoples. The alternative appears to be, that the combined worship of the Sun and the serpent-gods must have spread from a common centre, by the migration of, or communication with, the people who claim Solar descent." This is Elliot Smith's theory which would derive the entire cult from Egypt.

Oldham, however, differs from Elliot Smith in as much as he would make Asia and not Egypt the point of origin. Thus, p. 197: "The social customs and religious rites of the Egyptians were closely related to those of the Sun- worshipping people of Asia. There can, indeed, be little doubt as to the Asiatic origin of the Pharaohs and their followers." Nevertheless, {footnote p. 3} Wilfrid D. Hambly, in the case of serpent worship, at least, rejects the whole explanation. He finds in zoological evidence, sufficient reason for spontaneous origins of the serpent cult in various parts of the world.—Cfr. Wilfrid D. Hambly, *Serpent Worship in Africa*, Chicago, 1931, Chapter VII, p. 68 ff.

Cfr. also, John Bathurst Deane, *The Worship of the Serpent*, London, 1830, who states in his Preface, p. xii f.: "The plan of this treatise is simple. It professes to prove the existence of Ophiolatreia in almost every considerable country of the ancient world, and to discover in the mythology of every civilized nation, evidences of a recollection of the events in Paradise. If these facts can be established, the conclusion is obvious—that all such traditions must have had a common origin; and that the most ancient record, which contains their basis, must be the authentic history. The most ancient record containing this basis is the Book of Genesis, composed by Moses. The Book of Genesis, therefore, contains the history upon which the fables, rites, and superstitions of the mythological serpent are founded." The Reverend Mr. Deane, M.A., F.S.A. is recorded in the first edition of his work as "Late of Pembroke College, Cambridge: Curate of St. Benedict Finck; and evening preacher at the Chapel of the Philanthropic Society." His avowed purpose, the support of the Biblical narrative and his unquestioning acceptance of the Mosaic origin of Genesis, etc., effectively excludes him from the consideration of most so-called critical scholars. However, while admitting his partiality and bias, and even his lack of modern scientific methods, there is much that he has to say that is really worthy of serious consideration.

Reference should also be made to Professor Clemen of Bonn, who after stating: "Every possible kind of animal is regarded as a higher being by both primitive and civilized peoples, and it is not always easy to give a reason in the various cases," adds: "Especially frequent is the worship of the snake, whose power of locomotion without feet, as well as its repeated sloughing of its skin, its fixed gaze and its poisonous fangs, no doubt attracted special attention." Carl Clemen, *Religions of the World*, New York, 1931, p. 30. Finally, M. Oldfield Howey, *The Encircled Serpent*, Philadelphia, 1928, p. 17, asserts: "The origin of Egyptian Ophiolatry is lost in the mists of antiquity, but it is said to have been derived from Chaldea, which country is thought to have given it birth, and certainly produced enthusiastic adherents of its tenets. Put the serpent is everywhere in the mythologies and cosmogonies of Eastern lands, so that to trace out the ultimate source of its appearance in so ancient a civilization with any certainty is probably impossible."

5 Field Museum of Natural History Publication 289, Chicago, 1931, Anthropological Series, Vol. XXI, No. 1

6 Ditto, p. 74

7 Ditto, p. 75

8 Note:—Hambly remarks, p. 55: "My general conclusion is that Python worship is an indigenous factor of Negro culture; but on the contrary African ideas of rainbow-snakes, snake-monsters, and birth-snakes, are derived from Hamito-Semitic beliefs of southwestern Asia." And again, p. 64: 'I am reluctant to accept any statement with regard to. the Egyptian origin of snake-sun beliefs. There are, however, many Egyptian serpent beliefs, both ancient and modern, which may assist in tracing the origin of African beliefs and customs."

9 John Roscoe, *The Baganda, An Account of their Native Customs and Beliefs*, London, 1911, p. 320f

10 Hambly, l. c., Preface, p. 8

11 Ditto, p. 75. Cfr. also p. 48: "Python and snake worship were undoubtedly more firmly established in Africa years ago than they are at present." And, p. 55: "Python worship of West Africa is found to be strongly intrenched among people of Negro blood who speak non-Bantu languages, and of these the Ijaw are the best example. In East and West Africa the python is associated with success in agriculture and fishing. These occupations were followed by Negroes who were driven out by pastoral immigrants."

12 Cfr., however, Thomas J. Hutchinson, *Impressions of Western Africa*, London, 1858, p. 197. Writing from Fernando Po, where he was his Britannic Majesty's Consul, having spent eight years in West Africa, Hutchinson says: "The coronation of a king is a ceremonial that I have not yet had the pleasure of witnessing; but it has been reported to me as one possessing interesting features. It is so bound tip with their notions of a spirit or devil, that I deem it necessary to explain the peculiarity of their belief on this latter point. 'Maaon' is the title given to the devil, and the Botakimaaon (his high priest) is supposed to have influence with him through communication with the cobra-capella, the 'Roukarouko.' Their faith in God, to whom the name of 'Rupe' is given, is a loftier aspiration than that of the devil; but they believe that the Deity's favour can be only obtained by intercession through the 'Botakimaaon' with his master. At the ceremony of coronation, the Botakimaaon steps into a deep hole, and pretends to hold conversation with one of the Roukaroukos at the bottom; the candidate for regal honours standing alongside, and all his subjects, *in futuro*, being about. This conference is, I believe, carried on by means of ventriloquism,—a faculty with which many of the Fernandians are reported to me to be endowed. The Botakimaaon then delivers to the king the message from the Roukarouko for his guidance in his high station." The "Maaon" referred to is probably not the devil, but some ancestral or other spirit as happens elsewhere in the serpent worship.

13 Hambly, l. c., p. 18. Hambly further observes, p. 69: "Pythons of various kinds have a distribution ranging from the southern Sahara to Natal. The {footnote p. 7} Python *sebae*, the largest of all, may be found almost anywhere through the Sudan from Senegal to Dafur. Pythons of some species attain enormous size, have great crushing power, are non-poisonous, are easily tamed, seldom attack human beings, and are slow to bite if handled gently. With these points in view it is not difficult to understand why the python should have been selected as a suitable snake for captivity in temples. The reptiles are easily controlled by priests, and at the same time are harmless to those who come with petitions and sacrifices." He had already said, p. 44: "Most observers have remarked on the fearlessness with which priests and priestesses handle large pythons. These snakes are, however, non-poisonous, and their general harmlessness and domesticability are well attested.

Very seldom do they attack human beings. The question of immunity in handling poisonous snakes is another problem, but in this connection it must be admitted that many poisonous snakes, unless disturbed suddenly and startled, are reluctant to strike."

14 Hambly, l. c., p. 29 ff. Note:—He has already observed: "In Uganda the main ceremonies of supplication are carried out at new moon; to this I have found no parallel in the

ceremonies reported from West Africa."—l. c., p. 21

15 Hambly, l. c., p. 49
16 Note:—Later he states, p. 75: "Within the African continent itself migration of ideas
has probably played a more important part than has independent invention. Easy
communication from east to west, and from north to south; known Hamitic and Semitic
movements; also the appeal made by transmigration and fecundity ideas in all grades of
society, have assisted a ready diffusion."
17 Hambly, l. c., p. 50 f
18 A. L. Kitching, *On the Backwaters of the Nile*, London, 1912, Foreword, p. xi
19 Ditto, p. 256.
20 Ditto, p. 259
21 John Roscoe, *The Bakitara or Banyoro*, Cambridge, 1923, p. 42
22 Roscoe, l. c., p. 44. Note:—After twenty-five years of missionary work in Africa, Canon
Roscoe undertook an ethnological expedition there in 1919. He tells us, John Roscoe,
The Soul of Central Africa, London, 1922, Preface, p. vii: "For some time funds for such a
purpose were not available, but Sir James G. Frazer, who first aroused in me an interest
in anthropology, was unceasing in his attempts to find some means of financing the
work. At length, owing to his efforts, Sir Peter Mackie, of Glenreasdell, became interested
in the project, and most generously came forward and shouldered the whole financial
burden, handing over to the Royal Society ample sums for the purpose." It is interesting
then, to find Frazer writing from Cambridge on Feb. 5, 1908, to his friend Sir Spencer
Gillen in Australia, *Spencer's Scientific Correspondence Sir J. G. Frazer and others*, Oxford,
1932, p. 107: "I wish if possible to relieve J. Roscoe of his mission work in Central Africa,
and set him free there entirely for anthropology. We should learn very much from him.
I know no keener anthropologist than he." Particular value, then, is attached to the
following testimony of Roscoe, taken from the very book that we have quoted in the
text, *The Bakitara or Banyoro*, p. 21: "Though the Bakitara had a great number of objects
of worship, there was but one god, Ruhanga, the creator and father of mankind. With
him were associated the names Enkya and Enkyaya Enkya, whose identity it is not easy
to separate from that of Ruhanga. One man asserted that they were a trinity and yet one
god; but as he had been for some years a devout Christian, in constant attendance at the
Roman Catholic Mission Station his statement may have {footnote p. 11} been coloured
by Christian ideas. The general impression gathered, however, was that their belief was
entirely monotheistic, and that, if the three were not one deity, then Enkya and Enkyaya
Enkya were subordinate gods whose appearance in their theology was later than that
of Ruhanga, and more frequently, Enkya and Enkyaya Enkya were called upon by the
people in distress or need; prayers were made to them in the open, with hands and eyes
raised skywards."
In connection with East African Ophiolatry, the following citations might be noted.
"The only disquietude to a stranger in their houses arises from the snakes which rustle in
the straw roofs, and disturb his rest. Snakes are the only creatures to whom either Dinka
or Shillooks pay any sort of reverence. The Dinka call them 'brethren' and look upon their
slaughter as a crime. I was informed by witnesses which I have no cause to distrust, that

the separate snakes are individually known to the householder, who calls them by name, and treats them as domestic animals."—Georg Schweinfurth, *The Heart of Africa*, London, 1874, Vol. I, p. 158.

"When a medicine-man or a rich person dies and is buried, his soul turns into a snake as soon as his body rots; and the snake goes to his children's kraal to look after them."—Masai saying recorded by A. C. Hollis, *The Masai: Their Language and Folklore*, Oxford, 1905, p. 307.

"Under ordinary circumstances a snake is killed at sight. A snake is also killed if it enters a house, and a hole has to be made in the wall in order to eject the body, as it may not be thrown out of the door. But if a snake goes in to the woman's bed, it may not be killed, as it is believed that it personifies the spirit of a deceased ancestor or relation, and that it has been sent to intimate to the woman that the next child will be born safely."—A. C. Hollis, *The Nandi: Their Language and Folklore*, Oxford, 1909, p. 90.

"According to the belief of a great many Bantus, especially in South Africa, the dead appear chiefly in the form of snakes."—Lucien Lévy-Bruhl, *The "Soul" of the Primitive*, New York, 1928, p. 292.

"The Zulu . . . recognizes the soul of an ancestor in the snake which visits his kraal."—Frank Byron Jevons, *An Introduction to the History of Religion*, London, 1896, p. 303.

These instances refer rather to serpent cult than to formal Ophiolatry

23 Hambly, l. c., p. 34
24 Arthur Glyn Leonard, *The Lower Niger and its Tribes*, London, 1906, p. 327. Note:—In a Preface to Major Leonard's work (p. xii) Professor A. C. Haddon thus explains the author's general animistic theory. "We learn that the religion of the Niger delta natives is based on the adoration of ancestral spirits, materially represented by emblems, the latter being nothing more nor less than convenient forms of embodiment which can be altered or transferred according to circumstances. These objects, rude and senseless as they may be, are regarded as vehicles of spiritual influence, as something sacred because of their direct association with some familiar and powerful spirit, and not as objects which in themselves have, or carry with them, any so-called supernatural powers. It is not the object itself, but what is in or is associated with it. The object accordingly becomes nothing more nor less than a sacred receptacle, and its holiness is merely a question of association. The thing itself is helpless and powerless. it cannot do harm, just as it cannot do good; the spirit, which is invariably ancestral, even when deified, alone does the mischief and wrecks the vengeance in the case of neglect or impiety, or confers the benefits and the blessings when the ancestral rites are performed with due piety by the household."

According to Major Leonard, ancestor worship eventually postulated a Supreme Being. Thus he argues, p. 89: "Surrounded on all sides by evil, *i. e.* by people who were inimical to him, and spiritual influences, who sought his life on every opportunity, the family looked to its head for protection. But he, poor man, was to a greater extent then this family circumvented by enemies on all sides, and in spite of his skill, his strength, and his prowess, he felt himself powerless in the face of them all. So in his misery he turned to the spirit of his father, whom during his lifetime he had honoured and revered, and to whose spiritual aid, when he was victorious, he had once attributed the victory. But victory did not always shine upon him, for the race was not always to the swift, nor was the battle always to the strong. Therefore it was in these moments that be looked beyond his father to the first or spirit ancestor who had made every man and everything, good or evil. A moment this of supremest exaltation, arising out of the lowest depths of despair. Of supremest triumph also, for the Supreme One had once more asserted his power and given him the victory. Having recognized the existence and presence of a Creator, and evoked his aid, the next stage in the process was the formation of a system by which the victory of the Supreme One and his great influence were to be commemorated and kept alive." We cannot accept the Major's process of reasoning on the part of the so-called primitive. But it is sufficient for our purpose that he does require a Supreme Being in the present-day belief. To all appearances, Major Leonard is {footnote p. 13} only following Frazer who says: "The theology of the Bantu tribes, especially of such of them as have remained in the purely pastoral stage, appears generally to be of the most meagre nature: its principal element, so far as we can judge from the scanty accounts of it which we possess, is the fear or worship of dead ancestors, and though these ancestral spirits are commonly supposed to manifest themselves to their descendants in the shape of snakes of various kinds, there is no sufficient ground for assuming these snakes to have been originally totems."—J. G. Frazer, *Totemism and Exogamy*, London, 1910, Vol. IV, p. 32.

In his chapter on "The Gods of the Priests and People," Major Leonard states; p. 416: "This system of religion is based fundamentally—that is, purely and entirely—on the close and naturally inseparable ties and associations of family or ancestral relationships, which is regarded by these natives as a natural order, direct from the Supreme God."

25 Leonard l. c. p. 328
26 Located about N. 10º; E. 10º
27 C. K. Meek, *The Northern Tribes of Nigeria*, Oxford, 1925, Vol. I, p. 54
28 Ditto, p. 76 f
29 Meek, l. c., p. 174. Note:—In a later work, *Tribal Studies in Northern Nigeria*, London, 1931, Meek adds further details. Thus, Vol. I, p. 164, we read: "The Melim are natural objects worshipped publicly in the bush, but families and individuals protect themselves with minor objects known as 'habtu' which are amulets or 'fetishes,' according as the efficacy is transmitted from outside or is due to the presence of an indwelling spirit." He is referring to the Bura and Pabir tribes located around N. 12º½; E. 10º½. Again, p. 165; "Habtu Pwapu is a striking representation in iron of a snake (pwapu means 'snake') which is commonly seen in houses. Or it may be attached to the leg as an amulet. In the houses they may be seen set in pairs (male and female) in the shell of a baobab nut. They are said to ward off evil influences and appear to have a fertility signification. Their custodians are women, but every householder must at harvest offer benniseed and cotton and the blood of a chicken to his Habtu Pwapu, otherwise one of his household will be bitten by a snake. It may be noted here that the figure of the serpent appears as a personal or house-protecting amulet all through Egyptian history. A specimen of a Habtu Pwapu was obtained."

Writing of the Mumuye, located about N. 9°; E. 11°½, Vol. I, p. 468, Meek states: "The rain cult par excellence for all the Mumuye and surrounding tribes is that centred at Yoro. When a serious drought occurs all the senior priests of the tribe proceed with gifts to the rain-maker Yoro. To this cult even the chief of Kona appeals as a last resort, by sending numerous gifts. The rites are said to be as follows. The priest (the kpanti mi, *i.e.* rain-chief) removes from a large pot the symbol of the cult, which is a piece of iron fashioned like a snake. It is kept rolled up in a curtain of black string. The priest unwinds the curtain and fastens it to two pegs on opposite walls of the hut. Then taking a blacksmith's hammer in his right hand and a pair of iron scissors in his left, he says: 'What I am about to do my forefathers did before me. Grant that this drought may cease, and that we may have corn to eat.' He then chews a piece of the *vitis quadrangularis* creeper and spits it out on the implements. which he lays on the ground. Picking up the iron snake he says, 'You we received from Yoro in the East; a drought has come upon us, and if we do not have rain, how shall we obtain food to eat? Grant, therefore, that by your graciousness we may have rain in abundance. and that in due course we may reap a sufficient harvest.' He again takes a piece of the creeper, chews it and spits it out on the iron snake. He then hurls, the snake against the hammer and scissors, and it is said that as soon as this is done the first peal of thunder is heard. It is a sympathetic rite, the clanging of the iron being a simulation of thunder."

As regards the Hausa, C. G. Seligman, *Races of Africa*, London, 1930, p. 81 f., records the derivation of the word title which now signifies king or chieftain in the Hausa language. The founder of the royal line was said to have been a son of the King of Bagdad. On his arrival at Daura he found the well guarded by a serpent called Ki Serki, who prevented the drawing of water. He slew the serpent, married the Queen of the country, and was thereafter called Mai-Kai Serki, the man who killed Serki. Seligman adds: "This legend is recorded since. on the one hand, it seems to preserve some features of the older organization of the land (matrilineal descent, snake- worship): and on the other emphasizes the constant tendency to borrow and greatly exaggerate Eastern connections, due to the increasing prestige & pressure of Islam."

30 P. Amaury Talbot, *In the Shadow of the Bush*, London, 1912, p. 25. Note:—Of the religion of the Ekoi, Talbot says, p. 13: "The religion of the Ekoi is altogether a fascinating study. Its principal features are the Cult of Ancestors and of Nature Forces.... Of actual Deities there are only two, Obassi Osaw, the Sky God, and the Earth God Obassi Nsi."

Major A. J. N. Tremearne, *The Ban of the Bori*, London, 1914, p. 413, remarks: The names of many snake- worshipping tribes in the West Sudan consist of *sa* or *so*, in combination with other letters. But *sa* or *za* alone or in combination, also mean chief and rulers with these names are said to have come from the cast; Sa, a younger son of Misraim or Menes, the earliest historic king of Egypt, being given the district bordering the Fezzan route to the desert." He personally rejects the opinion of those who hold that the *Sa* in question really stands for serpent.

31 Oxford, 1926
31 Oxford, 1926
32 Ditto, Vol. II, p. 14 33 Ditto, Vol. II, p. 83 f 34 Ditto, Vol. II. p. 93

35 Ditto, Vol. II, p. 103

36 Ditto, Vol. II, p. 112

37 Ditto, Vol. II, p. 112.

38 Ditto, Vol. II, p. 126

39 London, 1932

40 Ditto, p. 78

41 Ditto, p. 92

42 S. S. Farrow, *Faith, Fancies and Fetish, or Yoruba Paganism*, London, 1926, p. 20

43 Note:—Here we should observe that in the case of this local cult the serpent chosen is a poisonous one; which fact immediately distinguishes it from the general acceptation of the non-poisonous python. Indeed if the origin of this local cult had not been preserved for us historically, the instance might have been quoted to weaken the claim that one of the characteristics of the serpent peculiar to African Ophiolatry is that it is of the non-poisonous type

44 A. B. Ellis, *The Tshi-Speaking Peoples of the Gold Coast of West Africa*, London, 1887, p. 40 ff

45 Note:—Cfr. C. Staniland Wake, *Serpent Worship*, p. 28: "The fact is that the serpent was only a symbol, or at most an embodiment of the spirit which it represented, as we see from the belief of several African and American tribes, which probably preserves the primitive form of this superstition. Serpents are looked upon by these peoples as embodiments of their departed ancestors, and an analogous notion is entertained by various Hindu tribes." Also, M. Oldfield Howey, *The Encircled Serpent*, p. 17: 'The religion of ancient Egypt is from the earliest times closely interwoven with the symbolic worship of sun and serpent. Not only was the serpent looked upon as an emblem of Divinity in the abstract, but it was connected with the worship of all the Egyptian gods." And a couple of pages later, p. 19: "Both serpent and sun were emblems of the Celestial Father and participated in the honours that through them were paid to the Supreme Being." And finally, J. B. Schlegel, *Ewe-Sprache*, p. xiv: "Serpents hold a prominent place in the religions of the world, as the incarnations, shrines or symbols of high deities. Such were the rattlesnake's worshipped in the Natchez temple of the Sun, and the snake belonging in name and figure to the Aztec deity Quetzalcoatl; the snake as worshipped still by the Slave Coast Negro, not for itself but for its indwelling deity!' As quoted by Edward B. Tylor, *Primitive Culture*, p. 241

46 Note:—In cases where the serpent cult of Africa may actually imply more than the invoking of the intercessory power of ancestors with the Supreme Being, and where seemingly perhaps the Deity himself is venerated in the reptile, before ascribing the act of worship to idolatry, it would be well to weigh carefully Father Hull's explanation of a similar phase of Hindu worship in India, where not serpents but figures of stone are the object of the cult.—Cfr. Ernest R. Hull, *Studies in Idolatry*, Bombay, 1912, p. 1 ff. He says: "A European just come out to India, if asked what he means by idolatry, will point at once to some Hindu salaaming or prostrating himself in front of a lump of stone. 'That man,' he says, 'is worshipping a stone. He is paying to it that supreme reverence which is due to God alone. Idolatry means worshipping a stock or stone as God, and instead of God.' "Now it is difficult to believe that idolatry of this crude kind exists. Could any man short

of an idiot believe that a stone—as such—is God?

"Those who think that the uneducated Hindus really regard the material object as God seem to be misled by the crude way in which simple Hindus express themselves. They certainly do call the stone object a God. But they must all know well enough that before certain ceremonies the stone was an ordinary stone; and in one of their festivals they actually drive the God out of the image before throwing it into the sea. This clearly shows that the God is rather an inhabitant of the stone than the stone itself. In short, all the facts we know about Hindu worship are totally against this view. . . .

"A second explanation current among the exponents of Hinduism, is as follows:—The man does not believe that the stone as such is God. What he believes is that a stone, when selected, and set up, and consecrated in some way, becomes the dwelling place of God. In this case, worship is directed, not to the stone as such, but to the God present in the stone, which is merely an outward and visible object marking that presence. . . . Hence the material stone is reverenced or respected as sacred on account of its connection with the divine presence. But no Hindu, they say, dreams of paying divine worship to the stone as such. . . . It is true that the common people do not think metaphysically on the subject. The divine presence is in the material object, and they venerate the object in the rough divine. Still there is. no difficulty in allowing that their worship is far removed from the utterly preposterous idea that God is the stone as such, or that the stone as such is God.

The real object to which their worship is directed, is sometimes as it were behind the stone-some preternatural being, real or imaginary, whom they believe to be God, whose special presence has been induced therein by certain religious rites.

"As far as one can see, the normal belief of the mass of Hindus, is of this kind. A fairly educated Hindu layman and a well educated Hindu priest may be quoted for this. The layman said:—'I believe in the divine presence in the image, and I suppose three-quarters of my fellow Hindus do the same.' The priest said:—'The common people believe that the image contains the God, but we educated men do not. What we believe is that the object is a representation of an avatar, i.e. the form under which God has manifested himself on earth; or, if not a representation of the actual form, it is a symbolic representation of some divine attribute manifested to man.' This introduces the third view, according to which the object is a mere stone unendowed with any divine presence; it is at most a symbol or representation embodying some divine fact. The image in this case is respected as sacred, being devoted to a sacred purpose; but worship is not directed to it. An educated Hindu praying towards it is really praying not to it but to his God; that is to say, his worship, which is outwardly directed towards the stone, is internally directed to the God in heaven, and not to the God as specially present in the stone." In the African serpent cult the second explanation holds true in such cases as the serpent itself seems to be venerated. Usually, however, the reptile is merely the habitation of some spirit, ancestral or otherwise, who acts as an intermediary with God and through whom the veneration is actually given to God himself.

Chapter II

1 P. Labat, *Nouveau Voyage aux Isles de l'Amérique*, Vol. II, p. 41 f.

2 Cfr. *Nouvelle Biographie Générale*, Paris, 1860, Vol. XXXIII, p. 467

3 P. Labat, *Voyage du Chevalier Des Marchais en Guinée, Isles Voisines, et à Cayenne, fait en 1725, 1726 & 1727, Amsterdam*, 1731, Vol. I, Preface, p. ii

4 Labat, *Des Marchais*, Vol. II, p. 133 f

5 Ditto, p. 134. Note:—For his own part, Des Marchais seems to be rather sceptical about the longevity of this serpent. He writes: "If he is still alive, and it has always been so believed since he was given to this people, he should be of prodigious length and thickness. But it is needful to pay attention to what these people say of it and then believe what one thinks proper. For it is only the chief Sacrificer who has the privilege of entering its secret apartments, the King himself can do so only once when he goes to present his offerings, three months after his coronation."—*Des Marchais*, l. c., Vol. II, p. 136.

6 Ditto, Vol. II, p. 36

7 Cfr. Antonius Francus, *Synopsis Annalium S. J. in Lusitania*, 1540-1725, Augsburg, 1726

8 Charles Chaulmer, *Le Tableau de l'Afrique*, Paris, 1661

9 Dapper, Naukeurige Beschrijvinge der Afrikaensche Gewesten, Amsterdam, 1668

10 John Ogilby, Africa, London, 1670

11 Labat, Des Marchais, Vol. II, p. 261

12 Ditto, Vol. II, p. 145 ff

13 Ditto, Vol. II, p. 144 ff

14 William Bosman, *A New and Accurate Description of the Coast of Guinea, divided into the Gold, the Slave, and the Ivory Coast*, London, 1705, p. 368

15 Ditto, p. 369

16 Ditto, p. 370

17 Ditto, p. 376

18 Ditto, p. 377

19 Ditto, p. 379

20 Ditto, p. 380

21 Ditto, p. 381

22 Ditto, p. 381

23 John Atkins, A Voyage to Guinea, Brasil, and the West Indies in His Majesty's Ships, the Swallow and Weymouth, London, 735, p. 110

24 Ditto, p. 113

25 William Snelgrave, *A New Account of some Parts of Guinea and the Slave-Trade*, London, 1734, p. 2

26 Ditto, p. 10 f

27 William Smith, *A New Voyage to Guinea*, London, 1745, p. I

28 Ditto, p. 190

29 Ditto, p. 192. Note:-According to Robert Norris, Memoirs of the Reign of Bossa Ahadee, King of Dahomy, London, 1789, p. 69: "The infatuated Whydahs contented themselves with placing, with great ceremony, the fetish snake in tile path, to oppose the invading

army, which not answering their hopes and expectations, they deemed all other resistance vain, and fled precipitately before the conqueror."

30 Ditto, p. 196 f. Note:—Speaking of Dahomey and vicinity he says, p. 213: "All the natives of this Coast believe there is one true God, the Author of them and all things." C. des Brosses, Du Culte des Dieux Fetiches, ou Parallèle de l'Ancienne Religion de l'Égypte avec la Religion de Nigritie, Paris, 1760, pp. 25-37, drawing his information principally from Atkins, Bosman and Des Marchais, gives us a detailed account of the serpent cult at Whydah which he calls by its old name Juidah. As the title of his book suggests, he would make Egypt the source of this Ophiolatry of West Africa.

31 Note:—Cfr. *Report of the Lords of the Committee of Council appointed for the consideration of all matters relating to trade and foreign Plantations, London, 1789. Part I, View of the Evidence that the Committee had obtained of the present state of those parts of Africa from whence slaves have been exported.*—This is a large folio volume of some twelve hundred pages which are unfortunately not numbered, thus making reference difficult

32 Norris, *Memoirs of the Reign of Bossa Ahadee, King of Dahomey*, p. 2

33 Ditto, p. 105, Note

34 Note:—Cfr. also, Archibald Dalzel, *History of Dahomey, an Inland Kingdom of Africa*, London, 1793, Introduction, p. vi: "Most of the savage nations {footnote p. 35} have some confused notion of a Supreme intellectual Being, the maker of the universe; but this idea not being easily understood among a people not much addicted to metaphysical reasoning, a variety of corporeal beings have been selected as objects of devotion, such as the sun, moon, living animals, trees, and other substances. The tiger is the fetish of Dahomey; the snake, that of Whydah."

35 John M'Leod, *A Voyage to Africa with some Account of the Manners and Customs of the Dahomian People*, London, 1820, p. 32. Note:—Dr. M'Leod had previously stated of Dahomey in general:—Snakes of the boa species are here found of a most enormous size; many being thirty to thirty-six feet in length, and of proportionate girth. They attack alike the wild and domestic beasts, and often the human kind."—l. c., p. 32. These are certainly not the sacred species, as he tells us on the very next page: "The bulk of the animals these serpents are capable of gorging would stagger belief, were the fact not so fully attested as to place it beyond doubt. The state of torpor in which they are sometimes found in the woods after a stuffing meal of this kind, affords the Negroes an opportunity of killing them"—l. c., p. 31. If they were of the sacred variety they would not be killed by the Negroes.
To this same period belongs Pierre Labarthe, who writes, *Voyage à la, Côte de Guinée*, Paris, 1893, p. 133: "They have here a kind of high-priest whom the Negroes call the Great Fetisher or Great Voodnoo; he claims to have descended from heaven and poses as the interpreter of the gods on earth; under this guise he demands the same honours as are shown to the King." And again: "Despite their superstitions, these people have a confused idea of a Supreme Being, all Powerful, immense; they seek to placate Him through their fetishers: they are persuaded that God is too good to do them harm: that is why they render Him no worship."—l. c., p. 135

36 John Duncan, Travels in Western Africa in 1845 & 1846, London, 1847, Vol. I, p. 126.

Note:—The Reverend Thomas B. Freeman, who visited Dahomey in 1843, to promote the interests of the Wesleyan Missionary Society under date of March 14th records in his journal, Journal of various *Visits to the Kingdoms of Ashanti, Aku, and Dahomi in Western Africa*, London, 1844, p. 265: "When we had proceeded about two miles and a half we passed one of the King's fetish-houses; from whence a fetishman came and pronounced a blessing, begging of the fetish a safe journey for us to Abomi. Though I pitied the people on account of their superstitions, yet I could not help admiring their apparent sincerity."

37 Ditto, Vol. I, p. 195
38 Frederick E. Forbes, *Dahomey and the Dahomans: being the Journals of two Missions to the King of Dahomey, and Residence at his Capital, in the years 1849 and 1850*, London, 1851, Vol. I, p. 43
39 Ditto, Vol. I, p. 32
40 Ditto, Vol. I, p. 108 f.
41 Ditto, Vol. I, p. 171
42 Ditto, Vol. I, p. 112
43 Ditto, Vol. I, p. 201
44 J. Lafitte, *Le Dahomé*, Tours, 1873, p. 101
45 J. Leighton Wilson, *Western Africa, Its History, Condition, and Prospects*, London, 1856, p. 207. Note:—Wilson says of himself, Preface, p. iv: "The writer has spent between eighteen and twenty years in the country. He has had opportunity to visit every place of importance along the seacoast, and has made extended excursions in many of the maritime districts. He has studied and reduced to writing two of the leading languages of the country, and has enjoyed, in these various ways, more than ordinary advantages for making himself acquainted with the actual condition of the people. He claims for his book the merit of being a faithful and unpretending record of African Society." Of West Africa in general, he asserts, p. 209: "The belief in one great Supreme Being, who made and upholds all things is universal. Nor is this idea imperfectly or obscurely developed in their minds. The impression is so deeply engraved upon their moral and mental nature, that any system of atheism strikes them as too absurd and preposterous to require a denial. Everything which transpires in the natural world beyond the power of man, or of spirits, who are supposed to occupy a place somewhat higher than man, is at once spontaneously ascribed to the agency of God. All of the tribes in the country with which the writer has become acquainted (and they are not few) have a name for God, and many of them have two or more, significant of his character as a Maker, Preserver, and Benefactor." And again, p. 218: "On some parts of the Gold Coast the crocodile is sacred; a certain class of snakes, on the Slave Coast, and the shark at Bonny, are all regarded as sacred, and are worshipped, not on their own account, perhaps, but because they are regarded as the temples, or dwelling-places, of spirits. Like every other object of the kind, however, in the course of time the thing signified is forgotten in the representative, and these various animals have long since been regarded with superstitious veneration, while little is thought of the indwelling spirit. . . . The snake at Popo has become so tame that it may be carried about with impunity, and is so far trained that it will bite, or refrain

from biting, at the pleasure of its keeper."

46 Richard F. Burton, *A Mission to Gelele, King of Dahome*, London, 1864, Vol. I, p. 146

47 Ditto, Vol. I p. 96. Note:—According to Burton, Vol. I, p. 61: "The word 'Whydah' is a compound of blunders. It should be written Hwe-dah, and be applied to the once prosperous and populous little kingdom whose capital was Savi. A 'bush town' to the westward, supposed to have been founded and to be still held by the aboriginal Whydahs, who fled from the massacres Dahome, retains the name Hwe-dah. The celebrated slave- station which we have dubbed 'Whydah' is known to the people as Gre-hwe or Gle-hwe, 'Plantation-house.'"— Cfr. also, Archibald Dalzel, History of Dahomey Preface, p. xii: "Whydah," as it is Pronounced by the natives who sound the *w* of it strong, like in whip, the French write Juida; the Dutch, Fida, &c."
Burton also asserts, Vol. I, p. 96: "Ophiolatry in our part of Africa is mostly confined to the coast regions; the Popos and Windward races worship a black snake of larger size; and in the Bight of Biafra the Nimbi or Brass River people are as bigoted in boa-religion as are the Whydahs. The system is of old date: Bosman at the beginning of the last century, described it almost as it is at present. It well suits the gross materialism of these races, and yet here men ought to be tired of it."

48 Burton, l. c., Vol. I. p. 94

49 Ditto, Vol. I, p. 95

50 Ditto, Vol. I, p. 93

51 Ditto, Vol. I, p. 98

52 Ditto, Vol. I, p. 71

53 Pierre Bouche, *La Côte des Esclaves et le Dahomey*, Paris, 1885, p. 389

54 E. Desribes, *L'Évangile au Dahomey et à la Cote des Esclaves*, Clermont-Ferrand, 1877, p. 184 f. Note:— Another instance of exaggerated deference to the serpent is given by Mary H. Kingsley, West African Studies, London, 1899, p. 483, as follows: "The python is the Brass natives' titular guardian angel. So great was the veneration of this Ju-Ju snake in former times, that the native kings would sign no treaties with her Britannic Majesty's Government that did 'lot include a clause subjecting any European to a heavy fine for killing or molesting in any way this hideous reptile."

55 J. A. Skertchley, Dahomey as it is; being a narrative of eight months' Residence in that Country, London, 1874, Preface, p. vii

56 Note:—This fact may strengthen the supposition that the cult came originally from the east.

57 Skertchley, l. c., p. 54. Note:—Skertchley later observes, p. 461: "The Dahoman religion consists of two parts, totally distinct from each other. First a belief in a Supreme Being, and second, the belief in a whole host of minor deities. The Supreme Being is called Man, and is vested with unlimited authority over every being, both spiritual and carnal. He is supposed to be of so high a nature as to care very little for the circumstances of men, and his attention is only directed to them by some special invocation. He resides in a wonderful dwelling above the sky, and commits the care of earthly affairs to a race of beings, such as leopards, snakes, locusts, or crocodiles, and also to inanimate objects, such as stones. nags, cowries, leaves of certain trees, and, in short, anything

and everything. This deity is said to be the same as the God of civilization; but the white man has a far freer access to Him than the Negro, who is therefore obliged to resort to mediators. Hence the origin of fetishism."

Cir. also, A. Le Herissé, *L'Ancien Royaume du Dahomey; Mœurs, Religion, Histoire*, Paris, 1911, p. 96: "The Dahoman believe in a Supreme Being whom they call Mahon (God) or Se (Beginning, Intelligence). They have neither statue nor symbol to represent Him, they dedicate no cult to Him; His name is only pronounced in some exclamations or invocations. Mahou has created the universe; He has in particular created the fetishes, Vodoun, and has given them certain forces, certain powers of which they made use in their own way to govern human destinies. These Vodoun moreover, are not, in the strict sense, intermediaries of Mahon, but rather his free and independent agents: 'The fetish is a creature of God'—'Vodoun e gni Mahounou.' Or, again: 'God possesses the fetish—'Mahou oue do Vodoun.' The Vodoun are innumerable for, to the Dahoman, every monstrosity or phenomenon which exceeds his imagination or his intelligence is fetish, a creature of God which demands a cult. The thunder, small-pox, the sea are all fetishes; the telegraph and our railways would most assuredly also be so, if they were not a 'machine of the whites.'" M. Le Herissé was writing as Administrateur des Colonies. He is dealing with ancient Dahomey and consequently independent of the Whydah influence

58 Skertchley, l. c., p. 56

59 Note:—We must here notice that in the case of the snake-house, the mud hut has given way to one of palm branches. This is another indication that decadence in the worship has begun

60 A. B. Ellis, *The Land of Fetish*, London, 1883, p. 43 f.

61 Ditto, p. 46

62 Abel Hovelacque, *Les Nègres de l'Afrique Sus-Équatoriale*, Paris, 1889, p. 403. Cfr. also M. Malte-Brun, Universal Geography, Philadelphia, 1827, Vol. III, p. 23: "In Whydah a serpent is regarded as the god of war, of trade, of agriculture, and of fertility. It is fed in a species of temple, and attended by all order of priests. Some young women are consecrated to it, whose business it is to please the deity with their wanton dances, and who are in fact a sort of concubines of the priests. Every new king brings rich presents to the serpent. (Des Marchais, II, p. 180. Oldendorp, p. 328)."

63 Édouard Foà, *Le Dahomey*, Paris, 1895, p. 226 f

64 L. Brunet, *Dahomey et Dépendances*, Paris, 1901, p. 353 f

65 Mary H. Kingsley, Travels in West Africa, p. 394 f

66 *History of Religions*, p. 129 ff

67 Robert Hammill Nassau, *Fetichism in West Africa: Forty Years' Observation of Native Customs and Superstitions*, London, 1904, p. 48

68 Ditto, p. 274. Note:—Cfr. also J. J. Cooksey and Alexander McLeish, *Religion and Civilization in West Africa*, London, 1931, p. 82, in reference to Dahomey: "The native fetish priests are not the simple, ignorant men, many in Europe suppose them to be, on the contrary, they belong to the *élite* of the people and are of more than average intelligence. Actually a cunning sage, the fetish priest uses uncanny tricks designed to lead the common people to believe that, by virtue of an initiation of which he holds

the secret, he can command the good or evil powers of the spirit world. On all sides in Dahomey, whether around Port Novo, the capital, or away in the northern bush country, wayside shrines, snake temples and sacred groves are seen, all furnished with fantastic objects of veneration. The terrific hold of fetishism which was responsible for the revolting butchery of 'The Annual Customs' still persists in Dahomey, and is the great obstacle alike to civilization and the progress of the Gospel." Then in a footnote is added the remark: "The tremendous hold which this Voodoo worship has over its votaries is seen in its persistence in the Republic of Haiti, in which many people from Dahomey are found."

69 P. Baudin, *Fétichisme et Féticheurs*, Lyon, 1884, p. 3
70 Ditto, p. 5
71 Ditto, p. 6 f
72 Ditto, p. 37
73 Ditto, p. 37
74 Ditto, p. 40
75 Ditto, p. 45. Note:—Against the tendency of those who would exclude from scientific consideration the testimony of missionaries, under the pretence that they must of necessity show bias in their views, let us quote Sir James George Frazer, who will scarcely be accused of being prejudiced in their regard. In connection with the anthropological study of still surviving savage or barbarous peoples, he says, *Garnered Sheaves*, London, 1931, p, 244: "The method is neither more nor less than induction, which after all, disguise it as we may under the showy drapery of formal logic, is the only method in which men can and do acquire knowledge. And the first condition of a sound induction is exact observation. What we want, therefore, in this branch of science is, first and foremost, full, true, and precise accounts of savage and barbarous peoples based on personal observation. Such accounts are best given by men who have lived for many years among the peoples, have won their confidence, and can converse with them familiarly in their native language; for savages are shy and secretive towards strangers, they conceal their most cherished rites and beliefs from them, nay, they are apt wilfully to mislead an inquirer, not so much for the sake of deceiving him as with the amiable intention of gratifying him with the answers which he seems to expect. It needs a peculiar combination of intelligence, tact, and good nature to draw out a savage on subjects which he regards as sacred; to very few men will he consent to unbosom himself.

"Perhaps the class of men whose vocation affords them the best opportunities for observing and recording the habits of savage races are missionaries. They are men of education and character; they usually live for many years among the people, acquire their language, and gain their respect and confidence. Accordingly some of the very best accounts which we possess of savage and barbarous peoples have been written by missionaries, Catholic and Protestant, English, French, Dutch, German and Spanish."

Chapter III

1 Snelgrave, *A New Account of some parts of Guinea and the Slave-Trade*, p. 2. Note:—On p. 159 of the same book, Snelgrave states that from the entire Guinea Coast, the Europeans of all nations "have in some years, exported at least seventy thousand."
Cfr. also, W. D. Weatherford, The Negro from Africa to America, New York, 1924, p. 33: "Dahomey, a small kingdom on the Slave Coast, has sufficient open country, to allow of cooperation and aggressive military operations. It is said that this state at one time had an army of 50,000 mien and its terrible fighting Amazons of 3,000 women were no inconsiderable military force. . . . This Dahomey kingdom flourished for centuries and was one of the most powerful allies of the slave traders during the seventeenth and eighteenth centuries. It is supposed that this country alone, at the height of the slave trade, delivered an annual quota of fifteen thousand slaves, most of which were captured from neighbouring tribes."

2 A. B. Ellis, *On Vodu-Worship*, POPULAR SCIENCE MONTHLY, Vol. XXXVIII (1891), p. 651 ff

3 A. B. Ellis, *The Ewe-Speaking Peoples of the Slave Coast of West Africa*, London, 1890, p. 29. Note:—The body- guard of Christophe was known as the "Royal Dehomays."—Cfr. Blair Niles, *Black Hayti*, New York, 1926, p. 289 4 Burton, *A Mission to Gelele*, King of Dahome, Vol. I, p. 98

5 Ditto, Vol. I. p. 79. Note:—In the opening number of the JOURNAL OF AMERICAN, FOLK-LORE issued in 1888, William W. Newell, under the caption *Myths of Voodoo Worship and Child Sacrifice in Haiti*, strives to annihilate the whole question of Voodoo in Haiti. He thus enunciates his purpose, p. 17 f.: "Although all the {footnote p. 58} writers who have alluded to these superstitions have assumed that they are an inheritance from Africa, I shall be able to make it appear first, that the Vaudoux, or Voodoo, is derived from a European source; secondly,, that the beliefs which the word denotes are equally imported from Europe; thirdly that the alleged sect and its supposed rites, have in all probability, no real existence, but are a product of popular imagination."
His own conjecture is even more fantastic than the most extreme tenets of his adversaries. He would have us believe that the word itself as used in Haiti was derived from the followers of Peter of Lyons who was condemned by the Council of Verona in 1184, and who came to be known as Waldenses or Vaudois. According to his theory, "the word vaudois, feminine vaudoise, had in fact come to mean a witch, as its abstract vauderie or vauldoverie signified sorcery," and was brought to Haiti in the seventeenth century when the rule of the island passed from Spain to France. He continues: "To establish my second proposition, that the characteristic practices ascribed to the alleged Haitian sect, as well as the name, are of European origin, it will only be necessary to compare the charges now made against the Vaudoux of Haiti with those which in the fifteenth century were made against the Vaudois of France and Switzerland." And as both accusations were groundless, according to his theory, although three centuries apart, the one must be the source of the other. It is difficult to see logic in such deductions. In fact in a subsequent issue of the JOURNAL OF AMERICAN FOLK-LORE, Vol. II, 1889, p. 41, Mr. Newell makes the suggestive confession: "A few days before the publication of the article in question appeared the

third volume of a history of the Inquisition of the Middle Ages by Mr. H. C. Lee in which a like derivation of the name Voodoo is incidentally set forth." "Incidentally," too, Mr. Newell makes the further admission, p. 45: "Whatever opinion may be entertained about the worship, which I consider as probably imaginary, there can be no doubt concerning the habitual practice, even at the present day in the United States, of sorcery under the name of Voodooism." Further while quoting Mr. B. F. Whidden, United States Minister to Haiti, as saying that the trial and conviction of certain Voodooists at Port-au-Prince in 1864, was unfair, since the "evidence was extracted by torture," p. 41; he adds, seemingly with approval: "Mr. Whidden is of opinion that, if the truth were ascertained, there would be found no more cannibalism in Haiti than in Jamaica. On the other hand he thinks that there is no doubt concerning the existence of a Vaudoux worship and dance, which latter he has frequently seen and heard."

6 Note:—We must crave pardon if we seem discursive in giving a brief outline of the principal events in the life of our witness on the difficult question of Voodoo as it existed in Haiti immediately before the slave insurrection.

Médéric Louis Élie Moreau de Saint-Méry was a West Indian by birth and through marriage a distant relative of the Empress Josephine of France. Born {footnote p. 59} in Martinique, January 13, 1750, he came to Paris at the age of nineteen to enlist in the King's Gendarmes. During his three years of service he continued his studies and qualified as a barrister. To recoup financial losses, he took up the practice of law at Le Cap in Haiti about 1772, and some eight years later he entered the Superior Council of the Island. Thenceforth he devoted the hours of leisure afforded by his office of magistrate, to classify and arrange the laws of the French Colonies. In 1780 the fruits of his earlier labours had appeared in Paris as a five volume work, which immediately attracted much attention. Louis XVI called him to Paris to assist in the colonial administration and he was received with acclaim by the learned world and was honoured by men of letters.

With the outbreak of the French Revolution, Moreau de Saint-Méry took a leading part in the political life of Paris. As President of the electors assembled there, he was twice called upon to address the King, and, it is said, it was he who prevailed upon his colleagues to place Lafayette at the head of the National Guard. The appreciation of his efforts was shown when the Assembly unanimously voted him a medal.

In 1790, he represented Martinique in the Constitutional Convention where he made the affairs of the colonies his chief concern, and in the following year he was a member of the Judicial Council established by the Minister of Justice.

While a partisan of liberty, he was the uncompromising adversary of licence, and as such he incurred the enmity of Robespierre. A few days before the fatal August 10th, the latter's partisans attacked and seriously wounded Moreau de Saint-Méry, who was thus forced to retire to a seaport town in Normandy. This accident probably saved his life, as on the dissolution of the Constitutional Assembly, he was immediately proscribed, but escaped the scaffold through the devotion of one of the local guard to whom he had done some favour in the past. Making his escape to the United States, he remained there until 1799, when he returned to France, and held several state and diplomatic posts until in 1806 he fell into disfavour with Napoleon. Thereafter until his death at the age of sixty-nine, he scarcely kept body and soul together, and even that: was made possible solely through the charity of the Empress Josephine, and later through the bounty of Louis XVIII. He died at Paris on January 28, 1819.—Cfr. *Nouvelle Biographie Générale*, Paris, 1861, Vol. XXVI, p. 498; F. X. doe Filler, *Dictionaire Historique*, Lyon, 1822, Vol. CII, p. 546

7 Note:—As the work that we are quoting is extremely rare, we feel justified in giving the entire passage especially as the description will enable us later in the final' analysis, to distinguish the other dances that are today so often mixed in with Voodoo in a most confusing manner. The full title of the work is: *Description topographique, physique, civile, politique, et historique de la partie Française de l'isle Saint-Domingue. Avec des observations générales sur la population, sur le caractère et les mœurs de ses divers habitants; sur son climat, sa culture, ses productions, son administration, &c. Accompagnées des détails les plus propres à faire connaître l'état de cette Colonie à l'époque du Octobre 1789; et d'une nouvelle carte de la totalité de l'isle. Par M. L. E. Moreau de Saint-Méry*, Philadelphia, 1797-98. Our quotation is from Vol. I, pages 44 to 51.

8 Cfr. also Pierre de Vaissière, Saint Domingue: *La Société et la vie Créoles sous l'Ancien Régime* (1629-1789), Paris, 1909, p. 177. In reference to the only rest days of the slaves, namely Sunday and Feast-days, he remarks how "some {footnote p. 60} spent them in a complete stupor, stretched out before their doors," while the greater number "passed their leisure in drinking and dancing, the only distraction from work with which they were familiar. The dance especially is with them a real passion!"

9 Père Labat, Nouveau Voyage aux Isles de l'Amérique, Vol. II, p. 51 f., writing of the year 1698, devotes a lengthy chapter to the West Indian slaves. While resident in Martinique at the time, his remarks are general. He says of the Negroes: "The dance is their favourite passion. I don't think that there is a people on the face of the earth who are more attached to it than they. When the Master will not allow them to dance on the Estate, they will travel three and four leagues, as soon as they knock off work at the sugar-works on Saturday, and betake themselves to some place where they know that there will be a dance.

"The one in which they take the greatest pleasure and which is the usual one is the Calenda. It came from the Guinea Coast and to all appearance from Ardra. The Spaniards have learned it from the Negroes and throughout America dance it in the same way as do the Negroes.

"As the postures and movements of this dance are most indecent the Masters who live in an orderly way, forbid it to theirs, and take care that they do not dance it; and this is no small matter; for it is so to their liking, that the very children who are as yet scarcely strong enough to stand up, strive to imitate their fathers and mothers whom they see dancing, and will spend entire days at this exercise." He then describes the two drums used as accompaniment in the Calenda, the larger to beat the time and direct the dance, while the smaller is beaten much more rapidly as all undertone with a higher pitch. Seemingly the one really directs the dance, the other arouses the passions. The dance itself is thus described by Père Labat. "The dancers are drawn up in two lines, one before the other, the men on the one side and the women on the other. Those who are waiting their turns and the spectators make a circle around the dancers and the drums. The more adept chants a song which he composes on the spur of the moment, on some subject which he deems appropriate, the refrain of which, chanted by all the spectators, is accompanied by a great clapping of hands. As regards the dancers, they hold their arms a little after the manner of those who dance while playing the castanets. They skip, make a turn right and left, approach within two or three feet of each other, draw back in cadence until the sound of the drum directs them to draw together, striking the thighs one against the other, that is to say the man against the woman. To all appearances it seems that the stomachs are hitting, while as a matter of fact it is the thighs that carries the blows. They retire at once in a pirouette, to begin again the same movement with altogether lascivious gestures, as often as the drum gives the signal, as it often does several times in succession. From time to time they interlock arms and make two or three turns always striking the thighs and kissing. One easily sees from this abbreviated description how the dance is opposed to decency." It will be noticed that this is not the real Calenda but rather a modified form of the Chica which as stated by Saint-Méry in the next paragraph of the text, was called Calenda in Martinique as one of the Windward Islands.

10 Saint-Méry, Vol. I, p. 29, explains that the word Arada is a corruption of the pronunciation of Ardra, the name of a kingdom on the Slave Coast, which was prior to its conquest by the Dahomans located between Dahomey and Whydah. The term Aradas, then, applies specifically to the people of Ardra, but generically to any tribes from the Gold or Slave Coasts. Here it seems to signifiy {sic} Dahomans, including those from Ardra proper and Whydah.

11 Moreau de Saint-Méry, l. c., Vol. I, p. 44 ff. Note:—Moreau de Saint-Méry, *Loix et Constitutions des Colonies Françoises de l'Amérique sous le Vent*, Paris, 1780, Vol. I, p. 4,5, shows that the Code Noir, published in March, 1685, by Article II prescribes that slaves must within a reasonable time be instructed and baptized as Catholics. By Article III, Masters who permit their slaves to gather for religious purposes other than Catholic service are as liable as if they took part themselves in such gatherings. By Article XVI, Gatherings of slaves belonging to different masters are forbidden "either by day or night, under pretence of weddings or otherwise, either on the premises of one of the masters or elsewhere, and even more so if on the public highway or in hidden places." Corporal punishment is prescribed for the first offence, with the death penalty for repeated infractions. By the next Article, Masters who permit such gatherings are liable to fines, etc.—Cfr. also: Vol. V, p. 384: Official Orders for the Police of Port-au-Prince, issued May 23, 1772. Article II forbids all kinds of assemblies and gatherings of slaves under pain of corporal punishment. And Article VI forbids even free Negroes and persons of color from holding night-dances or the Calenda. Even the dances that are allowed to them must stop at 9 P. M. Vol. IV, p. 234: On August 5, 1758, Sieur Lebrun, manager of the Carbon Estate at Bois de L'Anse is fined 200 pounds "for having permitted an assembly of Negroes, and a Calenda on the 23rd of July preceding, on the said Estate." Vol. IV, p. 829: *Order of the Governor General dated January 15, 1765*, for the formation of a Corps of Light Troops, to be known as the "First Legion of San Domingo." It assigns as one of their duties: "To break up the assemblies and Calendas of the Negroes."

That the Calenda was danced despite all legal restrictions, we have ample evidence.

Thus for example, the Baron Wimpffen, who spent two years in the island during the period of unrest that immediately preceded the actual uprising of the slaves, records in his diary in August, 1789, that the day of the {footnote p. 69} arrival of the French mail was celebrated as a festival for the Negroes who were dispensed from work, feasted and allowed to dance a Calenda. In the same entry of the diary we read that baptism meant practically nothing for the Negroes generally except a change of name, which was frequently thereafter ignored—the sole motive being to please the master and nothing else.—Cfr. Albert Savine, *Saint-Domingue à la Veille de la Révolution*, Paris, 1911, p. 93

12 Dr. Price-Mars, in setting out to prove that Voodoo is a religion, accepts as his definition of the word religion, that adopted by the "sociological school of Durkheim."—*Ainsi Parla L'Oncle*, Compeigne, 1928, p. 30. Then follows a quotation from J. Bricourt, *Où en est l'Histoire des Religions*, Paris, 1912, p. 15, which is ultimately taken from Durkheim's chapter on "Definition of Religions Phenomena and of Religion"—Emile Durkheim, The Elementary Forms of the Religious Life, London, 1926, p. 37. The words quoted really form no part of Durkheim's definition which is only formulated towards the end of the chapter, where it runs as follows: "A religion is a unified system of beliefs and practices relative to sacred things, that is to say, things set apart and forbidden—beliefs, and practices which unite into one single moral community called a Church, all those who adhere to them."—p. 47. However the two are perfectly compatible and Voodoo satisfies them both as well as most of the other definitions of religion, enunciated by standard authors. Thus for example, "Religion may be defined subjectively and objectively. Subjectively, it is the knowledge and consciousness of dependence upon one or more transcendental personal Powers, to which man stands in a reciprocal relation. Objectively, it is the sum of the outward actions in which it is expressed and made manifest, as prayer, sacrifice, sacraments, {footnote p. 70} liturgy, ascetic practices, ethical prescriptions, and so on."—W. Schmidt, *The Origin and Growth of Religion*, New York, 1931, p. 2.

Dr. Price-Mars, *Ainsi Parla l'Oncle*, p. 32, advances his claim as follows: "Voodoo is a religion because all the adepts believe in the existence of spiritual beings who live in part in the universe in close touch with human beings Whose activity they control. These invisible beings constitute a numerous Olympus of gods, of whom the highest among them bear the title of Papa or Great Master and have the right to special homage.

"Voodoo is a religion because the cult developed to its god, demands a hierarchical sacerdotal body, a congregation of faithful, temples, altars, ceremonies, and in fine, altogether an oral tradition which certainly has not come down to us unchanged, but thanks for it, has transmitted the essential part of the cult.

"Voodoo is a religion because through the medley of legends and the corruption of fables one can disentangle a theology, a system of representations, thanks to which, primitively, our African ancestors had an explanation for the natural phenomena and which in a hidden way lays the foundation of the anarchistic beliefs on which rests the hybrid Catholicism of the masses of the people."

Then after considering the other side of Voodoo which consists of magic or witchcraft, concludes, p. 37: "And now, if we summarize the results of this he brief discussion, we may draw a first conclusion, to wit, that Voodoo is a very primitive religion, founded partially on the beliefs in all powerful spiritual beings—gods, demons, disincarnated souls—partially on the beliefs in witchcraft and magic. If we evaluate this double character we will disclose in proportion to our researches the state more or less pure in its country of origin, and on our soil, modified by its more than a century of juxtaposition to the Catholic religion adapted to the conditions of life of our rural masses, fighting against legal statute of the nation which wished to free itself of all contact with this form of beliefs, from which it has nothing else to expect. And there you have in brief the position which Voodoo occupies in our social status."

13 J. C. Dorsainvil, *Manuel d'Histoire d'Haïti*, Port-au-Prince, 1925, p. 81 f. Note:—Cfr. also Thomas Madiou, *Histoire d'Haïti*, Port-au-Prince, 1922, vol. I, p. 102, who states briefly: "On the night of August 14, 1791, 200 delegates from the ateliers of the northern province assembled in the Lenormand plantation. There a coloured man harangued them about a pretended decree whereby the King granted them three days of freedom each week. It was decided then the 22nd of the same month the insurrection should be general." Concerning the originator of the Don Pédro, Dorsainvil asserts, *Vodou et Névrose*, Port-au-Prince, 1931, p. 46: "Popular tradition, well after Independence, speaks among others of a certain Don Pédro, a being of flesh and bone, who, at a certain time, had come from the Dominican Republic to take up his abode in the mountains of the Commune of Petit-Goave. This Don Pédro was the introducer of that violent dance which by corruption the people call: the Pétro. At his death, Don Pédro did not delay in taking all honourable place in the Voodooistic pantheon, drawing in his train an entire progeny, such as Jean Philippe Pétro, Criminel Pétro, etc."—Cfr. also, D. Trouillot, *Esquisse Ethnographique*: Le Vaudoux, Port-au-Prince, 1885, p. 28: "It was from the Dominican Republic, at the time a Spanish Colony, that there came to Haiti in the last century, the famous Don Pédro, an African who founded at Petit-Goave the infernal sect, known under the same name as its author. The Don Pédro is a dance of Vaudoux where the most unbelievable orgies are perpetrated; this sect, diminishing daily, is only found in the hills of the place of origin."

14 Spencer St. John, *Hayti or the Black Republic*, London, 1889, Introduction, p. vii
15 Ditto, p. xi
16 Ditto, p. xiii
17 Ditto, p. 192
18 Ditto, p. 199
19 Ditto, p. 229
20 Ditto, Introduction, p. xii
21 Ditto, p. 130
22 Ditto, p. 231
23 Ditto, p. 203 ff. Note:—St. John further quotes p. 243 from THE EVENING POST Of New York, for February 25, 1888: "Port-au-Prince, February, 1888. Recently the body of a child was found near this city; an arm and a leg had been eaten by the Vaudoux. During Christmas week a man was caught in the streets here with a child cut up in quarters for sale. Cannibalism still prevails, despite all the forced statements to the contrary. President Salomon, to please the masses, the Negro element, allows them to dance a

Vaudoux dance formerly prohibited." He also cites many "fully-authenticated" cases, some of them falling under his own observation, of the administering of drugs to induce apparent death. Subsequently the victims were brought back to consciousness, not infrequently after burial and disinterment, that they might be murdered and certain portions of them at least used in the ungodly sacrifices of Don Pédro. He concludes: "It was by these means that the Papalois probably were enabled to obtain their victims during the French colonial period."-1. c., p. 241.

The following quotation from St. John, p. 232, should also be noted: "Moreau de Saint-Méry, in naming the different tribes imported into Haiti during the last century, says:—'Never had any a disposition more hideous than the last (the Mondongoes) whose depravity has reached the most execrable of excesses, that of eating their fellow creatures. They bring also to Santo Domingo those butchers of human flesh, for in their country there are slaughter-houses where they Sell slaves as they would calves, and they are here, as in Africa, the horror of the other Negroes.'" Here we have additional evidence that whatever cannibalism may have existed in Haiti in connection with the Don Pédro rites, must not be {footnote p. 79} ascribed to Voodoo, but rather to other agencies, even as it was noticed in the decadent cult of the serpent at Grand Popo

24 James Anthony Froude, *The English in the West Indies; or, the Bow of Ulysses*, London, 1888, p. 343

25 Ditto, p. 344

26 Hesketh-Prichard, *Where Black Rules White: A Journey across and about Hayti*, Westminster, 1900, p. 76 ff.

27 French Edition; *Haïti. Son Histoire et ses Détracteurs*, New York, 1907

28 English Edition, p. 346; French Edition, p. 345

29 Moreau de Saint-Méry, *Description de la Partie Française de Saint-Domingue*, Vol. I, p. 33

30 Note:—Wilfrid D. Hambly here takes exception as follows, *Serpent Worship in Africa*, p. 59: "Johnston (1910) says that snake worship in Haiti is of doubtful occurrence owing to the rarity of the snakes there. Such harmless snakes as do exist are tolerated in some villages and fetish temples for their rat-killing propensities. The idea has therefore got abroad that they are kept as sacred animals by the voodoo priests and priestesses. Those seeking scientific truth on voodooism should doubt much of what has been written on this subject.

Johnston rather negatives his own cautionary remarks by stating that the python worship of Africa was no doubt introduced by slaves into Haiti, Cuba, Louisiana, Carolina, Jamaica, the Guianas, and Brazil. If this is admissible, it is difficult to understand why the evidences of St. John respecting the survival of snake cults in Haiti (1889) should be discountenanced. Furthermore, Johnston's idea that snakes are rare in Haiti is a misconception, as snakes are both abundant and conspicuous oil the island, though there are only a few species, and Haiti, like the rest of the Greater Antilles, has no poisonous snakes. There are boas, blind snakes, and also some Colubrine snakes."

31 Harry H. Johnston, *The Negro in the New World*, London, 1910, p. 193 f. Note:—He is giving the "official" explanation for the sound of the drums. As we have noted there should be no drumming at real Voodoo or Don Pédro rites, although in practice a dance

usually precedes the Voodoo function to "disguise" the purpose of the gathering, as an alibi for the local authorities who may have given tacit permission for the meeting which officially they should contravene.—Cfr. Seabrook, *Magic Island*, p. 54: "There was no reason to suppose that we might be disturbed, but as an extra precaution a gay *danse Congo* was immediately organized to cover the real purpose of our congregation."

32 Note:—Is not this condition verified, then, in Haiti, where Johnston's own estimate was, as noted above, *The Negro in the New World*, p. 193: "At least two out of the three millions of Haitian Negroes are only Christians in the loose statistics of geographers. They are still African pagans, etc." It really looks as if Johnston had done more harm than good to Haiti's cause

33 Johnston, l. c., p. 64 f.

34 Ditto, p. 66 f

35 Stephen Bonsal, *The American Mediterranean*, New York, 1912, p. 88 f.

36 Ditto, p. 90

37 Ditto, p. 101 f

38 Vol. VIII (1917), p. 123 f

39 Ditto, p. 12540 . George Mannington, *The West Indies with British Guiana and British Honduras*, New York, 1925, p. 267 f.

41 Dr. Price-Mars, *Ainsi Parla l'Oncle*, p. 107

42 Ditto, p. 113f

43 Ditto, p. 114

44 Dr. Price-Mars, *Une Étape de l'Évolution Haïtienne*, p. 127

45 Ditto, p. 139

46 Ditto, p. 141

47 Ditto, p. 142 f. Note:—After observing that the Dahoman rites have undergone great chances and adaptations in the process of absorption, he adds, p. 144: "One may remark, in passing the ritual gesture of the Mohammedan in the habitual salaam of the official who holds his hands towards the east before beginning each Voodoo ceremony. One finds there, too, taboo of the forbidden foods and the unlucky days." And he sums it all up on the next page, p. 145: "It is nothing less than a syncretism of beliefs."
Cfr. also, D. Trouillot, *Esquisse Ethnographique*: Le Vaudoux, p. 28: "The Creole Vaudoux is a syncretism of the different sects of the primordial Vaudoux and of the superstitions as well African as Aryan mingled together by slavery. It is certain that if an old Guinean was to return, he would not know what to do in the midst of the dance and Vaudoux ceremonies of today."

48 Note:—Dr. Price-Mars tells us that the word Hougan signifies fire or the warmth of fire, p. 144. It is derived from the Habbes of the Central Nigerian Plateau so well described by Louis Desplagnes.—Cfr. *La Plateau Central Nigérien*, Paris, 1907. Referring to the Hougans as "magico-religious leaders of our rural population of the north and southwest," he continues: "These leaders are constrained by the ceremonies of initiation to a life of austerity which bespeaks the great moral authority which they enjoy."—Cfr. Dr. Price-Mars, l. c., p. 130

49 Dr. Price-Mars, l. c., p. 172 f

50 Dr. Price-Mars, *Ainsi Parla l'Oncle*, p. 117 f

51 Ditto, p. 118 f

52 Note:—Prichard is not far wrong in his conclusions, Where Black Rules White, p. 81: "Vaudoux is so inextricably woven in with every side of the Haitian's life, his politics, his religion, his outlook upon the world, his social and family relations, his prejudices and peculiarities that he cannot be judged apart from them." Arthur W. Holly, *Les Daïmons du Culte Voudu*, Port-au-Prince, 1918, starts his Preface with a blatant profession of faith: "Without vanity or false shame, or cowardice, I declare that I am an esoterist— that is to say one initiated to the sciences whose roots are deep set in Ethiopic-Egyptian antiquity—sciences which allow one to recognize in the priestly writings the cosmogonic beginnings, to disengage from a symbol, a sign, a given letter the value of the idea, its metaphysical sense or its true scientific character." The work itself is merely an esoteric pretence of the most amateur type and of practically no real value. However, Dr. Holly stresses one point that may be significant, Preface, p. x: "Definitively I have good reason for asserting that the Negro initiated in the true Voodoo cult, in conformity with pure traditions, enters into no relations whatever with Satan. The demons to whom they accuse him of sacrificing are not tile spirits of darkness, and therefore malevolent. They are rather the Daimons according to the Greek concept, that is to say 'bright spirits.' Witchcraft, sordid magic, is incompatible with the great principles preconized {sic} by Voodoo morale."

53 A. J. Emerick, *Obeah and Duppyism in Jamaica*, Woodstock, 1915, p. 192 f

54 Seabrook, *Magic Island*, p. 12

55 Ditto, p. 3 1.

56 Ditto, p. 34. Note:—Gr. also Seabrook, p. 89: "In America the word Voodoo has come to mean indiscriminately any Negro sorcery, secret ceremony, or old African witch-doctor practice. In Haiti the word is similarly loosely used sometimes even by natives, so that when they wish to distinguish sharply they are likely to use the word Rada as the name of their religion, and Service Petro, or Service Legba for their ceremonial religious rites." P. 295: "Petro or Service Petro is the name given to the blood-sacrificial Voodoo ceremony. It derives from the name of a slave who was a famous papaloi in colonial times." p. 308: The following literally translated, is one of the formulas pronounced by the sorcerer over a death ouanga before hiding it in the secret place where it is to lie rotting: "Old master, now is the time to keep the promise you made. Curse him as I curse him and spoil him as I spoil him. By the fire at night, by the dead black hen, by the bloods, throat, by the goat, by the ruin on the ground, this ouanga be upon him. May he have no peace in bed, nor at his food, nor can he hide. Waste {footnote p. 98} him and wear him and rot him as these rot." But this is not Voodoo, it is undiluted witchcraft.

57 Ditto, p. 311

58 Ditto, p. 319 f.

59 Cr. also, J. C. Dorsainvil, *Vodou et Névrose*, p. 48: "We affirm that Voodooism satisfies a nervous racial habit firmly established by the belief in secular practices among many Haitian families. The proofs of such a condition are plentiful, if one will only take the trouble to observe well the facts." However, we cannot endorse Dr. Dorsainvil's

explanation of a "dual personality" even in the broad sense in which he uses the term. Trouillot, Esquisse Ethnographique: Le Vaudoux, p. 10, thinks that excessive alcoholism and feverish excitement induces a sort of hypnotic effect at the Voodoo dances so that it makes the participant insensible to pain as when he plunges his hand into the boiling caldron. He further observes, p. 10 f.: "It is a fact that the financial return of a dance and the orgiastic pleasures which it furnishes to dancers and spectators are the only and real perpetuation of Vaudoux. It is no longer a religion with its dogmas and rites, it is only a gross indulgence having preserved the empty form of a vanished belief." And it was as far back as 1885 that these words were written!

60 J. C. Dorsainvil, *Une Explication Philologique du Vòdú*, Port-au-Prince, 1924, p. 14 f.

61 Ditto, p. 18 f

62 Ditto, p. 20

63 Ditto, p. 29

64 Ditto, p. 37

65 Elsie Clews Parsons, *Spirit Cult in Hayti*, Paris, 1928, p. 1

66 Note:—Cfr. Seabrook, *The Magic Island*, p. 316 f.: "Eugène Aubin, a French writer who lived in Haiti for a number of years prior to 1898, interested himself in the study of Voodoo without ever apparently having wished to witness or participate in its sacrificial ceremonies. It is possible that he was restrained by moral scruples. He wrote, however, an excellent book called *En Haïti*, published in Paris in 1910, which shows he was on the friendliest terms with the leading papalois and hougans of that period. He discussed sympathetically and at length with the more intelligent ones the nature of their creed and was admitted to a number of their temples."

67 Eugène Aubin, *En Haiti*, Paris, 1910, pp. 43-51

Chapter IV

1 Note:—As mentioned before, this is a large folio volume of over twelve hundred unnumbered pages. As it is difficult of access, although a copy may be found in the Boston College Library, a somewhat lengthy citation may be permissible. Bryan Edwards says of this Report: "It was transmitted by the Agent of Jamaica to the Lords of the Committee of the Privy Council, and by them subjoined to their report on the slave trade; and, if I mistake not, the public are chiefly indebted for it to the diligent researches, and accurate pen, of Mr. Long."— Bryan Edwards, *The History, Civil and Commercial, of the British Colonies in the West Indies*, London, 1793, Vol. II, p. 88. As Edwards was writing less than four years after the publication of the Report, his statement may be relied upon as accurate. The Long referred to, was Edward Long, the historian, He was the great-grandfather of Sir Esme Howard, recently the British Ambassador to the United States. His own great-grandfather in turn, was at the age of sixteen attached as Lieutenant to the regiment of his kinsman Col. Edward Doyley when he set out on the original Cromwellian Expedition that seized Jamaica in 1655. The Secretary of the Commissioners dying, young Long succeeded him. This started him on a career that found him Speaker of the House of Assembly of Jamaica at the age of thirty-three and Chief Justice of Jamaica at thirty-eight. In the family tree with all its ramifications we find the names of nearly all the leading gentry of the island, and if we trace it back far enough it has a common origin with that of General Washington, the American patriot. Even Sir Henry Morgan, the notorious buccaneer, who on three separate occasions acted as Governor of Jamaica, was connected with the Long family by marriage. Edward Long, the historian, was born in England, but went to Jamaica in 1757 at the age of twenty-three. He was a member of the Jamaica Assembly from 1761 to 1768, and its Speaker for a time. Shortly afterwards he returned to England and died there in 1813.—Cfr. Robert Mobray Howard, *Records and Letters of the Family of the Longs of Longville, Jamaica, and Hampton Lodge*, Surrey, London, 1925, Vol. I, p. 119 ff. Bryan Edwards' supposition that the Report was chiefly the work of Edward Long is strengthened by a letter written by his daughter Jane Catherine Long to her brother Edward Beeston Long, under date of March 6, 1785, where we read in the postscript: "You must not expect to hear from my Father. He is obliged every day either to attend Mr. Pitt or a West India Committee."—l. c., Vol. I, p. 178

2 Note:—Cfr. also, *The Discoverie of Witchcraft: proving that the compacts and contracts of witches with devils and all infernal spirits or familiars are but erroneous novelties and imaginary conceptions. . . . By Reginald Scot Esquire. Whereto is added an. excellent discourse of the nature and substance of devils and spirits, in two books. . . .* London, 1665.— p. 71: "Book, VII. Chapter I. Of the Hebrew word Ob, what it signifieth where it is found: Of Pythonisses called Ventriloquae, who they be, and what their practices are; experience and examples thereof shewed. This word Ob. is translated Python, or Pvthonicus spiritus; sometimes, though unproperly, Magus. . . . But Ob signifieth most properly a Bottle. and is used in this place, because the Pythonists spoke hollow. as, in the bottom of their bellies; whereby they are aptly in Latin called Ventriloqui; . . . These are such as take upon them to give oracles, etc."

Reginald Scot's work first appeared in 1584. and provoked a reply from no less a personage than King James I of England, whose treatise *Demonologie, in forme of a Dialogue, Divided into three Bookes*, Edinburgh, 1587, expressly declared itself "against the damnable opinions of two principally in an age, whereof the one called Scot an Englishman, is not ashamed in public print to deny that there can be such a thing as Witchcraft: and so maintains the old error of the Sadducces, in denying of spirits, etc." Montague Summer, who edited a new edition of Scot in 1930, says in his introduction, p. xxviii: "That Reginald Scot's *The Discoverie of Witchcraft* is both historically and as a literary curiosity a book of the greatest value and interest, no one, I suppose, would dispute or deny."

While not quoted as such. Scot in all probability was the source from which is the entire theory of the Egyptian Ob being the origin of the term Obeah. However, as shown elsewhere, *Hebrewisms of West Africa*, p. 13 ff., the word Ob did not originate with the Egyptian but may he traced back to the Canaanites from whom the Egyptians as well as the Hebrews derived it and if there is any value at all in this suggested derivation. it would be at most the indication of an Hebraic influence on the parent stock of the Ashanti from whom, as we shall see shortly, West India Obeah is directly derived.

3 Note:—As this woman came from the Popo country, one would immediately classify her as a Dahoman, but there is every possibility that she may have been {footnote p. 115} an Ashanti or from some other tribe, brought from the interior after capture. A slave was generally spoken of, not by the name of the tribe from which he had originally come, but from the district of the African coast-line whence he had been shipped 4 Mary H. Kingsley, *West African Studies*, London, 1899, p. 139

5 Note:—Captain Rattray, *Ashanti*, p. 162, shows that Miss Kingsley was not familiar with the Ashanti language and attributes much to fetishism that has nothing whatever to do with the subject. in one place he naïvely remarks that it is fortunate that she could not understand what seemed to interest her very much. As to the information which she honestly thought that she was picking up from her West Indian informants, it is well to remember that the Jamaican, like our Southern Negroes, or I suppose any other child of Africa, is only too ready to furnish just the information that is most desired, especially if he is being paid for results. As a Resident Magistrate in Jamaica once said: "The real Jamaican in a Court of Law is essentially afraid of the truth, and seems to prefer to lose a case than abide by facts." When it comes to Obeah and the like he is even more reticent and deceptive with the "bockrah Masser"—white Master—and the real child of the "bush" will either assure you: "Me no belieb Obi, Sah!" or else will greet you with the laconic: "Me no no, Sah!"—I don't know

6 W. P. Livingston, *Black Jamaica*, London, 1890, p. 19 f. Note:—The power of fear is well illustrated by an example given by Lillian Eichler, *The Customs of Mankind*, London, 1925, p. 631: "Superstition caused Ferdinand IV to die of fright. The story is that in 1312 Peter and John Carvajal were condemned to death for murder on circumstantial evidence. They were sentenced to be thrown from the summit to jagged rocks below. Ferdinand IV, then King of Spain, resisted obstinately every attempt to induce him to grant a pardon. Standing upon the spot from which they were to be thrown, the two men called

upon God to witness their innocence, appealing to His high tribunal to prove it. They summoned the King to appear before this tribunal in thirty days. His Majesty laughed at the summons and gave the sign to proceed with the execution. In a few days the King fell ill. He retired to his country residence, ostensibly to rest, but really to shake off remembrance of the summons which somehow persisted. He could not be diverted. He became more and more ill, and on the thirtieth day he was found dead in bed—a victim to the mysterious dread which had gripped his heart from the moment the summons had been uttered." Some such fear works its effect in Obeah.

7 R. S. Rattray, *Ashanti Proverbs*, Oxford, 1916, p. 48

8 Williams, *Hebrewisms of West Africa*, p. 17 f.

9 Cfr. Rattray, *Ashanti Proverbs*, p. 54

10 Note:—Previously, Ellis, Dennett and Miss Kingsley held complete sway, despite the fact that they were utterly unqualified for the task that they had undertaken. Stephen Septimus Farrow well adjudges their claims to credibility in his thesis for the Degree of Doctor of Philosophy in the University of Edinburgh, in 1924. This Essay drew from Dr. R. R. Marett, Rector of Exeter College, Oxford, the encomium: "Dr. Farrow, I think, has disposed of the all-too-facile explanations of earlier investigators."—*Faith, Fancies and Fetish, or Yoruba Paganism*, p. vii. Of Col. Ellis, Farrow asserts, p. 5: "It is, unfortunately, not possible to exonerate the gallant colonel from a measure of anti-Christian bias, which at times leads him to jump to conclusions which are scientifically untrue." Concerning Dennett and Miss Kingsley, he writes, p. 5: "Mr. Dennett was intimately known to the writer, whose wife was first cousin {footnote p. 122} to this gentleman. Mr. Dennett never learned to speak the language, but wrote down Yoruba words as given to him by others; but, as he went openly to priests and keepers of shrines and asked direct questions, this thoroughly British and un-African method of inquiry was very likely, indeed certain, at times to lead to imperfect, and, not seldom untrue answers. Mr. Dennett's interpretations, deductions and conclusions are often at fault, owing to his poor acquaintance with the language, and also to the very free play he gave to his imagination. This is very prominent in his pamphlet, *My Yoruba Alphabet*. . . . It is also to be remembered that Dennett and Miss Kingsley alike borrow from Ellis and are influenced to some extent by his ideas."

Despite the fact that Ellis published grammars of more than one West African language, he was forced to do his work through an interpreter as he never acquired a conversational knowledge of any one of the languages about which he wrote

11 Rattray, *Ashanti Proverbs*, p. 18. Also, R. S. Rattray, *Ashanti*, Oxford, 1923, p. 139

12 Rattray, *Ashanti*, p. 140. Note:—Rattray had previously written, *Ashanti Proverbs*, p. 19 f.: "In Ashanti, in remote bush villages, buried away in impenetrable forest, and as yet even untouched by European and missionary influence, it would seem incredible that the Christian idea of a one and Supreme Being should, if a foreign element of only some two or three hundred years' growth, have taken such deep root as to effect their folklore, traditions, customs, and the very sayings and proverbs with which their language abounds. These proverbs and traditions, moreover, which speak of and contain references to a Supreme Being, are far more commonly known among the greybeards,

elders, and the fetish priestly class themselves than among the rising younger generation, grown up among the new influences and often trained in the very precincts of a mission. Fetishism and monotheism would at first sight appear the very antithesis of each other, but a careful investigation of facts will show that here in Ashanti it is not so." Of the Ashanti Proverbs given by Rattray we need quote only the following: Proverbs #1, 10, 15: p. 17 ff.: "Of all the wide earth, Onyame is the elder." "The words that Onyame had beforehand ordained, a human being does not alter." "All men are the children of Onyame, no one is a child of earth."

Rattray further shows that this Supreme Being has a temple and a regular priesthood, *Ashanti*, p. 144, for which a three years novitiate is required, *Religion and Art in Ashanti*, Oxford, 1927, p. 45, and the prayer of consecration uttered by the priest begins with the words, l. c., p. 45: "Supreme Being, Who alone is great, it is you who begat me, etc."

13 Bosnian, *New and Accurate Description of the Coast of Guinea*, p. 179 f

14 Rattray, *Ashanti*, p. 141

15 Rattray, *Ashanti*, p. 145 ff. Note:—Cfr. also Rattray, l. c., p. 182: "Grouped round the walls of the temple and raised a little from the floor upon their stools were several shrines-all but two of these, I was informed, were now mere empty receptacles. The priests who had formerly tended them when they were active shrines had died, and since then the spirit that had formerly manifested itself within them had ceased to do so. 'Some day this spirit might descend upon someone who would then become their priest.'

"Several priests and priestesses I had spoken to told me that this was how they had first become priests. They had been seized with a spirit and had either lost all consciousness or seemingly had become mad. A god would be consulted, and he might say it was an effect of an outpouring of such and such a spirit. in which case, if there were a shrine already, such as had been described, its cult would be once again revived. If no shrine existed, then a new abode would be prepared."

16 Rattray, *Ashanti*, p. 310

17 Rattray, *Ashanti Law and Constitution*, Oxford, 1929, p. 313. Note:—The association of poison with witchcraft is not peculiar to the Ashanti. It is recurrent throughout the history of magic. Thus Theocritus, writing in the third century B. C., describes a scene at Cos where a fire spell is laid against a neglectful lover by a maid whose affections have been spurned. Before a statue of Hecate, barley-meal, bay-leaves, a waxen puppet, and some bran are successively burned with appropriate incantations. Then follows a libation and the burning of herbs and a piece of the fringe of her lover's cloak. The ashes are to be rubbed by an attendant on the lintel of the lover. The maid's soliloquy shows that should her incantations fail to win back the faithless one, she has poisons in reserve to prevent his affections being bestowed elsewhere.—Cfr. J. M. Edmonds, *The Greek Bucolic Poets*, London, 1916, p. 24 ff.; Theocritus, *The Spell*.

18 Rattray, *Ashanti Proverbs*, p. 53

19 Rattray, Ashanti Proverbs, p. 47

20 Ditto, p. 53

21 Ditto, p. 47

22 Ditto, p. 47

23 Rattray, *Religion and Art in Ashanti*, p. 28

24 Rattray, *Religion and Art in Ashanti*, p. 39. Note:—Despite the fact, then, that in theory witchcraft is antagonistic to their religion, the Ashanti, as is so common elsewhere, in practical life blend the two without qualm or scruple. A further instance of this is found in the case of the talking drums. The first time a drummer uses them oil a particular day, he begins by pouring a few drops of wine on the edges as he invokes the various parts of the drums and invites them to drink and concludes: Rattray, *Ashanti*, p. 264 f.: "Obayifo, gye nsa nom (Witch accept wine and drink). Asase, gye nsa nom (Earth deity accept wine and drink). Onyankopon Tweaduampon Bonyame, gye nsa nom (Supreme Being Nyankopon, Tweaduampon Creator, accept wine and drink)." Then in connection with the drum history of the Mampon division of Ashanti, Rattray tells us, l. c.: "Before the serious business of drumming the name of the chiefs begins, the spirits of the various materials, which have gone towards the making of the composite drum, are each propitiated in turn, and these spirits are summoned to enter for a while that material which was once a portion of their habitation. The drums thus, for a time, become the abode of the spirits of forest trees and of the 'mighty elephant.' The deities of Earth and Sky are called upon in like manner. Even the hated and dreaded witches (abayifo), who prey upon the human body and gnaw the vitals and hearts of men (just as humans partake of meat and other food), are not forgotten, lest in anger they might seize upon the drummer's wrists and cause him to make mistakes. A drummer who falters and 'speaks' a wrong word is liable to a fine of a sheep, and if persistently at fault he might, in the past, have had an ear cut off."

The prelude referred to above precedes every drum "piece," and closes with the invocation of the witches which is thus translated by Rattray, *Ashanti*, p. 280: "Oh Witch, do not slay me, Adwo,*

Spare me, Adwo,
The divine drummer declares that,
When he rises from the dawn,
He will sound (his drums) for you in the morning,
Very early, Very early, Very early, Verly {*sic*} early,

Oh Witch that slays the children of men before they are fully matured,
Oh Witch that slays the children of men before they are fully matured,

The divine drummer declares that,
When he rises with the dawn,
He will sound his drums for you in the morning,
Very early, Very early, Very early, Verly {*sic*} early,
We are addressing you, And you will understand."

* Note:—"A title of respect given to chiefs, by women to their husbands, and children to their elders."

This same introduction of an evil influence into a good or "lucky" charm is indicated in the following news item taken from the PHILADELPHIA EVENING TELEGRAM for August 7, 1884: "The left hind foot of a graveyard rabbit, which has a potent influence among the Southern Negroes has been presented to Governor Cleveland as a talisman in the campaign. The rabbit from which the foot was taken was shot on the grave of Jesse James."

25 Note:—This would explain the statement of J. Leighton Wilson who when writing of the district of West Africa, between Cape Verde and the Cameroons, says: "Fetishism and demonology are undoubtedly the leading and prominent forms of religion among the pagan tribes of Africa. They are entirely distinct from each other, but they run together at so many points, and have been so much mixed up by those who have attempted to write on the subject, that it is no easy matter to keep them separated."—Cfr. Wilson, *Western Africa, Its History, Condition and Prospects*, p. 211

26 Note:—Among the Ashanti, it is true, the python is a totem of the Bosommuru, the most important of all the ntoro exogamous divisions on a patrilineal basis.—Cfr. Rattray, *Ashanti*, p. 47. In this connection Hambly remarks: "Rattray's description of reverence for the python in Ashanti includes statements which might reasonably be regarded as evidence of a decadent python cult. But the information is more correctly classified under totemism."—Hambly, *Serpent Worship in Africa*, p. 13. Furthermore, a complete absence of serpent cult seems to be implied by the Ashanti Proverb: "Wonho owe, to a, wommo no aba.—Unless you see a snake's head, you do not strike at it."—Rattray, Ashanti Proverbs, p. 72

27 Note:—W. G. Browne, *Travels in Africa, Egypt and Syria, from the Year 1792 to 1798*, London, 1806, p. go, notices at Kahira a similar distinction in connection with Egyptian magic which is divided into "halal, lawful, and haram, unlawful." This division of Magic into White and Black, as determined by its lawfulness or unlawfulness has since come to be generally recognized

28 Note:—Anyone who has lived for some time in Jamaica has come in contact with really marvellous "Bush remedies." For example, a throbbing headache is quickly relieved by the application of a particular cactus which is split and bound on the forehead; and a severe fever is broken effectively by a "bush tea" made from certain leaves and twigs known only to the old woman who gathers them, and whose only explanation is "Jes seben bush, Sah, me pick dem one one." Too frequently, the Obeah man makes use of this knowledge of herbals in connection With his art. In a particular case of Obeah poisoning that came under my personal notice, just as the victim was on the point of losing consciousness, the very individual who was for good reasons suspected of being the cause of the trouble, suddenly entered the sick room unannounced and administered the antidote. A change of heart or more probably fear of the consequences, had probably saved the life.

29 D. Amaury Talbot, *Woman's Mysteries of a Primitive People*, London, 1915, p. 138

30 Baudin, *Fétichisme et Féticheurs*, p. 86

31 Moreau de Saint-Méry, *Description de la Partie Française de Saint Dominigue*, Vol. I, p. 36

32 Louis p. Bowler, *Gold Coast Palava: Life on the Gold Coast*, London, 1911, p. 17

33 Ditto, p. 136 f

34 Note:—It is equally common in Ashanti, and is also found in Jamaica today. I never met with any case where it was administered to human beings, but I have known live stock to be destroyed in this way. I lost a horse myself on one occasion through this very means. The technical term is "obi-water" and it produces dysentery and a slow-wasting death.

35 Bowler, l. c., p. 137 f

36 Eustace Cameron, *The Evolution of the Negro*, Georgetown, Demerara, 1929, Vol. I. p. 179.

37 Johnston, *The Negro in the New World*, p. 253, Note 1

38 Philadelphia, 1894

39 Hesketh J. Bell, *Obeah; Witchcraft in the West Indies*, London, 1889, p. 9 f

40 Ditto, p. 14 f

41 Ditto, p. 17

Chapter V

1 Williams, *Hebrewisms of West Africa*, Introduction

2 Ditto, p. 9

3 Gardner, *History of Jamaica*, p. 184. Note:—Gardner further observes p. 184: "It is and ever has been very difficult to extract from an old Negro what his religious belief really was, but it seems probable that there was some idea that departed parents had influence with the supposed rulers of the world beyond the grave, and that prayers were offered to them in some such spirit as that of the Roman Catholic who appeals to the saints in his calendar."

4 Williams, *Hebrewisms of West Africa*, p. 16

5 Herbert G. De Lisser, *Twentieth Century Jamaica*, Kingston, 1913, p. 110 f

6 Gardner, *History of Jamaica*, p. 192. Note:—In this connection it is interesting to find A. W. Cardinall, *In Ashanti and Beyond*, London, 1927, p. 239, who had spent many years as a District Commissioner of the Gold Coast, when describing the initiation to a Bimoda secret society, observing: "If a Kussassi Youth wishes to become a member he has to undergo a rather frightening ordeal. He is cut with a knife and medicine is inserted in the wounds: thereby he is reduced to unconsciousness for a long time. 'He dies for five days' is the expression used. They then anoint him with medicine, and he returns to consciousness."

7 Note:—Lewis is evidently describing a Myal rite in the strict sense of the word. His reference to it as the opening of an Obeah ceremony is due to the common error of his day on the part of the whites who had not yet learned to distinguish between the functions of the Myalist Okomfo and the Obeah man, although it is clearly implied in the present instance by the subsequent reference to the officiating functionary whom he calls by his proper title "the chief Myal man" to whom he had previously misapplied the term "chief Obeah man."

8 Matthew Gregory Lewis, *Journal of a West India Proprietor, kept during a Residence in the Island of Jamaica*, London, 1834, p. 354 f

9 Gardner, *History of Jamaica*, p. 460

10 R. Thomas Banbury, *Jamaica Superstitions, or The Obeah Book*, Kingston, 1895

11 Rattray, *Religion and Art in Ashanti*, p. 152

12 Ditto, p. 53

13 As just noted, in my own experience that was the work of the Obeah man. The Myal man released them.

14 A. J. Emerick, *Jamaica Mialism*, Woodstock, 1916, p. 39 ff

15 Note:—On the contrary Bedwardism is an offshoot of Revivalism which dates back to the closing days of slavery.

16 A. J. Emerick, l. c., p. 47 f

17 De Lisser, *Twentieth Century Jamaica*, p. 134

18 London, 1684, p. 140 ff

19 Ditto, p. 142

20 *Acts of Assembly, passed in the Island of Jamaica from 1681 to 1737, inclusive*, London, 1743, p. 50 ff

21 Ditto, p, 55
22 Ditto, p. 55
23 *Acts of the Privy Council*, Vol. II, p. 834
24 *Acts of Assembly*, l. c., p. 108
25 *Acts of Assembly, passed in the Island of Jamaica front 1681 to 1754, inclusive*, London, 1756, p. 263 ff
26 Ditto, p. 264. ff
27 Gardner, *History of Jamaica*, p. 141
28 *Acts of Assembly, passed in the Island of Jamaica, from 770 to 1783, inclusive*, Kingston, 786, p. 256 ff
29 Ditto, p. 277
30 Stephen Fuller, *New Act of Assembly of the Island of Jamaica commonly called the New Consolidated Act*, London, 1789
31 Ditto, p. 10
32 Ditto, p. 11. Note:—This Act failed to receive the Royal Assent and we find no mention of its provisions in *An Abridgement of the Laws of Jamaica being an alphabetical digest of all the public Acts of Assembly now in force*, published at St. Jago de la Vega, in 1802. In fact there is no reference there in any way pertaining to assemblies of slaves, Obeah or poisonings.
33 John Lunan, *Abstract of the Laws of Jamaica relating to Slaves*, St. Jago de la Vega, 1819, p. 105
34 Ditto, p. 118
35 Ditto, p. 124 f
36 Ditto, p. 124
37 Lunan, l. c., p. 124, Note:—While the non-conformists have always felt that this legislation was aimed solely at their missionaries through motives of bigotry, more sincerity of purpose should be accredited to the Assembly than was generally accorded. The objective of the law is the Revivalist meetings initiated by the Methodists, it is true, but the real motive is self-protection against the rising spirit of Myalism fostered in these gatherings
38 Lunan, l. c., p. 124 f
39 Cynric R. Williams, *A Tour through the Island of Jamaica, from the western to the eastern end, in the year 1823*, London, 1826, p. 38 f
40 Ditto, p. 240
41 Ditto, p. 344
42 *Slave Law of Jamaica with Proceedings & Documents relative thereto*, London, 1828, p. 95 ff.
43 Ditto, p. 108
44 Ditto, p. 109
45 Ditto, p. 110
46 Ditto, p. 111
47 Ditto, p. 231
48 Ditto, p. 146
49 Ditto, p. 147

50 Ditto, p. 156
51 Ditto, p. 159
52 Ditto, p. 189
53 Ditto, p. 164 ff
54 Note:—Cfr. also D. Trouillot, *Esquisse Ethnographique: Le Vaudoux*, Port-au-Prince, 1885, p. 27, where Jamaica Revivalism is classified with the Haitian "Fandango," a Chica Dance and claimed to be a form of Voodoo in the wide sense of the word
55 Gardner, History of Jamaica, p. 358. Note:—The so-called "Native Baptist Churches" are not to be confused with the regular Baptists. They had their origin, it is said, in groups expelled from the older organization for superstition and immortality. They carried with them the name of Baptist and little more.—Cfr. Samuel Green, *Baptist Mission in Jamaica*, London, 1842, p. 19 f. Many of the leaders in the insurrection of 1831 in St. James' parish, as well as not a few of those who were associated with the Morant Bay Rebellion Of 1865, were connected with these Native Baptist Churches.
56 William Wilberforce, *An Appeal to the Religion, Justice, and Humanity of the Inhabitants of the British Empire, in behalf of the Negro Slaves in the West Indies*, London, 1823, p. 22
57 Ditto, p. 23
58 George Wilson Bridges, *A Voice from Jamaica; in reply to William Wilberforce*, London, 1823, p. 28 f
59 Stephen Fuller, *Two Reports from the Committee of the Honourable House of Assembly of Jamaica*, London, 1789, Appendix
60 60. Robert Hammill Nassau, *Fetishism in West Africa*, London, 1904, p. 25.
61 Ditto, p. 263. Note:—Nassau further states, p. 264: "An English traveller recently in the Igbo country of Nigeria, in discussing the native belief in occult forces, says: 'It is impossible for a white man to be present at the gatherings of "medicine men" and it is hard to get a native to talk of such things, but it seems evident to me that there is some reality in the phenomena one hears of, as they are believed everywhere in some degree by white men as well as black.' However that may he the native doctors have a wide knowledge of poisons; and if one is to believe reports, deaths from poison, both among the white and black men, are of common recurrence on the Niger. One of the white man's often quoted proverbs is. 'Never quarrel with your cook'; the meaning of which is that the cook can put something in your food in retaliation if you maltreat him. There is everywhere a belief that it is possible to put medicine on a path for your enemy, which when he steps over it, will cause him to fall sick and die. Other people can walk uninjured over the spot, but the moment the man for whom the medicine is laid reaches the place, he succumbs, often dying within an hour or two. I have never seen such a case myself; but the Rev. A. E. Richardson says he saw one when on the journey with Bishop Tugwell's house-party, He could offer no explanation of how the thing is done, but does not doubt that it is done. Some of the best educated of our native Christians have told me that they firmly believe in this 'medicine-laying.'"
62 Hans Sloane, *A Voyage to the Islands*, London, 707, Introduction, p. lii
63 Ditto, Introduction, p. lvi.
64 Note: Retribution falls heavily on the slave of his day, if we may judge by the following

statement of Sloane, Introduction, p. lvii: "The punishment for crimes of slaves, are usually for rebellions burning them, by nailing them down on the ground with crooked sticks on every limb, and then applying the fire by degrees from the feet and hands, burning them gradually up to the head, whereby their pains are extravagant. For crimes of a less nature gelding or chopping off half of the foot with an ax. These punishments are suffered by them with great constancy."

65 Charles Leslie, *New History of Jamaica*, London, 1740, p. 308

66 Note:—Dr. Patrick Browne, *The Civil and Natural History of Jamaica*, London, 1756, p. 25, like his predecessor, Dr. Sloane, remarks the presence of poisonous plants. However he ascribes the high death rate among the slaves not to poison but rather to the poor medical attendance on the island. Speaking of the diseases so prevalent among the slaves, he is decidedly outspoken: "These are indeed frequently of a peculiar nature, and require a consummate knowledge of symptoms and disorders, to discover the real forces of them; yet the owners, {footnote p. 181} whose interest depends chiefly on their welfare, will commit them to the care (f some raw youth, or ignorant assumer, that is hardly skilled enough to breathe a vein, or dispense a dose of physic; but this proceeds more from ignorance and vanity, than any real want of humanity; for few of them are judges of physic, and each would be thought to have a doctor of his own."

67 This is the common misconception, already noticed, of considering Myalism as an offshoot from Obeah

68 Edward Long, *History of Jamaica*, London, 1774, Vol. II, p. 416

69 Ditto, Vol. 1I, p. 420. Note:—In reference to the slave law of Jamaica, Long writes, p. 493: "The Negro code of this island appears originally to have copied from the model in use at Barbadoes; and the legislature of this latter island, which was the first planted by the English, resorted to the English villeinage laws, from whence they undoubtedly transfused all that severity which characterizes them, and shows the abject slavery which the common people of England formerly laboured under."

70 William Burdett, *Life and Exploits of Mansong, commonly called Three-finger Jack, the Terror of Jamaica*, Sommers Town, 1800, p. 34

71 Ditto, p. 17. Note:—Robert Renny published in London in 1807: *An History of Jamaica, ... To which is added an illustration of the Advantages, which are likely to result, from the Abolition of the Slave Trade*. He remarks, Preface, p. xi: "Perhaps an observation will be deemed requisite respecting the non-quotation of authorities, for the various historical facts, related in the Present volume. For this conduct, the conciseness requisite in a short history, will Probably account in a satisfactory manner." The entire work lacks originality and is little more than a reprint from others. Hence we may confine ourselves to the following brief quotation, p. 169 f.: "Whatever their notions of religion may have been, they, not unlike their European masters, seem to pay little regard to the ceremonies of any system in Jamaica. But they are not on that account, the less superstitious. A belief in Obeah, or witchcraft, is almost universal among them. The professors of this occult science, are always Africans, and generally old and crafty. Hoary heads, gravity of aspect, and a skill in herbs, are the chief qualifications for this curious office. The Negroes, both Africans and Creoles (*i. e.* those born in the island), revere, consult, and fear them." Then

follows an account which is little more than a paraphrase from the Report of 1780

72 J. Stewart, *An Account of Jamaica and its Inhabitants*, London, 1808, p. 256 ff. Note:—In
the second edition of this work which was published under the title, *A View of the
Past and Present State of the Island of Jamaica*, Edinburgh, 1823, for some unexplained
reason, this passage is rewritten and considerably changed with the element of
poison in Obeah introduced.—Cfr. p. 276 f.: "The most dangerous practice, arising from
the superstitious credulity, prevailing among the negroes is, what is called obeah, a
pretended sort of witchcraft. One negro who desires to be revenged on another, and
is afraid to make an open and manly attack on his adversary, has usually recourse to
obeah. This is considered as a potent and irresistible spell, withering and palsying, by
indescribable errors and unwonted sensations, the unhappy victim. Like the witches'
caldron in Macbeth, it is a combination of many strange and ominous things—earth
gathered from a grave, human blood, a piece of wood fashioned in the shape of a coffin,
the feathers of the carrion-crow, a snake's or alligator's tooth, pieces of eggshell, and
other nameless ingredients, compose the fatal mixture. The whole of these articles may
not be considered as absolutely necessary to complete the charm, but two or three are
at least indispensable. It will, of course, be conceived, that the practice of obeah can
have little effect, unless a negro is conscious that it is practiced upon him, or thinks so;
for as the whole evil consists in the terrors of a superstitious imagination, it is of little
consequence whether it be really practiced or not, if he can only imagine that it is. But
if the charm fails to take hold of the mind of the proscribed person, another and more
certain expedient is resorted to—the secretly administering of poison to him. This saves
the reputation of the sorcerer, and effects the purpose he had in view. (The negroes
practicing obeah are acquainted with some very powerful vegetable poisons, which
they use on these occasions.) An obeah-man or woman (for it is practiced by both sexes)
is a very wicked and dangerous person on a plantation; and the practice of it is made
a felony by the law, punishable with death where poison has been administered, and
with transportation where only the charm is used. But numbers may be swept off by its
infatuation before the crime is detected; for, strange as it may appear, so much do the
negroes stand in awe of those obeah professors, so much do they dread their malice and
their power, that, though knowing the havoc they have made, and are still making, they
are afraid to discover them to the whites; and others perhaps, are in league with them
for sinister purposes of mischief and revenge. A negro under this infatuation can only
be cured of his terrors by being made a Christian: refuse him this boon, and he sinks a
martyr to imagined evils. The author knew an instance of a negro, who, being reduced
by the fatal influence of obeah to the lowest state of dejection and debility, from which
there were little hopes of his recovery, was surprisingly and rapidly restored to health
and cheerfulness by being baptized a Christian. A negro, in short, considers himself
as no longer {footnote p. 186} under the influence of this sorcery when he becomes a
Christian. But, though so liable to be perverted into a deadly instrument of malice and
revenge, obeah—at least a species of it—may be said to have its uses. When placed
in the gardens and grounds of the Negroes, it becomes an excellent guard or watch,
scaring away the predatory runaway and midnight plunderer with more effective power

than gins and spring-guns. It loses its power, however, when put to protect the gardens and plantain-walks of the Buckras."

B. Pullen-Bury, *Jamaica as It Is, 1903*, London, 1903, p. 140, says of recent times: "Some planters adopt Obi to ensure themselves against thieving. They take a large black bottle, fill it with some phosphorescent liquid, and place within it the feather of a buzzard, the quill sticking uppermost. This they fasten to a tree on the outskirts of the coffee-patch or banana-field, where it can be well observed by all who pass near. The dusky population, firmly believing it to be the work of the Obeah man, refrain their thieving propensities accordingly."

73 Lewis, *Journal of a West India Proprietor*, p. 134
74 Ditto, p. 148 f
75 James Stephens, *The Slavery of the British West India Colonies, delineated*, London, 1824, Vol. I, p. 305
76 Alexander Barclay, *A Practical View of the Present State of Slavery in the West Indies*, London, 1828, p. 185 f
77 George Wilson Bridges, *Annals of Jamaica*, London, 1828, Vol. II. p. 404
78 Ditto, Vol. II, p. 404
79 R. R. Madden, *A Twelvemonth's Residence in the West Indies, during the Transition front Slavery to Apprenticeship*, London, 1835, Vol. I. Preface, p. vi
80 Ditto, Vol. I, p. 93
81 Ditto, Vol. I, p. 97
82 Ditto, Vol. I, p. 98. Note:—Dr. Madden later makes the observation on p. 108: "The Africans, like all other people who profess the Mohammedan faith, have an opinion that insanity and supernatural inspiration are frequently combined, and consequently, knaves and lunatics (partially insane) are commonly the persons who play the parts of santons and sorcerers. The Africans carried most of their superstitions to our colonies, and, amongst others their reverence for those either whose physical or mental peculiarities distinguished them from the multitude,—and such were the persons who in advanced age, usually took on themselves the Obeah character. It is evident to any medical man who reads these trials, that in the great majority of cases the trumpery ingredients used in the practice of Obeah were incapable of producing mischief except on the imagination of the person intended to be Obeahed." The good Doctor here overlooks the element of poison and greatly underrates the power of superstitious fear on the part of the Negro.
83 John Joseph Gurney, *Familiar Letters to Henry Clay of Kentucky, Describing a Winter in the West Indies*, New York, 1840, p. 76
84 James M. Phillippo, *Jamaica: Its Past and Present State*, London, 1843, p. 263
85 *Report of the Jamaica Royal Commission*, 1866, London, 1866, Vol. 1I, p. 52I, Items 26459-26540
86 Charles Rampini, *Letters from Jamaica*, Edinburgh, 1873, p. 131 f
87 Labat, *Nouveau Voyage aux Isles de l'Amérique*, Vol. II, p. 46
88 Note:—The real Negro who has remained uncontaminated by Mohammedan influence has a degree of morality that puts the average white to shame, *e.g.;*—Cfr. J. H. Driberg,

The Lango, London, 1923, p. 209f., especially the Notes. Here we find the death penalty for those sensual acts which are usually classified as being "against nature."

89 Rampini, l. c., p. 135

90 Ditto, p. 142

91 Note:—Cfr. also J. G. Wood, *The Uncivilized Races of Man*, Vol. I, p. 550: 'Sasabonsam is the friend of witch and wizard, hates priests and missionaries, and inhabits huge silk-cotton trees in the gloomiest forests; he is a monstrous being, of human shape, of red colour and with long hair."

92 Edwards, *History of the British Colonies in the West Indies*, Vol. II, p. 71. Note:—Trouillot, *Esquisse Ethnographique: Le Vaudoux*, p. 39, tells us that in Haiti Sassa-Boussa is recognized as "the devil of the Bambaras."

93 Banbury, *Jamaica Superstitions*

94 E. M. Cook, *Jamaica: The Lodestone of the Caribbean*, Bristol, 1924, p. 115 f

95 Ditto, p. 125

96 A. J. Emerick, *Obeah and Duppyism in Jamaica*, p. 190 ff

97 *Slave Law of Jamaica and Documents relative thereto*, p. 146

98 Ditto, p. 249

99 Note:—The full petition may be found, l. c., p. 252 f

100 Gardner, *History of Jamaica*, p. 188

101 Note:—Cfr. Martha Warren Beckwith, *Black Roadways; a Study of Jamaica Folk Lore*, Chapel Hill, 1929. Miss Beckwith opens her chapter on "Obeah," p. 104, with the following paragraph: "We have seen that all Jamaica Negroes believe in a spirit world. Many think that there are mischievous spirits who have the power to take animal shape and go about making themselves troublesome to men; these they say are the ghosts of evil men. Even the ghosts of good men, whose souls the Christian religion teaches them to look upon as happy in heaven, may come back to their friends on earth 'to keep holiday,' and may at times be hovering about the house where they have lived on earth. There is a general inclination today to associate these hauntings with the 'shadow' of the dead which lingers about the grave and which, if properly solicited may be persuaded to take a part in human affairs. This 'shadow,' which is the duppy, may be tempted out of the grave by a member of the dead man's family and 'set' upon someone against whom the exorciser has a grudge, or it may be made to perform other services to his disadvantage. The practice of this power over the shadow world is called obeah, and the so-called obeah religion depends on the belief that such spirits may be employed to work harm to the living or may be called off from such mischief. 'Working' obeah means to 'set' a duppy for someone; 'pulling' obeah means to extract the obeah set by another." Miss Beckwith tells us in her Foreword, p. vii: "Between the summers of 1919 and 1924 I made four visits to the island of Jamaica." If these four short visits had been lengthened out into four full years, she would not have been so ready to settle off-hand the difficult question of just what is Obeah, and her conclusions would unquestionably have differed greatly from what she has written. Again, p. 106, she asserts absolutely: "Obeah is merely sympathetic magic." In her foreword, too, p. vii, she states: "When the confidence of the people has been won

and my own knowledge widened, I could question them about beliefs and customs. To three such informants I am especially indebted—to Wilfrid Bonito of Richmond (but brought up in Manderville), etc." Her friend, then, must have been amusing himself at her expense at times, if we may judge from the following, p. 108: "The real Obeah man, says Wilfrid, must kill one of his own family—it may be an infant. Wilfrid did not say so, but I suppose in this way the Obeah man secures the duppy who acts as his 'familiar' or 'control.'"

Chapter VI

1 Moreau de Saint-Méry, *Description de la Partie Française de Saint Dominigue*, Vol. I, p. 24.

2 Note:—Commander Frederick E. Forbes, *Dahomey and the Dahomans*, London, 1851, Vol. II, p. 7 f., writes: "On the western and north-western side the stream of the Volta alone separates Dahomey from its great rival monarchy of Western Africa, the kingdom of Ashantee. Time alone can develop the consequences to Africa of such powerful and ambitious nations being divided by no more difficult boundary than the far from wide or impassable waters of the Volta. Already on that side the Attahpahms and Ahjabee have been defeated although not annexed to the rapidly increasing territory of Dahomey. If we turn to the East, we find the extensive provinces of Yoruhbah looked upon with cupidity, and marked out for devastation, slaver, and murder."

3 H. Osman Newland, *West Africa*, London, 1922, p. 94

4 Dr. Price-Mars, *Ainsi Parla l'Oncle*, p. 120

5 Note:—Dr. Price-Mars, however, goes too far when, in a lecture delivered before the Society of History and Geography in 1926, he allows his fervour and patriotism to carry him away and in an oratorical outburst asserts that Voodoo which he defines as an animistic religion is not "opposed to the religion of the one God, sovereign and supreme master of the Universe."—Cfr. *Une Étape de l'Évolution Haïtienne*, p. 115. He states specifically, p. 130: "This animism which deifies the forces of Nature renders homage to the spiritual genii which they incarnate, this animism, in fact, which renders to deceased ancestors a cult of veneration and implores their favour and protection, is it a religion in opposition to the religion of the one God, sovereign and supreme Master of the Universe? No, certainly not." It is monotheistic, yes, and in that restricted sense his statement might stand, and possibly that is all that he really meant to signify

6 Arthur C. Millapaugh, *Haiti, under American Control 1915-1930*, Boston, 1931, p. 20.

7 Ditto, p. 140, Note 27

8 Note:—Compare this scene with that described by Rattray on page 127

9 Note:—Cfr. Rattray, *Religion and Art in Ashanti*, p. 23

10 Cardinall, *In Ashanti and Beyond*, p. 224

11 Rattray, l. c., p. 25 f

12 A. J. Emerick, *Jamaica Duppies*, Woodstock, 1916, p. 342

13 Ditto, p. 342

14 Ditto, p. 343

15 Ditto, p. 343

16 Gardner, *History of Jamaica*, p. 192

17 Ditto, p. 193

18 Long, *History of Jamaica*, Vol. II, p. 235

19 Ditto, p. 236

20 Chambers's *Cyclopedia of English Literature*, London, 1899, Vol. II, p. 24

21 Leslie, *New History of Jamaica*, p. 303

22 Cfr. Stephen Fuller, *Original Letter Book, 1776-1784*, Boston College Library, MS. No. 6002

23 Wilberforce, *Appeal* etc., p. 19

24 Cundall, *Historic Jamaica*, London, 1915, p. 5.

25 Ditto, p. 372

26 Bridges, *Voice from Jamaica*, p.26 f

27 Gardner, History of Jamaica, p. 334

28 R. Bicknell, The West Indies as they are; or a Real Picture of Slavery; but more particularly as it exists in the island of Jamaica, London, 1825, p. 74

29 John Riland, *Memoir of a West India Planter*, London, 1827, p. 186 f

30 Bicknell, l. c., Flyleaf

31 Ditto, p. 67

32 Ditto, p. 73

33 Ditto, p. 71. Note:—The Home Government made futile efforts at times to check the growing abuses, if we may judge from a letter of the Duke of Halifax answering one from Stephen Fuller who had sought an extended leave of absence for the Rev. John Venn, at that time Rector of St. Catherine's, Jamaica, and dated April 17, 1764, wherein he states: "I shall be ready to move his Majesty to grant him that indulgence, upon being assured that Governor Lyttleton is satisfied of the necessity and approves of the curate who is to officiate in his stead. For I must acquaint you that, upon the complaints which have been made by the Bishop of London of the bad consequences arising from the general and frequent absence of the clergy from their livings in the West Indies, I have made it a rule never to procure any such indulgence, unless the application be so granted."—Cfr. Stephen Fuller, *Original Letter Book, 1762-1771*, Boston College Library, MS. No. 6001

34 Peter Duncan, *A Narrative of the Wesleyan Mission to Jamaica*, London, 1849 p. 7 f.

35 Claudius Buchanan, *Colonial Ecclesiastical Establishment*, London, 1812, p. 53

36 Ditto, p. 60 f

37 Peter Samuel, *The Wesleyan-Methodist Missions in Jamaica and Honduras*, Delineated, London, 1850, p. 9

38 Ditto, p. 10

39 Note:—Cfr. Duncan, *Wesleyan Mission to Jamaica*, p. 11

40 Note:—Cfr. Duncan, l. c., p. 8 f

41 Duncan, l. c., p. 16

42 Buchanan, *Colonial Ecclesiastical Establishment*, p. 76 ff

43 Gardner, *History of Jamaica*, p. 340

44 Note:—Cfr. *Further Proceedings of the Honourable House of Assembly of Jamaica, relative to a Bill introduced into the House of Commons for effectually preventing the unlawful importation of slaves and holding free persons in slavery in the British Colonies*, London, 1816, p. 40f

45 Ditto, p. 42

46 London, 1892, p. 191

47 Duncan, *Wesleyan Mission to Jamaica*, p. 223

48 Ditto, p. 273, Note 1

49 Note:—We might then have been spared this terrible arraignment: "The misdirected efforts and misguided counsel of certain Ministers of Religion, sadly so miscalled, if the Saviour's example and teaching is to be the standard, have led to their natural,

their necessary, their inevitable result (amongst an ignorant, excitable, and uncivilized population)—rebellion, arson, murder. These are hard and harsh words, gentlemen, but they are true; and this is no time to indulge in selected sentences, or polished phraseology."—Speech of His Excellency, Edward John Eyre, Governor of Jamaica, before the Legislative Council, Tuesday, November 7, 1865, at the opening of the first session after the Morant Bay Rebellion.—Cfr. Augustus Constantine Sinclair, *Parliamentary Debates of Jamaica*, Spanish-Town, 1866, Vol. XIII, p. 3. And the Assembly in their answering Address to the Governor, on the following day, state: "We desire to express our entire concurrence in Your Excellency's statement that, {footnote p. 236} to the misapprehensions and misrepresentations of pseudo philanthropists in England and in this country. . . . and to the misdirected efforts and misguided zeal of certain miscalled ministers of religion, is to be attributed the present disorganization of the colony, resulting in rebellion, arson, and murder."—Cfr. l. c., p. 13

Chapter VI

1 Moreau de Saint-Méry, *Description de la Partie Française de Saint Dominigue*, Vol. I, p. 24.

2 Note:—Commander Frederick E. Forbes, *Dahomey and the Dahomans*, London, 1851, Vol. II, p. 7 f., writes: "On the western and north-western side the stream of the Volta alone separates Dahomey from its great rival monarchy of Western Africa, the kingdom of Ashantee. Time alone can develop the consequences to Africa of such powerful and ambitious nations being divided by no more difficult boundary than the far from wide or impassable waters of the Volta. Already on that side the Attahpahms and Ahjabee have been defeated although not annexed to the rapidly increasing territory of Dahomey. If we turn to the East, we find the extensive provinces of Yoruhbah looked upon with cupidity, and marked out for devastation, slaver, and murder."

3 H. Osman Newland, *West Africa*, London, 1922, p. 94

4 Dr. Price-Mars, *Ainsi Parla l'Oncle*, p. 120

5 Note:—Dr. Price-Mars, however, goes too far when, in a lecture delivered before the Society of History and Geography in 1926, he allows his fervour and patriotism to carry him away and in an oratorical outburst asserts that Voodoo which he defines as an animistic religion is not "opposed to the religion of the one God, sovereign and supreme master of the Universe. "—Cfr. *Une Étape de l'Évolution Haïtienne*, p. 115. He states specifically, p. 130: "This animism which deifies the forces of Nature renders homage to the spiritual genii which they incarnate, this animism, in fact, which renders to deceased ancestors a cult of veneration and implores their favour and protection, is it a religion in opposition to the religion of the one God, sovereign and supreme Master of the Universe? No, certainly not." It is monotheistic, yes, and in that restricted sense his statement might stand, and possibly that is all that he really meant to signify

6 Arthur C. Millapaugh, *Haiti, under American Control 1915-1930*, Boston, 1931, p. 20.

7 Ditto, p. 140, Note 27

8 Note:—Compare this scene with that described by Rattray on page 127

9 Note:—Cfr. Rattray, *Religion and Art in Ashanti*, p. 23

10 Cardinall, *In Ashanti and Beyond*, p. 224

11 Rattray, 1. c., p. 25 f

12 A. J. Emerick, *Jamaica Duppies*, Woodstock, 1916, p. 342

13 Ditto, p. 342

14 Ditto, p. 343

15 Ditto, p. 343

16 Gardner, *History of Jamaica*, p. 192

17 Ditto, p. 193

18 Long, *History of Jamaica*, Vol. II, p. 235

19 Ditto, p. 236

20 Chambers's *Cyclopedia of English Literature*, London, 1899, Vol. II, p. 24

21 Leslie, *New History of Jamaica*, p. 303

22 Cfr. Stephen Fuller, *Original Letter Book, 1776-1784*, Boston College Library, MS. No. 6002

23 Wilberforce, *Appeal* etc., p. 19

24 Cundall, *Historic Jamaica*, London, 1915, p. 5.

25 Ditto, p. 372

26 Bridges, *Voice from Jamaica*, p.26 f

27 Gardner, History of Jamaica, p. 334

28 R. Bicknell, The West Indies as they are; or a Real Picture of Slavery; but more particularly as it exists in the island of Jamaica, London, 1825, p. 74

29 John Riland, *Memoir of a West India Planter*, London, 1827, p. 186 f

30 Bicknell, l. c., Flyleaf

31 Ditto, p. 67

32 Ditto, p. 73

33 Ditto, p. 71. Note:—The Home Government made futile efforts at times to check the growing abuses, if we may judge from a letter of the Duke of Halifax answering one from Stephen Fuller who had sought an extended leave of absence for the Rev. John Venn, at that time Rector of St. Catherine's, Jamaica, and dated April 17, 1764, wherein he states: "I shall be ready to move his Majesty to grant him that indulgence, upon being assured that Governor Lyttleton is satisfied of the necessity and approves of the curate who is to officiate in his stead. For I must acquaint you that, upon the complaints which have been made by the Bishop of London of the bad consequences arising from the general and frequent absence of the clergy from their livings in the West Indies, I have made it a rule never to procure any such indulgence, unless the application be so granted."—Cfr. Stephen Fuller, *Original Letter Book, 1762-1771*, Boston College Library, MS. No. 6001

34 Peter Duncan, *A Narrative of the Wesleyan Mission to Jamaica*, London, 1849 p. 7 f.

35 Claudius Buchanan, *Colonial Ecclesiastical Establishment*, London, 1812, p. 53

36 Ditto, p. 60 f

37 Peter Samuel, *The Wesleyan-Methodist Missions in Jamaica and Honduras*, Delineated, London, 1850, p. 9

38 Ditto, p. 10

39 Note:—Cfr. Duncan, *Wesleyan Mission to Jamaica*, p. 11

40 Note:—Cfr. Duncan, l. c., p. 8 f

41 Duncan, l. c., p. 16

42 Buchanan, *Colonial Ecclesiastical Establishment*, p. 76 ff

43 Gardner, *History of Jamaica*, p. 340

44 Note:—Cfr. *Further Proceedings of the Honourable House of Assembly of Jamaica, relative to a Bill introduced into the House of Commons for effectually preventing the unlawful importation of slaves and holding free persons in slavery in the British Colonies*, London, 1816, p. 40f

45 Ditto, p. 42

46 London, 1892, p. 191

47 Duncan, *Wesleyan Mission to Jamaica*, p. 223

48 Ditto, p. 273, Note 1

49 Note:—We might then have been spared this terrible arraignment: "The misdirected efforts and misguided counsel of certain Ministers of Religion, sadly so miscalled, if the Saviour's example and teaching is to be the standard, have led to their natural,

their necessary, their inevitable result (amongst an ignorant, excitable, and uncivilized population)—rebellion, arson, murder. These are hard and harsh words, gentlemen, but they are true; and this is no time to indulge in selected sentences, or polished phraseology."—Speech of His Excellency, Edward John Eyre, Governor of Jamaica, before the Legislative Council, Tuesday, November 7, 1865, at the opening of the first session after the Morant Bay Rebellion.—Cfr. Augustus Constantine Sinclair, *Parliamentary Debates of Jamaica*, Spanish-Town, 1866, Vol. XIII, p. 3. And the Assembly in their answering Address to the Governor, on the following day, state: "We desire to express our entire concurrence in Your Excellency's statement that, {footnote p. 236} to the misapprehensions and misrepresentations of pseudo philanthropists in England and in this country. . . . and to the misdirected efforts and misguided zeal of certain miscalled ministers of religion, is to be attributed the present disorganization of the colony, resulting in rebellion, arson, and murder."—Cfr. l. c., p. 13

Bibliography

BIBLIOGRAPHY FOR AFRICAN OPHIOLATRY

• ANONYMOUS.
Ophiolatreia or Serpent Worship (Printed Privately).
• ATKINS, JOHN.
A Voyage to Guinea, Brasil, and the West Indies in His Majesty's Ships the Swallow and Weymouth, London, 1735.
• BASDEN, G. T.
Among the Ibos of Nigeria, London, 1921.
• BAUDIN, PÈRE.
Fétichisme et Féticheurs, Lyon, 1884.
• BOSCH, F.
Le Culte Des Ancêtres chez les Banyamwezi—ANTHROPOS, Vol. XX (1925).
• BOSMAN, WILLIAM.
A New and Accurate Description of the Coast of Guinea, divided into the Gold, the Slave, and the Ivory Coast, London, 1705.
• BOUCHE, PIERRE.
La Côte des Esclaves et le Dahomey, Paris, 1885.
• BREASTED, JAMES HENRY.
History of Egypt, New York, 1905.
Development of Religion and Thought in Ancient Egypt, New York, 1905.
Ancient Records of Egypt, London, 1907.
History of Ancient Egyptians, London, 1908.
• BRIAULT, M.
Polytheism and Fetishism, London, 1931.
• BROSSES, CHARLES DES.
Du Culte des dieux Fétiches ou Parallèle de l'Ancienne Religion de l'Égypte avec la Religion de Nigritie, Paris, 1760.
• BROWNE, W. G.
Travels in Africa, Egypt and Syria, from the Year 1792 to 1798, London, 1806.
• BRUCE, JAMES.
Travels to Discover the Source of the Nile, Edinburgh, 1804.
• BRUGSCH, HENRI.
History of Egypt under the Pharaohs, London, 1879.
• BRUNET, L.
Dahomey et Dépendances, Paris, 1901.

- BUDGE, A. E. WALLIS.
  Egyptian Magic, London, 1908.
  Egyptian Ideas of the Future Life, London, 1908.
  The Book of the Dead, London, 1923.
  Short History of the Egyptian People, London, 1923.
  Dwellers on the Nile, London, 1926.
  Amulets and Superstitions, Oxford, 1930.
- BURTON, RICHARD F.
  A Mission to Gelele, King of Dahome, London, 1864.
- CLEMEN, CARL.
  Religions of the World, New York, 1931.
- COOKSEY, J. J. and McLEISH, ALEXANDER.
  Religion and Civilization in West Africa, London, 1931
- DALZELL, ARCHIBALD.
  History of Dahomey, an Inland Kingdom of Africa, London, 1793.
- DEANE, JOHN BATHURST.
  The Worship of the Serpent, London, 1830.
- DENNETT, R. E.
  At the Back of the Black Man's Mind, London, 1906.
- DESRIBES, E.
  L'Évangile au Dahomey et d la Côte des Esclaves, Clermont-Ferrand, 1877.
- DRIBERG, J. H.
  The Lango, a Nilotic Tribe of Uganda, London, 1923.
- DU CHAILLU, PAUL BELLONI.
  A Journey to Ashango Land, London, 1867.
- DUNCAN, JOHN.
  Travels in West Africa in 1845 and 1846, London, 1847.
- ELLIS, ALFRED BURTON.
  The Land of Fetish, London, 1883.
  The Tshi-Speaking Peoples of the Gold Coast of Africa, London, 1887.
  The Ewe-Speaking Peoples, London, 1890.
  The Yoruba-Speaking Peoples of the Slave Coast, London, 1894.
- FARROW, STEPHEN SEPTIMUS.
  Faith, Fancies and Fetish, or Yoruba Paganism, London, 1926.
- FERAUD, L.
  Les Peuplades de la Sénégambie, Paris, 1879.
- FOÀ, ÉDOUARD.
  Le Dahomey, Paris, 1895.
- FORBES, FREDERICK E.
  Dahomey and the Dahomans; being the Journals of two Missions to the King of Dahomey, and Residence at his Capital, in the Years 1849 and 1850, London, 1851.
- FRAZER, JAMES GEORGE.
  Totemism and Exogamy, London, 1910.

The Golden Bough, London, 1920.

Garnered Sheaves, London, 1931.

• FREEMAN, THOMAS B.

Journal of various Visits to the Kingdoms of Ashanti, Aku, and Dahomi in Western Africa, London, 1844.

• GARNIER, J.

The Worship of the Dead or the Origin and Nature of Pagan Idolatry, London, 1904.

• HADDON, A. C.

The Wanderings of Peoples, Cambridge, 1911.

Magic and Fetishism, London, 1921.

• HAMBLY, WILFRID DYSON.

History of Tattooing and Its Significance, London, 1925.

Serpent Worship in Africa, Chicago, 1931.

• HASTINGS, JAMES.

Encyclopedia of Religion and Ethics (Edited), New York, 1913-1922.

• HOLLIS, A. C.

The Masai: Their Language and Folklore, Oxford, 1905.

The Nandi: Their Language and Folklore, Oxford, 1909.

• HOPKINS, E. WASHBURN.

The History of Religions, New York, 1926.

• HOVELACQUE, ABEL.

Les Nègres de l'Afrique Sus-Equatoriale, Paris, 1889.

• HOWEY, M. OLDFIELD.

The Encircled Serpent, Philadelphia, 1928.

• HUREL, P. E.

Religion et Vie Domestique des Bakerewe—ANTHROPOS, Vol. VI(1911).

• HUTCHINSON, THOMAS

Impressions of Western Africa, London, 1858.

• JOHNSTON, HARRY HAMILTON.

The Uganda Protectorate, London, 1902.

The Nile Quest, New York, 1903.

Liberia, London, 1906.

• KINGSLEY, MARY H.

Travels in West Africa, London, 1897.

West African Studies, London, 1899.

• KITCHING, A. L.

On the Backwaters of the Nile, London, 1912.

• LABAT, PÈRE.

Nouveau Voyage aux Isles de l'Amérique, La Haye, 1724.

• LAFITTE, J.

Le Dahomé, Tours, 1873.

• LEONARD, ARTHUR GLYN.

The Lower Niger and its Tribes, London, 1906.

• LÉVY-BRUHL, LUCIEN.
The "Soul" of the Primitive, New York, 1928.
• LIPPERT, JULIUS.
The Evolution of Culture, London, 1931.
• LUBBOCK, JOHN.
Origin of Civilization and the Primitive Condition of Man, New York, 1912.
• MANGIN, ARTHUR.
L'Homme et la Bête, Paris, 1872.
• MANGIN, EUGÈNE P.
Les Mossi—ANTHROPOS, Vol. X (1915).
• MASPERO, GASTON.
The Dawn of Civilization, New York, 1894.
History of Egypt, New York, 1906.
Popular Stories of Ancient Egypt, London, 1915.
Études de Mythologie et d'Arcéologie Égyptiennes, Paris, 1916.
• M'LEOD, JOHN.
A Voyage to Africa with some Account of the Manners and Customs of theDahomian People, London, 1820.
• MEEK, C. K.
The Northern Tribes of Nigeria, Oxford, 1925.
Tribal Studies in Northern Nigeria, London, 1931.
• MEINHOF, C.
Die Dichtung der Afrikaner, Berlin, 1911.
• NASSAU, ROBERT HAMMILL.
Fetishism in West Africa, London, 1904.
Where Animals Talk, London, 1914.
• NORRIS, ROBERT.
Memoirs of the Reign of Bassa Ahadee, King of Dahomy, London, 1789.
• OLDHAM, C. F.
The Sun and the Serpent, London, 1905.
• PERRY, WILLIAM JAMES.
The Children of the Sun, London, 1927.
• PETRIE, W. M. FLINDERS.
History of Egypt, New York, 1896.
Religions and Conscience in Ancient Egypt, New York, 1898. *Personal Religion in Egypt before Christianity*, London, 1909. *Amulets*, London, 1914.
History of Egypt from the Earliest Kings of the XVIth Dynasty, New York, 1924.
• PRICHARD, JAMES COWLES.
Researches into the Physical History of Mankind, London, 1851,
• RATZEL, FRIEDRICH.
The History of Mankind, London, 1896-1898.
• REVILLE, A.
Les Religions des Peuples Non-Civilisés, Paris, 1883.

- ROSCOE, JOHN.
  The Baganda, An Account of their Native Customs and Beliefs, London, 1911.
  The Northern Bantu, Cambridge, 1915.
  Twenty-five Years in East Africa, Cambridge, 1921.
  The Soul of Central Africa, London, 1922.
  The Bakitara or Banyoro, Cambridge, 1923.
  The Banyankole, Cambridge, 1923.
- ROUGEMONT, FRÉDÉRIC DE.
  Le Peuple Primitif: Sa Religion, Son Histoire et Sa Civilisation, Genève, 1855.
- SAYCE, A. H.
  Ancient Empires of the East, London, 1886.
  Egypt of the Hebrews and Herodotus, London, 1896.
  The Religions of Ancient Egypt and Babylonia, Edinburgh, 1903.
- SCHWEINFURTH, GEORG.
  The Heart of Africa, New York, 1874.
- SCOT, REGINALD.
  The Discovery of Witchcraft, London, 1665.
- SELIGMAN, C. G.
  Races of Africa, London, 1930.
- SKERTCHLEY, J. A.
  Dahomey as it is; being a Narrative of eight months' Residence in that Country, London, 1874.
- SMITH, EDWIN W. and DALE, ANDREW MURRAY.
  The Ila-Speaking People of Northern Rhodesia, London, 1920.
- SMITH, GRAFTON ELIOT.
  The Evolution of the Dragon, Manchester, 1919.
  The Migrations of Early Culture, Manchester, 1929.
- SMITH, WILLIAM.
  A New Voyage to Guinea, London, 1745.
- SMITH, W. ROBERTSON.
  Lectures on Religion of the Semites, London, 1923.
- SNELGRAVE, WILLIAM.
  A New Account of some Parts of Guinea and the Slave-Trade, London, 1734.
- SPENCER, HERBERT.
  Descriptive Sociology: African Races: Compiled and abstracted by Prof. David Duncan, London, 1875.
  Reissue, entirely rewritten by E. Torday, London, 1930.
- STAM, N.
  The Religious Conceptions of the Kavirondo—ANTHROPOS, Vol. V (1910).
- SUMNER, WILLIAM GRAHAM and KELLER, ALBERT GALLOWAY.
  The Science of Society, New Haven, 1927.
- TALBOT, D. AMAURY.
  Woman's Mysteries of a Primitive People, London, 1915

• TALBOT, PERCY AMAURY.
In the Shadow of the Bush, London, 1912.
Life in Southern Nigeria, London, 1923.
The Peoples of Southern Nigeria, Oxford, 1926.
Tribes of the Niger Delta, London, 1932.
• THOMAS, NORTHCOTE W.
Anthropological Report on the Ibo-Speaking People of Nigeria, London, 1913-1914
• TREMEARNE, A. J. N.
Tailed Head-Hunters of Nigeria, London, 1912.
The Ban of the Bori, London, 1914.
• TYLOR, EDWARD B.
Primitive Culture, Boston, 1874.
• VAN GENNEP, ARNOLD.
L'État actuel du Problême Totemique, Paris, 1920.
• VINSON, JULIEN.
Les Religions Actuelles, Paris, 1888.
• WAKE, C. STANILAND.
Serpent-Worship and other Essays, London, 1888.
• WEEKS, JOHN H.
Among Congo Cannibals, London, 1913.
Among the Primitive Bakongo, Philadelphia, 1914
• WERNER, ALICE.
Natives of British Central Africa, London, 1906.
• WESTERMANN, DEITRICH.
Die Kpelle, Leipzig, 1921.
• WILSON, J. LEIGHTON.
Western Africa, Its History, Condition, and Prospects, London, 1856.

BIBLIOGRAPHY FOR HAITIAN VOODOO

• ANDRADE, MANUEL J.
Folk-lore from the Dominican Republic, New York, 1930.
• AUBIN, EUGÈNE.
En Haïti, Paris, 1910.
• BARSKEET, JAMES.
History of the Island of St. Domingo, from the Discovery of Columbus to the present Period, London, 1818.
• BIRD, M. B.
The Black Man; or, Haytian Independence, New York, 1869.
• BONNEAU, ALEXANDRE.
Haïti: Ses Progres—Son Avenir, Paris, 1862.
• BONSAL, STEPHEN.

The American Mediterranean, New York, 1912.
- BROWN, J.
History and present Condition of St. Domingo, Philadelphia, 1837.
- CHARLEVOIX, PIERRE FRANÇOIS XAVIER DE.
Histoire de l'Isle Espagnole ou de S. Domingue, Paris, 1830.
- DAVIS, H. P.
Black Democracy: The Story of Hayti, New York, 1928.
- DORSAINVIL, J. C.
Une Explication Philologique du Vòdú, Port-au-Prince, 1924.
Manuel d'Histoire d'Haïti, Port-au-Prince, 1925.
Vodou et Névrose, Port-au-Prince, 1931.
- ELLIS, ALFRED BURTON.
On Vodu-Worship—POPULAR SCIENCE MONTHLY, Vol. XXXVIII (1891).
- FROUDE, JAMES ANTHONY.
The English in the West Indies; or, the Bow of Ulysses, London, 1888.
- HAZARD, SAMUEL.
Santo Domingo: Past and Present with a Glance at Hayti, London, 1873.
- JOHNSTON, HARRY HAMILTON.
The Negro in the New World, London, 1910.
- LÉGER, J. N.
Haïti: Son Histoire et ses Détracteurs, New York, 1907.
Hayti: Her History and her Detractors, New York, 1907.
- MADIOU, THOMAS.
Histoire d'Haïti: Années 1492-1807, Port-au-Prince, 1922-1923.
Histoire d'Haïti: Années 1843-1846, Port-au-Prince, 1904.
- MANNINGTON, GEORGE.
The West Indies with British Guiana and British Honduras, New York, 1925.
- MERWIN, BRUCE W.
A Voodoo Drum from Hayti—UNIVERSITY OF PENNSYLVANIA MUSEUM JOURNAL, Vol. VIII (1917).
- MORAND, PAUL.
Magie Noire, Paris, 1928.
- MOREAU DE SAINT-MÉRY, MÉDÉRIC LOUIS ÉLIE.
Loix et Constitutions des Colonies Françoises de l'Amérique sous le Vent, Paris, 1780. *Description ... de la Partie Française de l'Isle Saint-Domingue*, Philadelphia, 1797-1798. *Topographical and Political Description of the Spanish Part of Saint-Domingo*, Philadelphia, 1798.
- NEWELL, WILLIAM W.
Myths of Voodoo Worship and Child Sacrifice in Hayti—JOURNAL OF AMERICAN FOLK- LORE, Vol. I (1888).
- NILES, BLAIR.
Black Hayti: A Biography of Africa's Eldest Daughter, New York, 1926.
- PARSONS, ELSIE CLEWS.
Spirit Cult in Hayti, Paris, 1928.

- PRICE-MARS, DR.
Le Sentiment et le Phénomène Religeux chez les Nègres de Saint-Domingue, Port-au- Prince, 1928.
Ainsi Parla l'Oncle, Port-au-Prince, 1929.
Une Étape de l'Évolution Haïtienne, Port-au-Prince, 1929.
- PRICHARD, HESKETH.
Where Black Rules White: A Journey across and about Hayti, Westminster, 1900.
- ST. JOHN, SPENCER BUCKINGHAM.
Hayti or the Black Republic, London, 1884. Second Edition (New Matter), London, 1889.
- SAVINE, ALBERT.
Saint-Domingue à la Veille de la Révolution. (Souvenirs du Baron Wimpffen), Paris, 1911.
- SEABROOK, WILLIAM BUCHLER.
The Magic Island, New York, 1929.
- TROUILLOT, D.
Esquisse Ethnographique: Le Vaudoux, Port-au-Prince, 1885.
- VAISSIÈRE, PIERRE DE.
Saint-Domingue: La Société et la Vie Créoles sous l'Ancien Regime, (1629-1789), Paris, 1909.
- WEATHERFORD, WILLIS DUKE.
The Negro from Africa to America, New York, 1924.
- WRIGHT, J.
Voyage to Saint Domingo in the Years 1788, 1789, and 1790, by Francis Alexander Stanislaus, Baron Wimpffen. *Translated front the original manuscript which has never been published*, London, 1817.

BIBLIOGRAPHY FOR JAMAICA OBEAH, MYALISM AND REVIVALISM

- ANONYMOUS.
Acts of Assembly, passed in the Island of Jamaica from 1681 to 1737, inclusive, London, 1743.
Acts of Assembly, passed in the Island of Jamaica from 1681 to 1754, inclusive, London, 1756.
Acts of Assembly, passed in the Island of Jamaica from 1770 to 1783, Kingston, 1786.
Consolidated Slave Law, passed 22 December, 1826, London, 1827.
Continuation of the Laws of Jamaica passed by the Assembly and confirmed by His Majesty in Council, December 26th 1695, London, 1695.
Further Proceedings of the Honourable House of Jamaica, relative to a Bill introduced into the House of Commons, London, 1816.
Hints respecting Christian Education of the Negro Population in the British Colonies, London, 1833.
Religious Instruction of the Coloured and Slave Population of Jamaica, London, 1832. Report of the Jamaica Royal Commission of Inquiry respecting Certain Disturbances in the Island of Jamaica and the Measures taken in the Course of their Suppression, London, 1866.
Report of the Lords of the Committee of the Council appointed for the Consideration of all Matters relating to Trade and Foreign Plantation, London, 1789.

Review of Hamel, the Obeah Man, London, 1827.

Slave Law of Jamaica and Documents relative thereto, London, 1828.

• BARCLAY, ALEXANDER.

A Practical View of the Present State of Slavery in the West Indies, London, 1828.

• BASTIAN, ADOLF.

Der Fetisch an der Küste Guineas, Berlin, 1884.

• BECKWITH, MARTHA WARREN.

Black Roadways; a Study of Jamaica Folk Lore, Chapel Hill, 1928.

• BELL, HESKETH J.

Obeah; Witchcraft in the West Indies, London, 1889.

• BICKNELL, R.

West Indies as they are; or a Real Picture of Slavery; but more particularly as it exists in the Island of Jamaica, London, 1825.

• BOWLER, Louis P.

Gold Coast Palava: Life on the Gold Coast, London, 1911.

• BRIDGES, GEORGE WILSON.

A Voice from Jamaica; in reply to William Wilberforce, London, 1823.

Annals of Jamaica, London, 1828.

• BROWNE, PATRICK.

Civil and Natural History of Jamaica, London, 1756.

• BUCHANAN, CLAUDIUS.

Colonial Ecclesiastical Establishment, London, 1812.

• BURDETT, WILLIAM.

Life and Exploits of Mansong, commonly called Three-finger Jack, the Terror of Jamaica, Sommers Town, 1800.

• CAMERON, NORMAN EUSTACE.

The Evolution of the Negro, Georgetown, Demerara, 1929.

• CARDINALL, A. W.

In Ashanti and Beyond, London, 1927.

• COOK, E. M.

Jamaica: The Lodestone of the Caribbean, Bristol, 1924.

• COOPER, THOMAS.

Facts illustrative of the Condition of the Negro Slaves in Jamaica, London, 1824.

• CUNDALL, FRANK.

Jamaica Negro Proverbs and Sayings, Kingston, 1927.

• DE LISSER, HERBERT G.

In Jamaica and Cuba, Kingston, 1910.

Twentieth Century Jamaica, Kingston, 1913.

White Witch of Rosehall, London, 1929.

• DUNCAN, PETER.

Narrative of the Wesleyan Mission to Jamaica, London, 1849.

• EDWARDS, BRYAN.

History, Civil and Commercial of the British Colonies in the West Indies, London, 1793.

- EMERICK, ABRAHAM J.
  Obeah and Duppyism in Jamaica (Printed Privately) Woodstock, 1915.
  Jamaica Mialism (Printed Privately) Woodstock, 1916
  Jamaica Duppies (Printed Privately) Woodstock, 1916.
- FULLER, STEPHEN.
  New Act of Assembly of the Island of Jamaica ... commonly called the New Consolidated Act, London, 1789.
  Two Reports from the Committee of the Honourable House of Assembly of Jamaica, London, 1789.
- GARDNER, WILLIAM JAMES.
  History of Jamaica from its Discovery by Christopher Columbus to the Present Time, London, 1873.
- GAUNT, MARY.
  Where the Twain Meet, New York, 1922.
- GREEN, SAMUEL.
  Baptist Mission in Jamaica, London, 1842.
- GURNEY, JOHN JOSEPH.
  Familiar Letters to Henry Clay of Kentucky, Describing a Winter in the West Indies, New York, 1840.
- JECKYLL, WALTER.
  Jamaica Song and Story; Anancy Stories, Digging Songs, Ring Tunes and Dancing Tunes, London, 1907.
- KNIBB, WILLIAM.
  Facts and Documents connected with the late Insurrection in Jamaica and the Violations of Civil and Religious Liberty arising out of it, London, 1832.
- LESLIE, CHARLES.
  New History of Jamaica, London, 1740.
- LEWIS, MATTHEW GREGORY.
  Journal of a West Indian Proprietor, kept during a Residence in the Island of Jamaica, London, 1834.
- LIVINGSTON, WILLIAM PRINGLE.
  Black Jamaica: A Study in Evolution, London, 1899.
- LONG, EDWARD.
  History of Jamaica, London, 1774.
- LUNAN, JOHN.
  Abstract of the Laws of Jamaica relating to Slaves, St. Jago de la Vega, 1819.
- MADDEN, RICHARD ROBERT.
  A Twelvemonth's Residence in the West Indies, during the Transition from Slavery to Apprenticeship, London, 1835.
- MARRYAT, JOSEPH.
  More Thoughts occasioned by two Publications, London, 1816.
- McCREA, HARRY.
  Sub-Officers' Guide, Kingston, 1903.

- NUGENT, LADY MARIA.
  Journal of a Voyage to, and Residence in, the Island of Jamaica, from 1801 to 1805. London, 1839.
- PHILLIPPO, JAMES MURCELL.
  Jamaica: Its Past and Present State, London, 1843.
- RAMPINI, CHARLES.
  Letters from Jamaica, Edinburgh, 1873.
- RATTRAY, R. SUTHERLAND.
  Ashanti Proverbs, Oxford, 1916.
  Ashanti, Oxford, 1923.
  Religion and Art in Ashanti, Oxford, 1927.
  Ashanti Law and Constitution, Oxford, 1929.
- RENNY, ROBERT.
  History of Jamaica, London, 1807.
- RILAND, JOHN.
  Memoir of a West India Planter, London, 1827.
- ROSE, G. H.
  Letter on the Means and Importance of Converting the Slaves in the West Indies to Christianity, London, 1823.
- SAMUEL, PETER.
  Wesleyan-Methodist Missions in Jamaica and Honduras, London, 1850.
- SCOTT, SIBBALD DAVID.
  To Jamaica and Back, London, 1876.
- SHORE, JOSEPH.
  In Old St. James, Kingston, 1911.
- SINCLAIR, AUGUSTUS CONSTANTINE.
  Parliamentary Debates of Jamaica, Vol. XIII, Spanish-Town, 1866.
  Chronological History of Jamaica, Jamaica, 1889.
- SLOANE, HANS.
  Voyage to the Islands ... and Jamaica, London, 1707-1725.
- STEPHEN, JAMES.
  The Slavery of the British West India Colonies, delineated, London, 1824.
- STEWART, J.
  Account of Jamaica and its Inhabitants, London, 1808.
  View of the Past and Present State of the Island of Jamaica, Edinburgh, 1817.
- UNDERHILL, EDWARD BEAN.
  West Indies: their Social and Religious Condition, London, 1862.
- WATSON, RICHARD.
  Defence of the Wesleyan Methodist Missions in the West Indies, London, 1817.
- WILBERFORCE, WILLIAM.
  An Appeal to the Religion, Justice, and Humanity of the Inhabitants of the British Empire, in behalf of the Negro Slaves in the West Indies, London, 1823.

- WILLIAMS, CYNRIC R.
  Tour through the Island of Jamaica from the Western to the Eastern End, in the Year 1823, London, 1826.
- WILLIAMS, JOSEPH JOHN.
  Whisperings of the Caribbean, New York, 1925.
  Hebrewisms of West Africa, New York, 1930.
- YOUNG, ROBERT.
  View of Slavery in connection with Christianity, London, 1825.

ost **P**S criptum

Williams, sorcery and witchcraft in the Caribbean...

About Joseph J. Williams

VAMzzz Publishing

Williams: Jesuit priest and anthropologist

Joseph J. Williams was born in Boston in 1875 as the son of Nicholas and Mary Jane Williams. He was educated at home by his mother, a former Boston school teacher, and later at Boston College High. In 1893 he entered the *Society of Jesus* at Frederick, Maryland. After two years of scientific and philosophical studies at Woodstock College he was assigned to Jamaica from 1906 to 1907.

Williams earned a doctorate in ethnology at Woodstock and was editor of *America* from 1910 to 1911. The next five years he served as a missionary in Jamaica. These years laid the groundwork for his subjects in anthropology and he collected a mass of archaeological and anthropological data during his stay. Williams loved Jamaica and he felt like "an exile" every time he left the island. His academic and personal interests came together when he started a collection of thousandths of books, maps, lithographs, woodcuts and engravings related to African and Caribbean cultures and Judaism.

In 1932 Williams began lecturing in Boston College's graduate school and helped to establish the Department of Anthropology at Boston College. He also established an ethnological library containing Africana and Caribbeana; the library is named in honour of his father, Nicholas M. Williams. By the mid-1930s, his health was failing and he asked to be sent to Shadowbrook in the Berkshires where he died in 1940. ■

'Williams loved Jamaica and he felt like "an exile" every time he left the island.'

Other publications:

- *Whispering of the Caribbean (1925)*
- *Hebrewisms of West Africa: From Nile to Niger With the Jews (1930)*
- *Voodoos and Obeahs: Phases of West India Witchcraft (1932)*
- *Whence the "Black Irish" of Jamaica? (1932)*
- *Psychic Phenomena in Jamaica (1935)*
- *Africa's God (1937)*

Paper books

VAMzzz Publishing is located in the very centre of old Amsterdam, in The Netherlands. Our publishing company creates high quality revised editions of five star occult, witchcraft, Gothic and esoteric classics, mostly written in the Fin de siècle-period and early 20th century.

As a publisher, we deeply respect the writer of any book we choose, so we join our forces (top level graphic design & thirty years of occult studies) to produce enchanting volumes which maximize the reading pleasure and inform, often with extra added information. In contrast to the current trend of digital screen addiction, we think, this variety of literature needs to be presented on paper. *No e-books, but real books!*

Apart from republications of valuable but forgotten books, we are also in the preparation of new publications on topics such as self-healing, magic, new astrology and more.

Previews of all books including a complete table of contents can be viewed on www.vamzzz.com. More books will be added to the list. *VAMzzz Publishing* strives to publish new volumes every month. Please visit our website regularly for the latest updates.

VAMzzz Publishing
P.O. Box 3340
1001 AC Amsterdam
The Netherlands
contactvamzzz@gmail.com
www.vamzzz.com

VAMzzz Publishing

OPHIOLATREIA
Rites and Mysteries
of Serpent Worship

Hargrave Jennings

Recommended

Ophiolatreia
*Rites and Mysteries of
Serpent Worship*
Author:
Hargrave Jennings
186 pages, Paperback,
ISBN 9789492355126

Ophiolatreia - Rites and Mysteries of Serpent Worship is one of the most
substantial and complete books written on this subject. It was published
anonymously in London in 1889 by the Freemason and Rosicrucian
Hargrave Jennings. In several voluminous works, Jennings developed the
theory that the origin of all religion is to be sought in phallic worship of
the Sun and fire, which he properly called "phallism." Ophiolatreia is just
one of its expressions. Unlike many modern authors, for whom he word
"phallic" implies the penis, Jennings used the word "phallic" in its non-
gendered sense, meaning "relating to the sexual organs".
Hargrave Jennings was a rival of Blavatsky and friend of the American
sex magician and occult writer Paschal Beverly Randolph and both
authors had a major influence on the twentieth century pioneers of sex
magic. This collectors item describes the rites and mysteries connected
with the origin of Ophiolatreia and its rise and development in many
parts of the world. The relation between snake worship, raw creation
force and sexual energy includes Jennings analyses of Bacchic orgies
and rites related to Saturn, Zoroaster, Abaddon, Dionysus and Osiris.

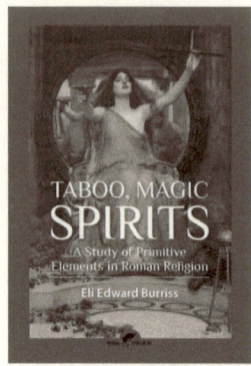

Taboo, Magic, Spirits
A study of primitive elements in Roman religion
by Eli Edward Burriss
200 pages, Paperback, ISBN 9789492355034

In Ancient Rome Mana was the term used for a mysterious, magical medium, which could be helpful or harmful (Taboo). Just like the Chinese qi, it could empower the positive and the negative. Contents: Mana, Magic and Animism – Positive and Negative Mana (Taboo) – Miscellaneous Taboos – Magic Acts: The General Principles – Removing Evils by - Magic Acts – Incantation and Prayer– Naturalism and Animism.

Chaldean Magic
It's Origin and Development
by François Lenormant
454 pages, Paperback, ISBN 9789492355027

The essentials of magic in Chaldea are presented inside a context of comparison or contrast to Egyptian, Median, Turanian, Finno-Tartarian and Akkadian magic, mythologies, religion and speech. Interesting is the Chaldean demonology, with its incubus, succubus, vampire, nightmare and many Elemental spirits, most of them coalesced with the primal powers of nature.

Amazons - *Two publications in one book* -
I. *The Amazons* by Guy Cadogan Rothery
II. *Religious Cults Associated With the Amazons*
    by Florence Mary Bennett
328 pages, Paperback, ISBN 9789492355089

Contents I: The Amazons of Antiquity – Amazons in Far Asia – Modern Amazons of the Caucasus – Amazons of Europe – Amazons of Africa – Amazons of America – The Amazon Stones. Contents II: The Amazons in Greek legend – The Great Mother – Ephesian Artemis – Artemis Astrateia and Apollo Amazonius – Ares.

Là-Bas
A Journey into the Self
by Joris-Karl Huysmans
378 pages, Paperback, ISBN 9789492355058

The plot of *Là-Bas* concerns the novelist Durtal, who is disgusted by the emptiness and vulgarity of the modern world. He seeks relief by turning to the study of the Middle Ages. Through his contacts in Paris, Durtal discovers that Satanism is not a thing of the past but alive and kicking in turn of the century France. The novel culminates with a description of a black mass.

Devil-worship in France
Or The Question of Lucifer
by Arthur Edward Waite
240 pages, Paperback, ISBN 9789492355065

In *Devil-Worship in France*, Waite attempts to discern what is genuine from what is fake in the evidence of 19th century Satanism. To get the answers he spends a great deal of time investigating the French Masonic echelon, debunking a "conspiracy of falsehood" and determining what should be understood by Satanism and what not. Huysmans' diabolical novel *Là-Bas* (1891) inspired Waite to write this sceptical analysis.

Testament of Solomon
A First Century AD Grimoire
76 pages, Paperback, ISBN 9789492355041

A first century AD grimoire, and therefore the oldest, and least known, of all grimoires (magical instruction books) in the occult tradition. The book describes health inflicting demons of zodiacal decans, summoned by King Solomon, and how he controlled them to use their forces to build his temple and more. Translated by F. C. Conybeare, appeared first in the *Jewish Quarterly Review* of October, 1898.

Fairy Mythology *(Volume 1)*
Romance and Superstition of Various Countries 1
by Thomas Keightley
404 pages, Paperback, ISBN 9789492355096

Fairy Mythology *(Volume 2)*
Romance and Superstition of Various Countries 2
by Thomas Keightley
404 pages, Paperback, ISBN 9789492355102

The term Fairy covers all kinds of nature spirits, not just the tiny sugarsweet creatures hovering around flowers. A unique and impressive book on this subject, published in a revised 2 volume-edition. No wiccan or pagan can afford to leave these books unopened. About Elves, Dwarfs, Kobolds, Trolls, Changelings, Meremaids, Nisses, Fairies, Brownies, Puck and other Elemental spirits all over the world.

Etruscan Magic & Occult Remedies
(Two volumes in one book)
Charles Godfrey Leland
628 pages, Paperback, ISBN 9789492355003

Part One of the book gives us a complete and detailed insight in the Etruscan and Roman rooted pantheon of the Tuscan Streghe (witches). Part Two describes many of their spells, incantations, sorcery and several lost divination methods. Much information in this book, Leland received first hand from the Tuscan witches Maddalena and Marietta.

Aradia
Gospel of the Witches
by Charles Godfrey Leland
174 pages, Paperback, ISBN 9789492355010

This wonderful book describes the creation according to
Italian witch-lore. We also read about the witch-meeting
or sabbath (treguenda) and the book contains many
original magical recipes, like spells for love and good
fortune. Diana is further connected to the Moon and
the fairy world.

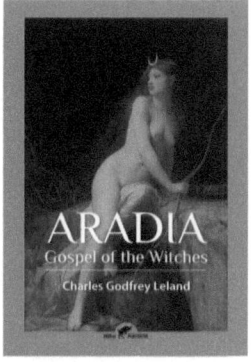